Product Liability Prevention

A Strategic Guide

Product Liability Prevention

A Strategic Guide

By Randall L. Goodden

ASQ Quality Press
Milwaukee, Wisconsin

Library of Congress Cataloging-in-Publication Data

Goodden, Randall L., 1951-
    Product Liability Prevention : a strategic guide / by Randall L. Goodden.
        p. cm.
    Includes bibliographical references and index.
    ISBN 0–87389–482–0
    1. Products liability—United States.   I. Title.

    KF1296.Z9 G663 2000
    346.7303´8—dc21   00–025299

© 2000 by ASQ

10 9 8 7 6 5 4 3 2 1

ISBN 0-87389-482-0

Acquisitions Editor: Ken Zielske
Project Editor: Annemieke Koudstaal
Production Administrator: Shawn Dohogne
Special Marketing Representative: Matthew Meinholz

ASQ Mission: The American Society for Quality advances individual and organizational performance excellence worldwide by providing opportunities for learning, quality improvement, and knowledge exchange.

Attention: Bookstores, Wholesalers, Schools and Corporations:
ASQ Quality Press books, videotapes, audiotapes, and software are available at quantity discounts with bulks purchases for business, educational, or instructional use. For information, please contact ASQ Quality Press at 800-248-1946, or write to ASQ Quality Press, P.O. Box 3005, Milwaukee, WI 53201-3005.

To place order or to request a free copy of the ASQ Quality Press Publications Catalog, including ASQ membership information, call 800-248-1946. Visit our web site at www.asq.org. or qualitypress.asq.org.

Printed in the United States of America

 Printed on acid-free paper

American Society for Quality

Quality Press
611 East Wisconsin Avenue
Milwaukee, Wisconsin 53202
Call toll free 800-248-1946
www.asq.org
http://qualitypress.asq.org
http://standardsgroup.asq.org

*To an outstanding woman who will serve
as an inspirational role model
for many family generations to come,
my Mother.*

TABLE OF CONTENTS

ACKNOWLEDGEMENTS

The author would like to give a special thanks to a few renowned individuals for their special contributions to this book. Attorney Kenneth Ross, of Minneapolis, MN, who has spent more than 20 years in the field of product safety and liability prevention; Attorney Christopher Hodges, of London, England, who has been a leading expert on product liability throughout the U.K. and Europe; and Attorney Helena Haapio, of Helsinki, Finland, who is a recognized expert in the field of international industrial contract law.

INTRODUCTION

The United States is the most litigious country in the world. Lawsuits are a preoccupation with our population. Manufacturers who faced multimillion dollar lawsuits yesterday face record setting billion dollar suits today. Even companies exporting products into the United States need to fear the potential risks they face from product liability lawsuits.

Foreign manufacturers have a difficult time understanding this American preoccupation, as they have never faced such legal problems within their own countries. Unfortunately, this activity is so lucrative that it is fast becoming a cancer to other countries around the world.

The end result is that many corporations are required to pay substantial risk insurance premiums or defense costs, forcing what might have been healthy organizations into major deficits, or even bankruptcy.

Insurance, defense costs, and out of court settlements impact the bottom line and drain funds that would otherwise go into profit sharing, investment, and growth. And yet, many corporate executives fail to see that there is something they can do about this, and often view the costs associated with product liability and lawsuits as the unavoidable costs of doing business in the United States.

Today, companies are open to learning about product liability prevention. Law firms, insurance companies, corporations, and manufacturing executives across the United States are taking an interest in this new area of corporate improvement. With all the movements that have pounded on the door of corporate America in the past 20 years, this is one that all the professions of management recognize as being the most credible. All they need to hear are the facts, and they begin to realize their shortcomings.

This book deals with this new corporate focus, recognizing the challenges, opportunities, and paybacks that equal or exceed other popular corporate trends in the past decade, but proving to be much more meaningful.

Corporations must look at this area in a whole new light. They must fully understand the legal aspects of product liability and slowly become as well versed as lawyers. Just like the other areas of total quality, continuous improvement, and improved efficiencies, corporations must focus on product liability. This isn't an area that will just make a manufacturer more competitive, it can make the difference as to whether they remain in business. They must recognize the need to become principal players in order to ensure their own future. They must recognize that each time a product liability lawsuit occurs, although they may have insurance that initially covers the loss, the corporation will inevitably pay the price.

This book thoroughly describes how a manufacturer can put a comprehensive *Product Liability Prevention* program and effort in place, and move their existing quality program to a new level. It demonstrates step-by-step how your company with its own nonlegal staff, typically led by the head of quality, can institute effective new programs and safeguards which will make a substantial difference in helping to avoid future legal actions and losses. In addition, you will learn how to become significantly involved in product liability litigation management and substantially increase your chances of winning future cases.

These new efforts will significantly increase the safety and reliability of the company's products and put into place proper procedures and practices in other areas of the operation which could contribute to additional legal problems. Once initiated, the company will not only gain a new level of awareness and education, but will also have in place their own product liability teams and experts that can help steer them clear of any future problems.

Finally, this newly dedicated effort will generate more profit by reducing the expenses and premiums associated with product liability losses and insurance costs, without increasing manpower or overhead.

This is a new frontier for manufacturers, with more reward than any other area of total quality. It is *The Next Dimension in Quality*.

The Current State
of Law and Litigation

INTRODUCTION

We are living in the most litigious age in our country's history. Civil lawsuits flourish in the country's courts, and one of the major areas is that of product liability. It is estimated that product liability costs the government, manufacturers, and insurance companies over $100 billion annually, more than the profits of the United State's top 200 corporations, and it continues to mount. The impact of this is reflected not only in the insurance premiums paid by manufacturing corporations, but also in the profits lost, the costs added to products marketed to cover these expenses which then affects global competitiveness, the products that are pulled from the market for fear of possible liability, and the jobs lost because of product liability settlements and impact on manufacturers.

The United States is the most litigious nation in the world. Everyone sues everyone here. It is part of the American *get rich quick* program and many recognize the opportunity. Every year more product manufacturing corporations become painfully aware of this problem. Unfortunately for some, they may not recognize it until it is too late and they are substantially involved in one or more devastating lawsuits. It is easy to find young companies with promising futures that were suddenly taken out of business because of the devastating effects of multiple product liability lawsuits. Even the largest and highly recognized corporations can be knocked to their knees by the effects of either multiple lawsuits or record judgements.

Even with all the reform bills that are brought to the legislature, the impact of product liability lawsuits continues to be devastating, with record awards recorded every year. Manufacturing corporations aren't likely to see changes that will lessen this effect, with the Legal lobby as strong as it is and half the Congress comprised of lawyers. It is too lucrative a field for those who stand to gain 30 to 40 percent of the judgements awarded. Life will continue to go on as normal.

PRODUCT LIABILITY PREVENTION

Seminars

Associations for defense attorneys hold conferences and seminars to study successful defense strategies in product liability litigation. Seminars and conferences are also provided for manufacturing executives who seek out new knowledge and direction as it relates to product liability prevention. Typically those who attend the product liability prevention seminars are product engineers, risk managers, and a few in-house attorneys.

Other members of management are beginning to realize that these seminars are important for everyone within the organization. Quality professionals, manufacturing management, finance, research and development, and even the presidents of companies are beginning to attend the seminars. They are discovering the roles they play in this new focus and are learning that they can't just leave product liability prevention up to one group. For example, the product engineers normally focus just on those elements which they control, such as safety in design and the development of warnings, and pass over the other elements of concern, largely because they felt they couldn't control those issues. Consequently, the rest of the organization wouldn't gain the awareness or the opportunity of knowing what they should be doing to prevent product liability.

Books

Hundreds of management and quality improvement books are published each year. They explain how the corporation can improve its efficiencies, style of management, profitability, processes, level of quality, and customer satisfaction. The books expound on many of the same points year after year, wrapping them in different packages and calling them different buzzwords.

Simultaneously, a number of Legal reference books and monographs are published every year to assist attorneys in various areas of business, trade, manufacturing, and corporate business practice. Books are published devoted to helping attorneys in product liability cases. They explain the laws that exist in different states and aspects of manufacturing defects, trial techniques, and defense strategies. These books aren't normally found in the same bookstores as the management books, but instead are offered directly from the Legal publishers or law associations.

What is missing is a marriage of the two: books that help manufacturers understand the laws and issues surrounding product liability, and books that teach attorneys how to proactively help their manufacturing clients in the area of product liability avoidance. Defense attorneys have always been in a *reactionary* mode, working for manufacturers once they get in trouble. They will be much more beneficial once they become proactive to manufacturers, and function as consultants in the effort to teach manufacturers how to avoid liability.

Manufacturers and Defense Attorneys

Manufacturers need all the help they can get from experienced defense attorneys in learning where others have gone wrong and where they need to improve their own efforts. They need guidance in making some of the day-to-day decisions, and expert opinions before the products and support programs are launched.

From the opposite perspective, defense attorneys need to gain a better understanding of how manufacturers work, the roles members of management play, what the systems and procedures are, and how the systems work. For instance, it is common for an experienced product liability defense attorney not to know what total quality management (TQM) is, or to have heard of ISO 9000. For defense attorneys to be as effective as manufacturing consultants, they should learn all the things manufacturers deal with every day.

Even when manufacturers get involved in a product liability lawsuit, defense attorneys need assistance from their manufacturing clients in understanding the technical intricacies of the product in question, as well as assistance in dealing with the phases of the litigation process. Manufacturers must know that the assigned defense attorney, especially those assigned by the manufacturer's insurance carrier, will be under constant cost constraints, which makes such help and assistance even more critical. Otherwise, the defense attorney will do their best with the resources available, the manufacturer will do what is requested, and when the case is over both parties will go their separate ways.

Insurance Companies

There is quite an incentive for insurance companies to enthusiastically endorse this new focus and to recognize that such programs would impact their own profitability. When the manufacturing client loses a case or is forced to settle, the insurance carrier will be the first to foot the bill, even though they will ultimately try to recoop their expenses during the annual renewal. In addition to endorsing and promoting this educational process, the carriers could eventually certify manufacturers in the area of product liability prevention and offer them a premium reduction for the programs and efforts in place. For what is truly available here is a win/win/win proposition.

IN-HOUSE LEGAL DEPARTMENTS

Few manufacturing corporations have legal departments. The largest corporations which do maintain them involve them in customer contracts and acquisition negotiations rather than in product liability lawsuits. Few corporate legal department, if any, get involved in the internal quality effort, much less drive anything like product liability prevention. Larger corporations that have legal departments commonly tend to *farm out* the handling of their defense to various law firms across the country.

Even more significant is the growing trend of corporate America to actually employ less full-time departments and executives in all areas, in favor of contract employees. It is becoming common practice for corporations to subcontract their finance, data processing, design, and engineering demands to specialized outside companies, as opposed to maintaining the departments internally. That way the corporations don't have to deal with the added costs of benefits and overhead, or layoffs due to work slowdowns, and if they aren't satisfied with the effort they can take their business elsewhere. Another advantage is that the outside experts are more likely to be on the leading edge because of their wide range of experience.

The small amount of corporate legal departments that do exist could someday be on their way out as opposed to actually growing in number. So manufacturers, along with their entire management team, need to learn all they can about product liability in order to effectively function as their own in-house Legal team.

THE LATE '90S EFFORTS TO OVERHAUL THE LAW—THE NEW RESTATEMENT OF TORTS

One of the most ambitious projects in the product liability field this decade, which reached conclusion in 1997, was the writing of the Restatement (Third) of Torts: Products Liability (Restatement Third) by the American Law Institute. Thirty years earlier the Institute published § 402A of the Restatement Second which served as the basis for product liability law.

In its time, the Restatement Second and § 402A represented a major turn in tort law. Section 402A imposed strict liability for products considered to be *defective* or *unreasonably dangerous,* but the definitions were ambiguous. Because of this, many states enunciated their own definitions of the terms which led to an array of variations across the country.

The writers of the Restatement Third overhauled the Restatement Second and developed the standards for liability as they relate to defects in manufacturing, design, and warnings, which had little distinction in the 1964 version of the Restatement. The Restatement Third addresses general product liability for commercial product sellers as well as liabilities for special products like drugs and food. It addresses the liabilities for distributors, post-sale duties, failure to recall, successor liability, causation, affirmative defenses, disclaimers, and apportionment of fault. After almost six years of work and 12 drafts, the new 300-page Restatement was finally approved in May 1997.

What follows is a summary of the Restatement Third by Attorneys Hildy Bowbeer and Kenneth Ross. Ms. Bowbeer is Senior Counsel at 3M in St. Paul, Minnesota. She is a member of the American Law Institute, was a member of the ALI's Consultative Group, and was a Liaison to the project for the Product Liability Advisory Council. Mr. Ross has been well recognized for over two decades as a leading authority on the subject of product safety and liability prevention throughout the United States and abroad. He is a member of the American Law Institute and was a member of the ALI's Consultative Group. He was also Liaison to the project for the American Bar Association's Section of Litigation.

An Analysis of the Restatement Third by Kenneth Ross and Hildy Bowbeer

⌐

In 1965, the American Law Institute published the Restatement of Torts (Second). This document contained § 402A, which articulated the concept of strict liability in tort for product defects. Most states in the United States adopted § 402A and incorporated some version into their own law. Over the years, product liability law and § 402A were expanded and interpreted thousands of times. As a result of these developments, many persons came to believe that the present form of §402A had become outdated. Furthermore, some literal and conceptual inconsistencies and confusion had developed in product liability law in general and in the application of §402A in particular.

Accordingly, the American Law Institute (ALI) decided to undertake a revision of the sections of the Restatement of Torts (Second) dealing with product liability. The project was completed in May 1997 when the ALI members approved the new Restatement of the Law, Third, Torts: Products Liability (referred to as *Restatement*).

The process of developing this new Restatement began in 1992. Professors Aaron Twerski and James Henderson, both with distinguished careers in teaching and writing about the law of product liability, were appointed the Reporters of the new Restatement. Furthermore, to assure broad-based input, *liaison groups* were formed to provide a formal mechanism for communicating the comments of groups outside the ALI who had a special interest in the terms of the Restatement. In addition, the Reporters received comments and suggestions through the traditional channels of the ALI Members Consultative Group, Advisors, and Council.

In early 1993, the Reporters circulated Preliminary Draft No. 1, which included the first group of *black-letter*[1] sections, plus comments and *reporters' notes* on various aspects of the law related to product liability. Various meetings and revisions occurred and finally Council Draft No. 1A was approved by the ALI Council and became Tentative Draft No. 1 in April 1994. This Tentative Draft was distributed to the full ALI membership and debated at the ALI annual meeting in May 1994. While the specific provisions of the Draft were not submitted for approval at that time, the members debated the structure and approach taken by the Reporters, and ultimately took a vote which indicated that a majority of the membership approved the overall direction of the project.

Tentative Draft No. 1 was substantially amended and became Tentative Draft No. 2 in early 1995. This document was debated at the May 1995 ALI meeting and key sections concerning the basic approach were approved by the members. Additional sections and revisions to earlier sections were published in Tentative Draft No. 3 in early 1996 and most of these sections were approved at the May 1996 meeting.

---

[1]Having wide acceptance and great authority.

Finally, Tentative Draft Nos. 2 and 3 were combined and revised in accordance with various comments and direction from the ALI members and various advisory groups in a document called Proposed Final Draft issued in April 1997. This draft was voted on and approved with revisions in May 1997.

Although the Final Draft of the Restatement was approved, the Reporters made minor revisions to the *black-letter* text, Comments and Reporter's Notes to reflect the votes and comments at the May meeting. The final version of this document was published on May 6, 1998, in both hardbound and soft-cover editions.

The Restatement contains twenty-one sections of law divided into four chapters:

> Chapter 1 (Sections 1–8) deals with liability for product defects at the time of sale;
>
> Chapter 2 (Sections 9–11) deals with liability for defects not existing at the time of sale;
>
> Chapter 3 (Sections 12–14) covers liability of successors and apparent manufacturers; and
>
> Chapter 4 (Sections 15–21) deals with causation, affirmative defenses, and definitions.

Section 1 states the basic premise that a commercial seller or distributor is liable for harm to persons or property caused by defects in its products. Section 2 then provides definitions and commentary for determining whether there are defects in manufacturing, design, and warnings and instructions.

Section 2(a) provides that a manufacturer is subject to liability for manufacturing defects if ". . . the product departs from its intended design. . . ." It contains no requirement that the plaintiff prove the departure rendered the product "unreasonably dangerous."

By contrast, § 2(b) states that a product is defectively designed if the foreseeable risks ". . . could have been reduced or avoided by the adoption of a reasonable alternative design . . . and the omission of the alternative design renders the product not reasonably safe." In other words, the plaintiff may not recover simply by criticizing the design of the subject product; the plaintiff must also prove that a feasible alternative design would have prevented the accident.

In Comment d to § 2, which addresses § 2(b) liability for defective design, the Reporters adopt a risk-utility balancing test that requires a comparison between a proposed alternative design and the product design that caused the injury, undertaken from the viewpoint of a reasonable person.

However, Comment f to § 2 makes it clear that this alternative design must be practical and technologically feasible, although the plaintiffs need not present a prototype to the jury. The alternative design must also be evaluated with respect to overall safety, not only its safety in the circumstances of the plaintiff's accident. The comments further provide that the alternative design does not necessarily have to be commercially available so long as there is expert testimony that it could reasonably have been adopted at the time the subject product was sold.

A possible exception to the requirement that the plaintiff prove a feasible alternative design is found in Comment e to § 2, which provides that a court may permit liability even in the absence of an alternative where a product has such extreme danger and such negligible utility that no reasonable person who understood the risks would use the product. The Reporters have stated that the black-letter law and comments which adopt the risk-utility approach are supported by "very substantial authority." Thus, they have sought in this section not to create new law but to enunciate a clearer description of what they believe is occurring in most courts.

Comment g to § 2 makes it clear that "consumer expectations" are no longer an independent standard for judging the defectiveness of product designs, although they remain an important factor to consider in determining whether an alternative design should have been adopted. In addition, the Reporters list a number of factors in Comment f that are relevant in determining whether the omission of a reasonable alternative design renders a product not reasonably safe, including the magnitude of foreseeable risks of harm, the effects of the alternative design on cost and product function, marketability, and product longevity.

Section 2(c) deals with warnings and instructions, and runs essentially parallel to § 2(b). It states that there is a defect in warnings and instructions if the foreseeable risks ". . . could have been reduced or avoided by the provision of reasonable instructions or warnings . . . and the omission of the instructions or warnings renders the product not reasonably safe."

Comment i to § 2 points out some of the factors that should be considered in determining whether an alternative warning should have been used, including the likelihood of the risk and the importance of not providing so many warnings that the consumer will ignore them. In addition, Comment j states that a seller will not be liable for failure to warn of an "obvious" risk of harm. On the other hand, the "obviousness" of a design or manufacturing defect will not shield the manufacturer from liability for that defect.

The remainder of Chapter 1 comprises a section concerning the use of circumstantial evidence to support an inference of product defect (res ipsa loquitur); a section that says that noncompliance with a product safety statute or regulation can be the basis of a finding of defect if the noncompliance caused the injury or damage; a section dealing with the liability of a manufacturer of components, raw materials, and incomplete products; and sections on the liability of manufacturers of prescription drugs and medical devices, food products, and used products. These sections are generally consistent with the current law in the United States and, in some cases, are clarifications of current law.

Chapter 2 contains sections concerning defects occurring at some time other than sale—either before or after sale. Section 9 sets forth the law concerning misrepresentations that occur in connection with the sale of a product. Sections 10 and 11 deal with liability based on a seller or distributor's liability for harm caused by a post-sale failure to warn or failure to recall a product.

Sections 10 and 11 are noteworthy in that they establish a post-sale duty that has not been accepted or even decided by a majority of states in the United States. However, the Reporters and the membership felt that there were enough decisions in various jurisdictions accepting a post-sale duty, and that this duty contributes to product safety and is consistent with government regulations which encourage manufacturers to identify and deal with post-sale problems.

Chapter 3 deals with liability of business entities that are successors to the manufacturer or that are apparent manufacturers (e.g., a product seller whose name is on the product but whose product is manufactured by someone else). Sections 12 and 13 deal with liability of a successor for the predecessor's products and a successor's liability for failing to issue a post-sale warning concerning hazards that it learns of in the predecessor's product. These sections are generally consistent with existing law or with the new post-sale section in this Restatement.

Section 14 says that an apparent manufacturer is subject to the same liability as though it were the product manufacturer. However, in practice, an apparent manufacturer will not be liable if the actual manufacturer protects the apparent manufacturer from liability through a contractual agreement or insurance coverage.

Chapter 4 contains sections on causation, affirmative defenses, and definitions. Section 15 says that causation, one of the required elements of establishing liability, is to be determined by the applicable law of the place of the litigation. The possible defenses of product misuse, alteration, and modification are discussed in the Comments to this section.

Section 16 deals with crashworthiness or enhanced-injury liability. This is liability that arises when an alleged product defect does not cause the initial accident or harm, but is claimed to have made the harm worse than it otherwise would have been. Section 16(a) makes it clear that the plaintiff must prove that a defect was a substantial factor in causing increased harm beyond that which would have been suffered by the plaintiff from non-defect released causes.

Under § 16(b), the manufacturer is liable only for the actual increase in harm so long as there is proof from which the jury can make a finding about the extent to which the harm was increased by the defect as compared with the harm that would have been suffered if the product had not been defective. However, § 16(c) takes the controversial position that if there is no proof from which the jury can determine the actual amount of the increase in harm, the manufacturer will be liable for the entire harm suffered by the plaintiff so long as the plaintiff meets the burden imposed by § 16(a) of proving that a defect was a substantial factor in causing some increased harm.

Sections 17 and 18 discuss the affirmative defenses of apportionment of liability and contractual disclaimers. Section 17 will simply characterize current product liability case law on apportionment but will not take a position on what direction that law should take. This is because the ALI is working on a separate part of the Restatement of Torts, Third which will deal exclusively with apportionment. Section 18 confirms that contractual disclaimers do not bar or otherwise reduce valid products liability claims.

The last three sections are definitions of the terms *product, one who sells or otherwise distributes,* and *harm to persons or property.* Section 19 discusses when tangible and intangible personal property and real property are products under this Restatement and how to distinguish between services and products. Section 20 discusses when product giveaways, leases, bailments, and other activities related to the distribution of products fall within the Restatement.

Section 21 discusses when economic loss is included in coverage of this Restatement. Pure economic loss is governed by contract law and the remedies set forth in the Uniform Commercial Code. Economic loss such as loss of earnings suffered by the plaintiff and damage to the plaintiff's property other than the product itself are covered by the Restatement. Damage to the defective product is covered under contract law.

Many plaintiff's lawyers and law professors have expressed concern that the Restatement is too pro-defendant, that the requirement of proof of a reasonable alternative design makes the burden of proof too great and too costly, and that it eliminates theories of recovery for allegedly negligent conduct by a manufacturer where there is no reasonable alternative design. These arguments will certainly be emphasized to courts who are asked in the future to consider whether to adopt the new Restatement's approach to design defect.

Defense attorneys, by contrast, have expressed concern that the Comments to Section 2 dilute the plaintiff's burden to prove a feasible, safer alternative by stating that the plaintiff does not need to prove the specific effects of the proposed alternative on the cost, utility, and benefits of the product. These same defense attorneys are also troubled by the prospect that a plaintiff may propose an alternative design without actually building or testing it, or even proving that it was within the state of the art at the time the product was manufactured. Defense attorneys and manufacturers have also expressed concern about the possibility that a court could find an entire product category defective under Comment e to § 2.

Some manufacturers have also been disturbed about the § 2(a) definition of liability for a manufacturing defect, which, by contrast with Restatement(2d) § 402A and the current section on design defect, does not require a plaintiff to prove that the product was "unreasonably dangerous" or "not reasonably safe."

The Reporters have carefully studied the comments of all participants in this process, and in many cases have made changes to reflect expressed concerns. Nevertheless, the Reporters have acknowledged that because of the widely divergent views of interested parties, it is likely that no faction will be completely satisfied with the final product.

Since the ALI has no authority to establish law, it could take a few years for these sections to be incorporated by courts into the common law. However, now that this Restatement is finished, it will be cited by more courts and attorneys, and courts may incorporate this language into the common law. It is also possible for state legislators to revise their statutory laws to reflect this new Restatement.

It is difficult to say what effect adoption of these new sections will have on litigating product liability cases in the United States. Since the final document contains more than 300 pages, there is a lot of material for courts to accept, reject, and interpret. Furthermore, because so much of the substance of the Restatement is in the comments rather than in the specific *black-letter* text, the practical effect of the views expressed may be limited unless courts and attorneys can find a way to distill not only the *black-letter* sections but also the accompanying comments into meaningful jury instructions so that jurors can understand and apply the concepts and considerations as intended by the Institute.

Whatever happens, many believe that adoption of this new Restatement will be much less revolutionary than adoption of the Restatement (2d) of Torts in the 1960s. In its final form, this new Restatement is, with some notable exceptions, truly closer to a *restatement* of existing law than the Restatement (2d) was. It does not create any new, significant basis of liability, such as the adoption of strict liability thirty years ago. On the other hand, to the extent it encourages courts to move away from semantic morasses and move toward a practical, systematic approach to the analysis of product liability claims, it serves a highly important function.

⌐

PRODUCT LIABILITY LITIGATION IN EUROPE

As stated at the start of the chapter, the United States is the most litigious country in the world. In no other country (at the time of this publication) is the opportunity for suing a company as simple and possibly as lucrative as it is in the United States. In Europe, manufacturers don't face the threat of potential product liability lawsuits as their counterparts do in the United States. For one thing, with national health programs in place, many potential plaintiffs lack a primary reason (uncovered hospital expenses) for initiating a lawsuit. Secondly, the United States is one of the only countries that allows attorneys to work off a contingency basis, so all an injured plaintiff has to do is pick up the phone and they might be on the road to riches. They don't even have to worry about expenses. Even stronger deterrents in other countries are the laws which stipulate the *loser pays* rules, which means you not only have to pay an attorney to represent you, but if you lose the case against the manufacturer, you may end up responsible for their legal fees too. How many parties claiming constant headaches or loss of sex drive are going to gamble with those odds? Not many, unless they live in the United States. Foreign manufacturers exporting their products into the United States are astounded by what they face, for good reason.

Unfortunately, the practice is so lucrative for attorneys and lawfirms that eventually attorneys in foreign countries will lobby for changes that will allow them to prosper like their American counterparts. As a result, their manufacturing companies will suffer the same fate as ours.

The following sections—product liability law, access to justice issues, the incidence of product liability claims, and Table 1.1 EU product direction and their relative numbers—give an overview on the state of product liability litigation and practice in Europe. They were written by Attorney Christopher Hodges, a partner at the London firm of Cameron McKenna. Attorney Hodges is well recognized as a leading expert on prevention in the UK and throughout Europe. The section is written in the British-English manner.

An Analysis of Product Liability Litigation in Europe by Christopher Hodges

⌐

Certain aspects of law and practice vary considerably between the different European Union (EU) member states, so the information given here should

⌐ Table 1.1	EU product directives and their relative numbers
• Medicinal products	65/65/ 75/318, 75/319
• Cosmetics	76/768
• Motor vehicles	70/156, 92/53 and many others
• Active implantable medical devices	90/385
• Medical devices	93/42
• In-vitro diagnostics	98/79
• Electro-magnetic compatibility (EMC)	89/336
• Gas appliance	90/396
• Low voltage	7/23
• Machinery	89/392
• Lifts	93/44, 95/16
• Personal protective equipment	89/689
• Simple pressure vessels	87/404
• General product safety- consumer products	92/59

be regarded as a generalised overview rather than an attempt to be forensically accurate, which would require a considerable amount of detail.

It is first necessary to understand the nature of the legal systems within Europe. The law which applies in each country is the national law of that country. However, as a result of the (European Community) Treaty (originally the Treaty of Rome 1957 but subsequently amended on a number of occasions, most recently by the Treaty on European Union and Economic and Monetary Union at Maastricht in 1991 and the Treaty of Amsterdam 1997), member states of what is now the European Union have agreed that certain aspects of their national legislation will be subject to laws created by EU institutions. The principal relevant EU institutions are the Commission of the European Communities (which is the civil service of the EU and has the power to propose legislation), the European Parliament (which has the ability to influence but not originate legislation), and the Council of Ministers (comprising ministers of national governments). Decisions on constitutionality and legality of EU legislation are ultimately made by references by national courts or the Commission to the Court of Justice of the European Communities, based in Luxembourg.

Many aspects of product regulation and product liability are now governed by EC Directives, which are then implemented into the national law of each member state. Sometimes the legislative instrument is a

Regulation, which has direct effect and does not require implementation. There is a truly vast number of Directives dealing with product regulation in different sectors (some of which are listed in Table 1.1), anti-trust provisions, environmental protection, and health and safety in the workplace.

Product Liability Law

Product liability claims in Europe are generally based on one of three legal theories: breach of contract, negligence (fault liability), or strict liability. In general, the national laws of member states on contract law and negligence law are not harmonised by Directives but are in general terms very similar (although details may differ considerably, for example in relation to remedies and limitation periods). Directives do govern certain aspects of sale of goods or consumer contracts, for example:

Directive 1999/44/EC which requires goods delivered to consumers to be in conformity with the contract of sale, fit for relevant purposes and to have appropriate quality and performance; specifies consumer rights for lack of conformity; and provides for the enforceability of consumer guarantees;

Directive 93/13/EEC on unfair terms in consumer contracts, which prohibits the use of various terms, including terms which exclude or limit legal liability of a seller or supplier in the event of the death or personal injury of a consumer resulting from an act or omission of the seller or supplier;

Directives 84/450/EEC and 97/55/EC on misleading and comparative advertising.

Whilst liability for negligence (fault) of a manufacturer or supplier is reasonably standard in any modern first world country, being based on breach of a duty of care involving reasonable conduct and reasonable foreseeability of damage, the burden of disproving negligence has been reversed and is placed on the defendant in some EU states, such as Germany, Netherlands, France, and Italy. Otherwise the claimant has the burden of proving damage and causation.

Strict liability was a concept that was introduced into most EU states for the first time under Directive 85/374/EEC (referred to as the Product Liability Directive). Under this Directive, a producer is strictly liable for damage caused by his defective product. The claimant has the burden of proving defect, damage, and causation. By anomaly, damages for pain and suffering are not claimable under the strict liability laws in Germany and Norway, although this is subject to reform. A supplier or importer into the EC may be liable where the producer cannot be identified, or where the supplier cannot identify the person who supplied him. There are certain defences under the Directive, including where the defendant proves:

a. that he did not put the product into circulation;

b. that it is probable that the defect did not exist when the product was put into circulation by him;

c. that the state of scientific and technical knowledge at the time when he put the product into circulation was not such as to enable the existence of the defect to be discovered (referred to as the "development risks" defence, similar to the state of the art concept in negligence: this defence is currently optional and varies between member states);

d. in the case of a manufacturer of a component, that the defect is attributable to the design of the product in which the component has been fitted or to the instructions given by the manufacturer of the product.

There are certain other provisions in the Directives such as on contributory negligence and limitation. Limitation rules vary between member states sometimes to a considerable degree in relation to contract or negligence liability. Under strict liability, a limitation period of 3 years applies from the claimant's date of knowledge of the injury, but this is subject to a repose of 10 years from the date when the particular product was put into circulation.

Access to Justice Issues

National rules of court and mechanisms for funding the claimant's lawyer are subject to national provisions and not harmonised by any Directive. The Civil Procedure Rules in England and Wales have been dramatically reformed in 1999 to make litigation simpler, quicker, cheaper, and more proportionate as between the amount of money at stake and the costs. Concepts have been introduced of pre-action disclosure of evidence, pressure to mediate and settle early, strong judicial case management, transparency of costs being incurred, and strong costs penalties in case of noncompliance. This system is similar to that which operates in Singapore and is likely to be influential in other EU states. A European claimant who wishes to bring a claim may first be subject to national protocols in relation to pre-action disclosure, as in the UK.

The rules in most states on disclosure of documents do not, in the first instance at least, require full disclosure of all relevant materials but this can be subject to further specific inquiry. Cases in the United Kingdom and Ireland proceed to be final, integral trial. In most other states there is no single integral hearing but a succession on shorter hearings in which the court receives evidence on particular issues. Many states rely on expert evidence only from single court-appointed experts.

A claimant generally needs to have a mechanism of funding his lawyer. Contingency fees (linked to a percentage of the damages) are illegal or contrary to lawyers' professional codes in almost every European jurisdiction, and generally not used. However, mere no win-no fee agreements, without a success fee element, are permissible in a number of jurisdictions, although very rare. Lawyers are not permitted to advertise in most EU jurisdictions, with the exception of the UK. A strong claimants' bar is only readily identifiable in the UK and Ireland. Since 1995, conditional fee agreements have been permissible in England and Wales, under which the winning lawyer would be paid in the event of success his normal fee based on his normal hourly rates and work done, plus a success fee based on a percentage of the normal fee. The percentage must reflect the degree of risk in the case and may not be greater than 100 percent. In some jurisdictions, notably Germany and Austria, lawyers' fees are regulated by professional rules on a tariff basis related to the amount at stake and the stage which the case reaches: these are restrictive and make many small claims uneconomic propositions.

A most important structural difference between USA and EU jurisdictions is that most of the latter have a rule that the losing party in litigation must pay the legal costs of the winning party. This does not apply evenly across every jurisdiction and is subject to the discretion of the court, but it is a major disincentive to bringing speculative claims. Under the English Conditional Fee Agreement[2] (CFA) system, the claimant's risk has been provided for by the development of after-the-event insurance policies. The insurance market has not, however, yet reached equilibrium between affordable premiums and lawyers' and insurers' ability accurately to assess chances of success in claims.

The cost of litigation and the *loser pays costs* rules have meant that many people have been unable to afford the cost and accept the risk of litigation from their own resources. In the second half of the twentieth century, most EU states have introduced public funding of claimants through legal aid systems. These vary considerably in their availability and effectiveness between countries: in some states, junior lawyers are appointed on a pro bono basis, whereas in other countries, notably the UK, extensive government funding is available to pay private lawyers. The UK legal aid system, together with the ability of UK lawyers to advertise, are widely credited as having been one of the fundamental criteria permitting the development of multi-party actions for product liability cases from the 1980s onwards.

---

[2]The English version of a contingency fee.

Calculation of damages and levels of damages vary between EU states (Ireland is generally considered to be the most generous) but are generally considerably below levels awarded by U.S. courts. In virtually every EU state, decisions on liability and quantum[3] are made by judges; it is very rare for juries to be involved in civil claims. Punitive damages are in effect unavailable in virtually every EU state, although there is some pressure to raise levels of damages and introduce punitive damages.

The Incidence of Product Liability Claims

The preceding factors provide far less incentives for European consumers or lawyers to bring legal claims for compensation in the event of injury. European national healthcare and social security systems generally cover virtually all of the population, irrespective of private insurance provisions. In general there are very few product liability claims across Europe. Most of these are relatively small claims which are dealt with reasonably quickly by manufacturers' customer service departments and insurance arrangements. Very few claims reach trial. The exception to this is that there has been a particular phenomenon of multi-party claims in the United Kingdom since the 1980s. These have principally involved pharmaceutical and medical device products for which U.S. courts would not accept jurisdiction. The phenomenon has latterly spread to Ireland but not yet to other EU countries. An alternative no fault insurance mechanism exists for pharmaceutical claims in Germany (the Pharmapool system).

⅃

PRODUCT LIABILITY LAWS IN CANADA

In 1978 the Supreme Court of Canada established a cap of $100,000 on general damages for pain and suffering, which was raised to $250,000 in the '90s. Higher amounts can be awarded for past and future loss of income, future care costs, and special damages. Damage awards tend to be much smaller than in the United States, and punitive damages have never been awarded.

In Canada, matters of civil law are controlled by the individual provinces. Unlike the United States, the majority of trials are heard by judges and don't include juries. Successful litigants are also entitled to recover legal costs from the loser, referred to as *party costs*.

---

[3] A claim or count grounded on an implied contract that the defendant would pay the plaintff as much as deserved for services or materials provided.

In most of the provinces a lawsuit is commenced with the filing of a statement of claim, and the defendant responds with a statement of defense. All of the provinces except Quebec are considered to be common law jurisdictions. Quebec is a civil law jurisdiction. Issues of discovery, procedural matters, contingencies, class actions, periods of limitation and other matters are governed by the laws of the province in which the lawsuit is commenced.

When a manufacturer gets involved in a product liability suit in Canada, they typically end up retaining legal defense from an attorney within the province, for most attorneys are only allowed to practice within their own province. Most provinces require that each claim contain material facts which the party relies, as well as the extent of the relief sought. If the defense feels the allegations are too vague, the laws of the province allow the party to seek the specifics of the allegations, prior to responding.

The number of experts that can appear in a case are normally limited, along with their testimony. In most jurisdictions, experts are not deposed, but instead are required to furnish a report just prior to trial. At trial, the expert's evidence cannot go beyond what they disclosed in their report.

In addition, most jurisdictions also limit the number of corporate representatives the plaintiff can examine to one. Because of this, that individual is more likely to be questioned on behalf of the whole corporation, and what the corporation knew and did, as opposed to just being questioned on their own personal knowledge or opinions.

Regarding discovery, each party is obligated to create a list of all documents in the party's possession or control that contain any matter relevant to the matter in issue. The list is normally presented as part of a sworn affidavit by a representative of the corporation. The list, broken into privileged and nonprivileged, will show the author, recipient, date, and type of document. The lists must be delivered before the parties can enter into depositions, which they refer to as *examinations for discovery.*

PRODUCT LIABILITY LAWS
IN THE FAR EAST

Japan

The first product liability laws of any type went into effect in Japan in 1995. Prior to that, manufacturers in Japan could not be sued by the users of their products. The new Law adopts a strict liability standard that requires the plaintiffs only to prove the existence of a product defect and the occurrence of damage from the defect.

The Law covers only products that are moveable and manufactured or processed. This includes standard products such as food, cosmetics, electronics, baby goods, toys, health products, and home appliances. It also covers second-hand goods and recycled goods. It does not include intangible things such as electricity, energy, software, or sound, nor does it cover immovable products such as real estate and other land-related things (trees, etc.).

Importation of a product into Japan or the brand labeling of a product will bring the entity that undertakes those actions under The Law [Article 3]. The new product liability Law defines a *defect* in the following manner:

Ⴠ

As used in this Law, the term 'Defect' means lack of safety that the product ordinarily should provide, taking into account the nature of the product; the ordinary foreseeable manner of use of the product; the time when the manufacturer, etc., delivered the product; and other circumstances concerning the product. [Article 2(2)]

⅃

Article 4 of the Law identifies two important exemptions. A manufacturer will *not* be held liable if:

- The state of scientific or technical knowledge at the time when the manufacturer delivered the product did not allow the defect to be discovered; or
- If the product is used as a component or raw material of another product, that the defect is substantially attributable to compliance with the instructions concerning the specifications given by the manufacturer of the said other product, and that the manufacturer is not negligent on the occurrence of the defect.

Under Article 5, damage claims are statute-barred after 3 years as of the date the damaged party learned who the party was who had caused the damage and what actual damage incurred. Any claim is excluded from being brought after the lapse of 10 years after the respective product had been put into circulation.

Special agencies in Japan offer certain safety approvals for many products sold in Japan. Among these are the "safety goods" (SG) mark for consumer products from the *Seihin Anzen Kyokai* (Product Safety Association), the "better living" (BL) mark for housing products from the *Jutaku Buhin Kaihatsu Center* (Center for Housing Product Development), and the "safety toy" (ST) mark for toys from the *Nihon Gangu Kyokai* (Japan Toy Association).

The ultimate impact of the Law will depend upon the manner in which the case law develops. Japan is a culture in which mediation and negotiation are greatly preferred to litigation. It is also interesting to note that up to this point an attorney played a pretty minor role in Japan, typically handling matters like corporate contracts. They earned a typical middle management salary. Over the years many even came to the United States in order to take advantage of the wider range of opportunities and income. In 1998 with Japan's population of 125 million, Japan not only had substantially less attorneys than the one million practicing in the United States, but in actuality had fewer attorneys than even the state of Minnesota.

Some unique aspects of the Japanese legal system include: the absence of pretrial discovery, tendency not to use juries, and lack of punitive damages. With this in mind, manufacturers didn't start out facing any real serious threat of lawsuits, even when the laws were enacted. Nevertheless, two recent trends are of particular interest. The first is the fact that the Law has sparked a boom in the sale of product liability insurance in Japan. At the time the Law first came into existence, only 5 percent of the Japanese manufacturers even carried product liability insurance. The second is that many Japanese companies have increased their efforts in warning labeling. Japanese companies are taking this threat seriously, and will find ways to avoid the courts by covering their risks and by making their products safer.

This new law increases the importance of product manuals and other appropriate literature that describes the proper installation and use of products. It is also important for exporters to Japan to keep in mind that all user manuals should be in Japanese. Exporting manufacturers should also ensure that their products are properly labeled with appropriate warnings in Japanese.

The use of indemnification agreements can allocate the risks associated with this new law. While Japanese importers and distributors of products may want stringent indemnification agreements from U.S. manufacturers, businesses should carefully analyze their risks in Japan before agreeing to such provisions.

All exporters of products to Japan should confirm with their insurance carriers that they are covered in the event of a product-related liability in Japan. If current policies do not cover this liability, the businesses should carefully weigh the advantages of acquiring additional coverage against the cost.

In the event a U.S. company gets involved in a product liability dispute in Japan, U.S. businesses should carefully consider all available methods for resolution of the dispute before taking any action. U.S. businesses may wish to employ traditional Japanese alternative dispute resolution techniques rather than attempting to automatically fight such cases or resolving disputes through U.S. style litigation.

China

Any person selling products *in China* is required to comply with the requirements of China's *Product Quality Law,* which came into force in 1993. Claims can also be based on contracts between foreign sellers and Chinese buyers, which are growing in number against domestic retailers, manufacturers, and importers.

The sale of products will have to comply with the law at some point as they move down the distribution chain to sellers in China. A seller of products in China has the following obligations:

- To implement an inspection and acceptance system for products supplied by manufacturers or suppliers to verify product quality using certificates and marks.
- To adopt measures to maintain the quality of the products it sells.
- Not to sell expired and deteriorated products.
- To ensure that the marks on the products are in compliance with the law.
- Not to falsify the place of origin of the products and not to falsify or pass off the name and/or address of another party's factory.
- Not to forge or pass off quality marks such as certification marks, famous brand marks, and marks of excellence.
- Not to adulterate or mix improper elements with the products, and not to pass off fake products as genuine products or products of poor quality as quality products, and not to pass off substandard products as up-to-standard products.

Furthermore, the *Consumer Protection Law,* enacted in 1993, imposes the following obligations on a seller of products:

- To ensure its products are in conformity with personal and property safety standards, and to give true instructions and clear warnings if its products pose a danger to personal or property safety, indicating the correct use of the products and measures to prevent damages; and immediately to report to relevant administrative departments and inform consumers upon discovery of serious defects in a product which may pose a danger to personal or property safety even if used correctly, and to take preventive measures to avoid injuries.

- To provide accurate information about its products to consumers and not to make misleading advertisements; and to provide true and clear answers to questions raised by consumers regarding the quality and use of the products. Clearly to indicate its true names and marks.

- To ensure that its products possess reasonable quality, function, usage, and dates of expiration required for normal use of the products, unless consumers have knowledge of defects prior to the purchase of the products.

- To ensure that the actual quality of its products is consistent with the quality indicated in its advertisements, product descriptions, samples, or in any other manner.

In their mutually agreed sale contract, the foreign seller and the Chinese buyer may spell out their rights and obligations concerning product warranties and may apportion liability. Chinese law will respect the intent of the parties to the contract. If the contract does not spell out the product warranties, Chinese law will supply some of the terms. If the seller breaches either the expressed or written warranties set forth in the contract, or breaches the standards imposed by Chinese law, the seller may be subject to claims for specific performance.

A person who suffers personal injury or damage to property due to defects in a product may sue both the manufacturer and the seller of the product under the principles of Chinese tort law. Compensation for personal injury may include payment of medical expenses, loss of income due to absence from work, a living allowance, mental suffering, and others. In case of death, compensation may also include funeral expenses, a pension to the family of the deceased, living expenses of the descendants of the deceased, and others. Compensation for damage to property includes payment for actual, direct damage and may include indirect losses as well.

The State Technological Supervision Bureau and the State Administration of Industry and Commerce have jurisdiction to protect the public from defective products. Businesses which sell, distribute, or manufacture defective products may be subject to administrative sanctions, including orders to cease sales, orders requiring the repair, replacement, and return of products sold, warnings, confiscation of products, confiscation of illegal income gained, destruction or the ordering of technical rectification of products, the levying of fines, ordering the closure of businesses, and revocation of the business license, depending on the seriousness of the violation.

The seller and the manufacturer of a defective product may also be subject to criminal liability. For example, the following acts constitute crimes under Chinese law:

1. Manufacturing and/or selling products knowing that the quality of the products does not meet the mandatory State or industry quality standards for the protection of health and personal or property safety of others; selling expired and deteriorated products; adulterating or mixing improper elements with products; passing off fake products for genuine products or products of poor quality as quality products, and substandard products as up-to-standard products.

2. Manufacturing and/or selling products, the defects of which have caused personal injury or death.

To constitute a crime under China's Criminal Law, the seller must commit a criminal act specifically listed in the law, and such act must be committed with criminal intent or through negligence.

CONCLUSION

Product liability is becoming a real issue to manufacturers worldwide. Although the laws in some countries, such as Europe and the UK, still contain certain aspects that may deter potential plaintiffs, there is probably a good chance that eventually they'll follow the practices of the United States. As stated, product liability lawsuits are far too lucrative for plaintiff attorneys in the United States. It will only be a matter of time before attorneys in other countries succeed in westernizing their own laws.

Understanding the Legal Process

PRODUCT LIABILITY LAWSUITS

One of the first things that should be identified here is that attorneys are not all the same. Attorneys involved in the area of product liability normally align themselves in one of two camps: attorneys for defendents, or attorneys for plaintiffs. Although some of the smaller firms or individuals may act in either capacity, most firms will normally be aligned as one or the other. For manufacturers, defense attorneys and their associations are *the good guys*.

Notice of Complaint

One of the first steps in a product liability lawsuit is for an outside party (plaintiff) to file a complaint in the courts against a named product manufacturer (defendant) alleging injuries or losses stemming from their product. The official complaint might be served to a key individual within the manufacturing corporation in the form of a summons, demanding that the said individual formally respond.

Receiving a notice from the court that you have been named as the defendant in a product liability lawsuit can be a very sobering experience for a product manufacturer, especially if it is the first time. Different from a threatening letter, the other party has already formally filed the case with (typically) their local court. This could be the first step in getting acquainted with the legal process.

Although the court notice will appear as though it will only be a matter of time before the company is pulled into court, in reality it is just the beginning of a process that will likely drag out for a number of years. Nothing seems to happen instantly in any aspect of this process. Nonetheless, it is a very serious situation and has to be treated as such. It is also the time to secure a defense attorney.

Receiving a formal complaint from the courts is just one of the ways the process can start. In accident and fire cases the manufacturer is more likely to receive a letter from the party's insurance carrier making them aware of the incident and losses, and requesting that the company compensate them. It is even common for the insurance company to explain the incident in a simple letter, how it was positively determined that the manufacturer's product was the cause of the fire, the extent of the damages (for example, "losses to the building and content amounted to $198,540"), and asking that the company immediately send them a check for the amount. It is unknown how many companies actually do cut such checks, but apparently some do or it wouldn't be such a common practice. Of course if the loss was a significantly lesser amount, say in the neighborhood of $1000—$5000, and the evidence looked pretty compelling, and especially if the manufacturer knew they had product problems, they just might decide to write the check and close the case. But in other typical situations, it is just the first step in what might be a long drawn-out process, which could eventually grow into a court case.

In some situations the first notice of a complaint may come from an attorney representing the other party. In these situations insurance companies may not be involved, or may not have started their own actions. The attorney may solely be representing a client or part of a client's interests. In a small personal injury case for instance, or in a fire case where the owner of the business suffered losses that weren't insured, an attorney may be retained to pursue reimbursement or compensation for that part of the loss. The attorney may send the corporation a letter explaining that he or she is representing the other party, and that they are looking for the corporation to compensate for the losses. Typically the letter will include a closing recommending that the manufacturer cooperate, so as to avoid formal legal action.

Because the outside party isn't familiar with the company's organizational chart, such notices and letters could be sent to almost anyone within the corporation, even to just the company itself. A notice from the courts is most likely to be hand delivered by a local sheriff, or at least arrive by certified mail, and is going to be sent to the *Registered Agent* which may be the owner, CEO, or president. Other types of letters could be sent to the heads of finance, human resources, the Legal department (even if there isn't one), or numerous others within the organization.

Normal Practices in Fire Cases

The first notice of an incident that a company is likely to receive regarding a fire will be a letter from an insurance company. They will be pursuing subrogation for a claim of damages they are likely to have already paid. It is also very common in fire cases for the manufacturer to first gain knowledge of the incident 6 to 12 months after the fire already happened, and even after the entire place has been rebuilt. Manufacturers may find this incredible if it is their first experience, but it is common practice. The insurance carrier's first objective is to get their client back on their feet, minimizing losses due to business interruption (in cases that involve fires to commercial establishments), and then afterward, pursue reimbursement from the party believed to be responsible. This is when the suspected product's manufacturer is finally notified.

The claim may be based on an expert's investigative report, a brief fire department report, the claimant's own account of the incident, or possibly just the report of an eyewitness. In many instances the surrounding proof may be substantially lacking, but will be presented by the insurance carrier in such a way to appear impressive and conclusive.

As an example, a store is devastated by a fire, and the insurance company presents the manufacturer with a fire report which states that the fire appears to have originated with the manufacturer's product. The insurance carrier hires a cause and origin investigator to inspect the site immediately after the fire, and the investigator determines beyond a shadow of a doubt that the manufacturer's product caused the fire.

Sometimes there may be an investigative company involved as well as an independent expert. In addition, there may be the fire department report which points at the likely cause of the fire as seeming to have originated in the area of the product. However, in many cases the fire report is vague and speaks in general terms rather than specific allegations. Many times the local fire department is a volunteer fire department and lacks expertise in cause of origin inspections. They don't want to appear as experts and be dragged into a legal fight, so they typically state that the fire appears to have started in the area of a specific product, and might include the possibility that it could have been the result of an electrical short or some other general comment.

The usual problem with many *on the scene* reports is that the fire report is written by a volunteer fire chief who has done little real investigation of probable cause, but was probably more interested in ruling out arson. Or the report was written by a (questionable) cause of origin expert hired by the insurance company to quickly find fault so they would have someone to go after for subrogation and hope their finding wouldn't be challenged. Often the insurance carrier may have already identified what *they* think was the cause and merely steer the expert in that direction so their allegation becomes more credible. Many times such *experts* may have been hired for under $1000, are in and out of the location within an hour or two, and give the insurance carrier the *expert report* they're looking for. Or in the case where the other party hires what appears to be a highly credible expert, such as a professor, the individual may not in fact have any real technical product knowledge. They are banking on the individual's credentials to persuade the manufacturer and especially the manufacturer's insurance company that they're right.

Cause of origin experts will photograph the inside of the building immediately following the fire, possibly even videotape it, and will secure the remains of the product alleged to have started the fire. The expert will write a full report on their findings and submit it to the insurance carrier which hired them. The cause and origin experts will normally hold the evidence until the claim has been resolved. In situations where the alleged product was mounted to a wall, or partially contained in a wall, the experts may even have the remains of the wall in storage.

In many fire cases the claimant may have only had limited insurance coverage, such as for the structure and/or for a portion of the content, but may not have been covered for the full content or for loss of business or business interruption. In those situations the claimant will hire an attorney to pursue reimbursement for the unprotected losses. Although the insurance carrier for the claimant may have shared the information that a certain product is believed to have been the cause of the fire, the insurance company itself may not have notified the manufacturer. The attorney representing the claimant for the uninsured loss may initiate the first notification to the manufacturer, which may only be a letter from the law firm. So it becomes important to understand the full size of the claim, the potential number of parties involved, and who is representing what interests.

Even though a fire case may initially begin with correspondence from the claimant's insurance carrier, if the manufacturer doesn't appear to be honoring the claim rather quickly, the claim will soon be handed over to attorneys representing the carrier. These may be attorneys working within the insurance carrier's domain, or they may be an outside firm retained by the carrier. Up to this point the manufacturer could have been handling the claim with only their own carrier involved, or in self-insured situations the manufacturer may have been solely communicating with the claimant's insurance carrier. Once the claimant's insurance carrier turns the file over to attorneys, the manufacturer needs to get attorneys involved too. If the manufacturer is fully insured for a product liability incident, then the manufacturer needs to ask their carrier to retain an attorney for them. The appointed attorney will likely be someone who is near the city where the incident happened.

Normal Practices in Personal Injury Cases

Personal injury cases are more likely to start with a claim filed in the courts and less likely to start with a letter from an attorney. Typically the corporation will receive an official notice that a complaint has been filed against them in a court somewhere in the country. The complaint will identify the parties filing the official complaint, the court where the complaint was filed, a description of the product and possibly how it functions, the incident or injury, and a list of allegations against the manufacturer. The list will normally include the product cited as dangerous and defective, an absence of adequate warnings, the product being unsafe when used in the manner intended or a reasonably associated manner, the negligence of the manufacturer the breach of expressed or implied warranties by the manufacturer and many other possibilities. The complaint requires a response from the manufacturer's legal defense, which will involve denying all the allegations. At this point the manufacturer has entered into litigation.

In some situations the manufacturer might merely receive a letter from an attorney regarding a personal injury incident. In these cases the attorney is hoping to talk to the manufacturer and reach some sort of compensation agreement. This might also be a good indication that the attorney has done little work on the case and is hoping that the manufacturer will be willing to settle out of court, thereby making life easier for the attorney.

Even when the attorney has filed a complaint with the courts and has had papers served on the manufacturer, they may not actually have much of their case together. They are still hoping for a settlement even though they are obviously indicating that they're ready to go all the way.

The Interrogatory

The next stage, following the official court complaint, involves receiving the interrogatory. The interrogatory is basically a questionnaire from the plaintiff's attorney, asking pages of questions about the company and the product. Through the interrogatories the plaintiff's attorney hopes to gain enough information to help them build their case, or at least gain an insight into the inner workings of the company which may help them at a later stage.

In most cases the manufacturer will have 20 days to answer the interrogatories. It is extremely important to keep in mind when answering these questions that you're under a court order to do so, and your answers must be truthful.

The Request for Documents, or the Discovery Stage

In addition to the interrogatories, and normally accompanying them, will be a request for documents. This will also be a multi-page form requesting numerous documents related to all aspects of the company, the product, the development of the product, sales and distribution channels, and many other elements. The request for documents is referred to as the *discovery* process, largely because the attorney for the plaintiff is hoping that in the review of all the documents demanded more inside information will be *discovered* which will help them with their case. As with the interrogatory, the manufacturer will have a specific time frame to respond to the request and forward all the documents demanded. Once again it needs to be understood that the manufacturer is under a court order to produce the documents, so nothing is considered to be confidential.

Federal Rule 34 states the following:

⌐

Any party may serve on any other party a request (1) to produce and permit the party making the request, or someone acting on the requestor's behalf, to inspect and copy, any designated documents (including writings, drawings, graphs, charts, photographs, phonorecords, and other data compilations from which information can be obtained, translated, if necessary, by the respondent through detection devices into reasonably usable form), or to inspect and copy, test, or sample any tangible things which constitute or contain matters within the scope of Rule 26(b) and which are in the possession, custody or control of the party upon whom the request is served; or (2) to permit entry upon designated land or other property in the possession or control of the party upon whom the request is served for the purpose of inspection and measuring, surveying, photographing, testing, or sampling the property or any designated object or operation thereon, within the scope of Rule 26(b).

Procedure
The request shall set forth, either by individual item or by category, the items to be inspected, and describe each with reasonable particularity. The request shall specify a reasonable time, place, and manner of making the inspection and performing the related acts. Without leave of court or written stipulation, a request may not be served before the time specified in Rule 26(d).

The party upon whom the request is served shall serve a written response within 30 days after the service of the request. A shorter or longer time may be directed by the court or, in the absence of such an order, agreed to in writing by the parties, subject to Rule 29. The response shall state, with respect to each item or category, that inspection and related activities will be permitted as requested, unless the request is objected to, in which event the reasons for the objection shall be stated. If objection is made to part of an item or category, the part shall be specified and inspection permitted of the remaining parts. The party submitting the request may move for an order under Rule 37(a) with respect to any objection to or other failure to respond to the request or any part thereof, or any failure to permit inspection as requested.

A party who produces documents for inspection shall produce them as they are kept in the usual course of business or shall organize and label them to correspond with the categories in the request.

⅃

Depositions

The next stage of the process involves the depositions of parties on both sides. The deposition is a testimony under oath, prior to the trial, which will be recorded by a court stenographer. Depositions involve the questioning of key manufacturing employees, experts involved in the case for both parties, and witnesses to the incident. The plaintiff's attorney will depose the manufacturer's employees and hired experts, and the manufacturer's attorney will depose experts and witnesses supporting the plaintiff.

In fire cases, where several parties might have interests, it isn't uncommon to have three to five different attorneys present at the deposition, all of which will take turns questioning key individuals under oath.

Pretrial Conferences

The interrogatory, request for documents, and deposition process of a product liability action can take months, even years, to finish. In all probability, there will be long periods of inactivity during this process which adds to its longevity.

Once these have been completed to both parties' satisfaction, the plaintiff will secure a court date and move toward trial. Prior to the trial, the courts may require pretrial conferences for such purposes as the following:

1. Expediting the disposition of the action
2. Establishing early and continuing control so that the case will not be protracted due to lack of management
3. Discouraging wasteful pretrial activities
4. Improving the quality of the trial through more thorough preparation
5. Facilitating the settlement of the case

The last item in many cases is the most significant. Keeping in mind that 96 percent of the product liability cases settle out of court, here then is a final opportunity. Many times the attorneys for both parties will agree to a settlement during these pretrial conferences, one day or even hours before starting the jury selection process.

Additional objectives addressed in the pretrial conference include:

1. To join other parties and to amend the pleadings
2. To file motions
3. To complete discovery

The scheduling order may also include:

4. Modifications of the times for disclosures under Rules 26(a) and 26(e)(1) and of the extent of discovery to be permitted
5. The date or dates for conferences before trial, a final pretrial conference, and trial
6. Any other matters appropriate in the circumstances of the case

The order shall issue as soon as practicable but in any event within 90 days after the appearance of a defendant and within 120 days after the complaint has been served on a defendant. A schedule shall not be modified except upon a showing of good cause and by leave of the district judge or, when authorized by local rule, by a magistrate judge.

At any conference under this rule consideration may be given, and the court may take appropriate action, with respect to:

1. The formulation and simplification of the issues, including the elimination of frivolous claims or defenses
2. The necessity or desirability of amendments to the pleadings
3. The possibility of obtaining admissions of fact and of documents which will avoid unnecessary proof, stipulations regarding the authenticity of documents, and advance rulings from the court on the admissibility of evidence
4. The avoidance of unnecessary proof and of cumulative evidence, and limitations or restrictions on the use of testimony under Rule 702 of the Federal Rules of Evidence
5. The appropriateness and timing of summary adjudication under Rule 56
6. The control and scheduling of discovery, including orders affecting disclosures and discovery pursuant to Rule 26 and Rules 27 through 37
7. The identification of witnesses and documents, the need and schedule for filing and exchanging pretrial briefs, and the date or dates for further conferences and for trial
8. The advisability of referring matters to a magistrate judge or master
9. Settlement and the use of special procedures to assist in resolving the dispute when authorized by statute or local rule
10. The form and substance of the pretrial order
11. The disposition of pending motions
12. The need for adopting special procedures for managing potentially difficult or protracted actions that may involve complex issues, multiple parties, difficult legal questions, or unusual proof problems
13. An order for a separate trial pursuant to Rule 42(b) with respect to a claim, counterclaim, cross-claim, or third-party claim, or with respect to any particular issue in the case
14. An order directing a party or parties to present evidence early in the trial with respect to a manageable issue that could, on the evidence, be the basis for a judgement as a matter of law under Rule 50(a) or a judgement on partial findings under Rule 52(c)
15. An order establishing a reasonable limit on the time allowed for presenting evidence

16. Such other matters as may facilitate the just, speedy, and inexpensive disposition of the action

At least one of the attorneys for each party participating in any conference before trial shall have authority to enter into stipulations and to make admissions regarding all matters that the participants may reasonably anticipate may be discussed. If appropriate, the court may require that a party or its representatives be present or reasonably available by telephone in order to consider possible settlement of the dispute.

Final Pretrial Conference

Any final pretrial conference shall be held as close to the time of trial as reasonable under the circumstances. The participants at any such conference shall formulate a plan for trial, including a program for facilitating the admission of evidence. The conference shall be attended by at least one of the attorneys who will conduct the trial for each of the parties and by any unrepresented parties.

Pretrial Orders

After any conference held pursuant to this rule, an order shall be entered reciting the action taken. This order shall control the subsequent course of the action unless modified by a subsequent order. The order following a final pretrial conference shall be modified only to prevent manifest injustice.

Sanctions

If a party or party's attorney fails to obey a scheduling or pretrial order, or if no appearance is made on behalf of a party at a scheduling or pretrial conference, or if a party or party's attorney is substantially unprepared to participate in the conference, or if a party or party's attorney fails to participate in good faith, the judge, upon motion or the judge's own initiative, may make such orders with regard thereto as are just, and among others any of the orders provided in Rule 37(b)(2) (B), (C), (D).

In lieu of or in addition to any other sanction, the judge shall require the party or the attorney representing the party or both to pay the reasonable expenses incurred because of any noncompliance with this rule, including attorney's fees, unless the judge finds that the noncompliance was substantially justified or that other circumstances make an award of expenses unjust.

Trial

Of course the last stage of the process is actually going to trial. The day before the trial actually starts, or even the morning of the trial, jury selection will take place. Immediately following the jury selection, the trial will start. A manufacturer should never fear going to trial and having their day in court, unless they fear they have good odds of losing.

UNDERSTANDING COMMON LEGAL TERMS

As one enters into the legal world, there will be a number of terms used that must be understood. Two of the most significant, and initially the most confusing, are those of *plaintiff* and *defendant*. Although these terms along with many others are properly defined in the section that follows, some word associations will help you keep them in their proper perspective. The person or group that is *complaining* to the court about you is the *plaintiff*. Plaintiffs complain. You, and your company, will always be trying to *defend* yourselves against the *complaints* being made, so you will always be the *defendants*. If your company were to lose a lawsuit and decide to sue a supplier whose component part was really the cause of the accident or loss, your company would become the *plaintiff* in the case that would follow.

Most of the following terms will be used within this book, so this is a section that you may want to mark. Unique to the legal field, some definitions may change as the legal system itself goes through constant changes. It is recommended that the in-house product liability expert maintain a legal dictionary, such as *Black's Law Dictionary*.

◢ **Affidavit**—A written or printed declaration or statement of facts, made voluntarily, and confirmed by the oath or affirmation of the party making it, taken before a person having authority to administer such oath or affirmation. *State v. Knight*, 219 Kan. 863, 549 P.2d 1397, 1401.

Attorney-client Privilege—In law of evidence, client's privilege to refuse to disclose and to prevent any other person from disclosing confidential communications between him and his attorney. Such privilege protects communications between him and his attorney. Such privilege protects communications between attorney and client made for purpose of furnishing or obtaining professional legal advice or assistance. *Levingston v. Allis-Chalmers Corp.*, D.C. Miss., 109 F.R.D. 546, 550.

That privilege which permits an attorney to refuse to testify as to communications from client to him though it belongs to client, not to attorney, and hence client may waive it. In federal courts, state law is applied with respect to such privilege. Fed.Evid. Rule 501.

Breach of Warranty—In real property law and the law of insurance, the failure or falsehood of an affirmative promise or statement, or the nonperformance of an executory stipulation. As used in the law of sales, breach of warranty, unlike fraud, does not involve guilty knowledge, and rests on contract. Under Uniform Commercial Code consists of a violation of either an express or implied warranty relating to title, quality, content or condition of goods sold for which an action in contract will lie. U.C.C. 2-312 et seq.

Case Law—The aggregate of reported cases as forming a body of jurisprudence, or the law of a particular subject as evidenced or formed by the adjudged cases, in distinction to statutes and other sources of law. It includes the aggregate of reported cases that interpret statutes, regulations, and constitutional provisions.

Civil Action—Action brought to enforce, redress, or protect private rights. In general, all types of legal actions other than criminal proceedings. *Gilliken v. Gilliken,* 248 N.C. 710, 104 S.E.2d 861, 863. In the great majority of states which have adopted rules or codes of civil procedure as patterned on the Federal Rules of Civil Procedure, there is an action known as a *civil action.* The former distinctions between actions at law and suits in equity, and the separate forms of those actions and suits, have been abolished. Rule of Civil Proc. 2; New York CPLR 103(a).

Compensatory Damages—Amount of money determined adequate to compensate for any actual damages caused by the party against whom they awarded. Also awarded for things that are harder to measure, such as pain and suffering (as opposed to punitive damages).

(In patent cases) Amount of money adequate to compensate for any infringement, but in no event less than the amount of money the plaintiff would have received if the defendant had been paying the plaintiff a reasonable royalty for using the patent during the period of infringement. The law does not permit the award of a greater sum than the monetary loss the plaintiff suffered as a result of the defendant's infringement. 35 U.S.C.

Complaint—The original or initial pleading by which an action is commenced under codes or Rules of Civil Procedure.Fed.R. Civil P. 3. The pleading which sets forth a claim for relief. Such claimant shall contain: (1) a short and plain statement of the grounds upon which the court's jurisdiction depends, unless the court already has jurisdiction and the claim needs no new grounds of jurisdiction to support it, (2) a short and plain statement of the claim showing that the pleader is entitled to relief, and (3) a demand for judgement for the relief to which he deems himself entitled. Relief in the alternative or of several different types may be demanded. Fed.R. Civil P. 8(a).

Contributory Negligence—The act or omission amounting to want of ordinary care on part of complaining party, which, concurring with defendant's negligence, is proximate cause of injury. *Honacker v. Crutchfield*, 247 KY.495, 57 S.W.2d 502. Conduct by a plaintiff which is below the standard to which he is legally required to conform for his own protection and which is a contributing cause which cooperates with the negligence of the defendant in causing the plaintiff's harm. *Li v. Yellow Cab Co. of California*, 13 Cal.3d 804, 119 Cal.Rptr. 858, 864, 532 P.2d 1226.

Curriculum Vitae—A resume or summary of one's curricular background and experience. When used to qualify an expert witness, would include the expert's educational background, experience in the field, job history, and professional affiliations as it relates to the subject at hand. (When being deposed, the cross examining attorney will commonly ask for your curriculum vitae, or *CV*, in order to establish your knowledge and experience regarding the technical product in question.)

Defendant—The person defending or denying; the party against whom relief or recovery is sought in an action or suit or the accused in a criminal case.

Deposition—The testimony of a witness taken upon oral question or written interrogatories, not in open court, put in pursuance of a commission to take testimony issued by a court, or under a general law or court rule on the subject, and reduced to writing and duly authenticated, and intended to be used in preparation and upon the trial of a civil action or criminal prosecution. A pretrial discovery device by which one party (through his or her attorney) asks oral questions of the other party or of a witness for the other party. The person who is deposed is called the deponet. The deposition is conducted under oath outside of the courtroom, usually in one of the lawyer's offices. A transcript—word for word account—is made of the deposition. Testimony of the witness, taken in writing, under oath or affirmation, before some judicial officer in answer to questions or interrogatories. Fed.R. Civil P. 26 et seq.; Fed.R. Crim.P. 15.

Disclaimer—The repudiation or renunciation of a claim or power vested in a person or which he had formerly alleged to be his. The refusal, or rejection of an estate or right offered to a person. The disavowal, denial, or renunciation of an interest, right, or property imputed to a person or alleged to be his. *Disclaimer of warranties* is means of controlling liability of seller by reducing number of situations in which seller can be in breach of contract terms. *Collins Radio Co.,* Del.Super., 515 A.2d 163, 171.

Discovery—The pretrial devices that can be used by one party to obtain facts and information about the case from the other party in order to assist the party's preparation for trial. Under Federal Rules of Civil Procedure (and in states which have adopted rules patterned on such), tools of discovery include: depositions upon oral and written questions, written interrogatories, production of documents or things, permission to enter upon land or other property, physical and mental examinations, and requests for admission. Rules 26–37. Term generally refers to disclosure by defendant of facts, deeds, documents, or other things which are in his exclusive knowledge or possession and which are necessary to party seeking discovery as a part of a cause of action pending, or to be brought in another court, or as evidence of his rights or title in such proceeding. *Hardenbergh v. Both,* 247 Iowa 153, 73 N.W.2d 103, 106.

Et al.—Meaning *and others.* Often affixed to the name of the person first mentioned, where there are several plaintiffs, grantors, persons addressed, etc. Where the words are used in a judgement against defendants, the quoted words include all defendants. *Williams v. Williams,* 25 Tenn.App. 290, 156 S.W.2d 363, 369.

Expert Witness—One who by reason of education or specialized experience possesses superior knowledge respecting a subject about which persons having no particular training are incapable of forming an accurate opinion or deduct-ing correct conclusions. *Kim Mfg., Inc. v. Superior Metal Treating, Inc., Mo.App., 537 S.W.2d 424, 428.* A witness who has been qualified as an expert and who thereby will be allowed to assist the jury in understanding complicated and technical subjects not within the understanding of the average lay person. One skilled in any particular art, trade, or profession, being pos-sessed of peculiar knowledge concerning the same, and one who has given subject in question particular study, practice, or observation.

Express Warranty—A promise, ancillary to an underly-ing sales agreement, which is included in the written or oral terms of the sales agreement under which the promisor assures the quality, description, or performance of the goods. It is not necessary to the creation of an express warranty that the seller use formal words such as *warrant* or *guarantee* or that he have a specific intention to make a warranty, but an affirmation merely of the value of the goods or a statement purporting to be merely the seller's opinion or commendation of the goods does not create a warranty. U.C.C. 2-313.

Full Warranty—A warranty as to full performance cov-ering generally both labor and materials. Under a full war-ranty, the warrantor must remedy the consumer product within a reasonable time and without charge after notice of a defect or malfunction. 15 U.S.C.A. 2304.

Implied Warranty—A promise or contract not written or stated. Exists when the law derives it by implication or inference from the nature of the transaction or the relative situation or circumstances of the parties. *Great Atlantic & Pacific Tea Co. v. Walker,* Tex.Civ.App., 104 S.W.2d 627, 632.

Indemnification—The practice by which corporations agree to, or require, that other corporations or suppliers of products hold them harmless and accept their defense in the event of a product liability lawsuit.

Indemnify—To restore the victim of a loss, in whole or in part, by payment, repair, or replacement. To save harmless; to secure against loss or damage; to give security for the reimbursement of a person in case of an anticipated loss falling upon him. (If you as the manufacturer of the product agree to *indemnify* your customer or seller of your product, should the product ever be suspected of causing an injury or loss, then your company would be the only party ultimately found financially responsible for whatever costs and losses are determined by the court, and the indemnified party would be cleared of loss.)

Interrogatories—A pretrial discovery device consisting of written questions about the case submitted by one party to the other party or witness. The answers to the interrogatories are usually given under oath, i.e., the person answering the questions signs a sworn statement that the answers are true. Fed.R. Civil P. 33.

Litigation—A lawsuit. Legal action, including all proceedings therein. Contest in a court of law for the purpose of enforcing a right or seeking a remedy. A judicial contest, a judicial controversy, a suit at law.

Negligence—The failure to use such care as a reasonably prudent and careful person would use under similar circumstances; it is the doing of some act which a person of ordinary prudence would not have done under similar circumstances or failure to do what a person of ordinary prudence would have done under similar circumstances. Amoco Chemical Corp. v. Hill, Del.Super., 318 A.2d 614, 617.

Plaintiff—A person who brings an action; the party who complains or sues in a civil action and is so named on the record. A person who seeks remedial relief for an injury to rights; it designates a complainant. City of Vancouver v. Jarvis, 76 Wash.2d 110, 455 P.2d 591, 593.

Privity of Contract—That connection or relationship which exists between two or more contracting parties. It was traditionally essential to the maintenance of an action on any contract that there should subsist such privity between the plaintiff and defendant in respect of the matter sued on. However, the absence of privity as a defense in actions for damages in contract and tort actions is generally no longer viable with the enactment of warranty statutes, acceptance by states of doctrine of strict liability, and court decisions (e.g., MacPherson v. Buick Motor Co. 217 N.Y. 382, 111 N.E. 1050) which have extended the right to sue for injuries or damages to third-party beneficiaries, and even innocent bystanders. Elmore v. American Motors Corp., 70 Cal.2d 578, 75 Cal.Rptr.652, 451 P.2d 84.

Punitive Damages—The purpose of punitive damages is to punish a defendant and to deter a defendant and others from committing similar acts in the future. Plaintiff has the burden of proving that punitive damages should be awarded, and the amount, by a preponderance of the evidence. Punitive damages may be awarded only if defendant's conduct was malicious, or in reckless disregard of plaintiff's rights. Conduct is malicious if it is accompanied by ill will, or spite, or if it is for the purpose of injuring another. Conduct is in reckless disregard of plaintiff's rights if, under the circumstances, it reflects complete indifference to the safety and rights of others.

Sanctions—Penalty or other mechanism of enforcement used to provide incentives for obedience with the law or with rules and regulations.

State of the Art—In context of products liability case means level of pertinent scientific and technical knowledge existing at time of manufacture. *Wiska v. St. Stanislaus Social Club, Inc.,* 7 Mass. App. 813, 390 N.E.2d 1133, 1138, 3 A.L.R.4th 480.

Statute of Limitations—Statutes of the federal government and various states setting maximum time periods during which certain actions can be brought or rights enforced. After the time period set out in the applicable statute of limitations has run, no legal action can be brought regardless of whether any cause of action ever existed.

Statute of Repose—Statutes of limitations extinguish, after period of time, right to prosecute accrued cause of action; statute of repose, by contrast, limits potential liability by limiting time during which cause of action can arise. *Kline v. J.I. Case Co.,* D.C.Ill., 520 F.Supp. 564, 567.

Strict Liability—A concept applied by the courts in product liability cases in which seller is liable for any and all defective or hazardous products which unduly threaten a consumer's personal safety. This doctrine poses strict liability on one who sells product in a defective condition unreasonably dangerous to user or consumer for harm caused to ultimate user or consumer if seller is engaged in business of selling such product, and product is expected to and does reach user or consumer without substantial change in condition in which it is sold. *Davis v. Gibson Products Co.,* 68 N.J. 1, 342 A.2d 181, 184.

Subpoena—A subpoena is a command to appear at a certain time and place to give testimony upon a certain matter.

Subrogation—The substitution of one person in the place of another with reference to a lawful claim, demand, or right, so that he who is substituted succeeds to and its rights, remedies, or securities. *Gerken v. Davidson Grocery Co.,* 57 Idaho 670, 69 P.2d 122, 126. Insurance companies . . . generally have the right to step into the shoes of the party whom they compensate and sue any party whom the compensated party could have sued.

Summons—Instrument used to commence a civil action or special proceeding and is a means of acquiring jurisdiction over a party. Upon the filing of the complaint the clerk is required to issue a summons and deliver it for service to the marshal or to a person specially appointed to serve it. Fed.R.Civil P. 4(a)

Tort—A private or single wrong or injury, including action for bad faith breach of contract, for which the court will provide a remedy in the form of an action for damages. *K-Mart Corp. v Ponsock,* 103 Nev. 39, 732 P.2d 1364, 1368.

Warranty—A promise that a proposition of fact is true. An assurance by one party to an agreement of existence of fact upon which other party may rely. It is intended precisely to relieve promisee of any duty to ascertain facts for himself, and amounts to promise to indemnify promisee for any loss if the fact warranted proves untrue. *Paccon, Inc. v. U.S.,* 399 F.2d 162, 166, 185 Ct.Cl. 24.

Work Product Rule—Under this rule any notes, working papers, memoranda, or similar materials, prepared by an attorney in anticipation of litigation, are protected from discovery. Fed.R.Civ.Proc. 26(b)(3).

Understanding Quality

From 1990 forward the *quality* focus worldwide was given a major boost and endorsement by corporations, countries, academic associations, and every other type of organization affiliated with the business world. For those with positions in quality, it was recognition and support that was long overdue. Quality departments and quality professionals had been long looked at as a necessary evil, not as a benefit.

TOTAL QUALITY MANAGEMENT: THE EARLY YEARS

Prior to the '90s, sales and production volume took precedent over product quality, which ended up being the fatal mistake of many manufacturers. Starting in the middle '80s, the competitive marketplace in the United States began to be won over by overseas manufacturers of high-quality, reliable products. Companies not only began to recognize the demand for and importance of selling high-quality products, but also recognized the potential profits achieved by having every member of their organization focus on quality in everything they did. Hence, the total quality management effort was born, along with countless new gurus and prophets of quality, all claiming to be the chosen one to follow.

The countless gurus, consultants, and numerous quality program models soon lead to confusion and corporations found it difficult to figure out which to follow. Eventually the European community developed the ISO 9000 standard for quality programs, and the United States developed standard programs of its own. The teachings of named quality gurus faded as a new breed of industry leaders and quality consultants, who focused on these new internationally recognized standards, emerged.

Impact of the Quality Effort on Quality Positions

Corporations were not only sold on adopting these new total quality practices (many of which were required by key customers), but challenged themselves to compete for them. It wasn't enough to recognize the virtues of having a comprehensive quality program and effort in place, there were now trophies to win and flags to fly outside the corporate headquarters. At first such support and worldwide recognition was a quality professional's dream, but as time went on it slowly became a quality nightmare. CEOs were driven to win these *Oscars* in quality to such an extent that large teams were formed with the sole objective of driving the effort. This was especially true with the Malcolm Baldrige Award, but existed with other top quality acknowledgements as well.

Eventually, this corporate acceptance of quality, and especially the focus on total quality management, began to lead to the demise of many quality positions within industry. Now that the manufacturing executive groups were finally in complete support of these total quality programs, and the roles and responsibilities for ensuring quality were incorporated into every job description, they mistakenly felt they no longer needed any titled *quality* positions. Even the quality consultants, who began to propagate in the early '90s, would come into a corporation and state to the management team that once their programs were fully integrated, they would put the quality department out of business.

It was ludicrous for any corporation to think that just because they were finally cooperating with and highly endorsing the overall quality effort, there was no longer a need for the *quality* professional. Members of management always were fully responsible for assuring quality. That shouldn't have changed the role and contributions of quality managers, quality engineers, and other positions within the quality organization. Quality people still need to drive the overall programs and efforts, routinely perform statistical studies, conduct reliability tests, and spearhead other valuable programs. But the quality effort nonetheless began to lead to the downfall of the profession.

The future of quality professionals was questioned even by their own associations. Articles appeared in quality periodicals questioning the future of the quality profession. With all of this impending doom, people moved out of their quality assurance positions and into other areas of management. As the years went by, many corporations realized the need to have the quality champions in place driving the programs and supplying the needed performance data and educational programs.

Increase in Product Liability Lawsuits

Ironically, while all this focus on improved quality was taking place, another plague was affecting the health of American manufacturers. The whole area of product liability and the numerous lawsuits involved had grown out of control in the United States and became a major threat to every other industrial country in the world. The impact of product liability lawsuits had a wide array of effects on all types of companies.

Numerous manufacturing corporations went out of business because of the impact of multiple product liability lawsuits, even with their certifiable quality programs in place. They may have ensured that the products produced complied with every specification, but no one thought to challenge the specification itself. In many other cases it was much more than that. Customers misused and abused the products and held the manufacturer responsible. The highly lucrative nature of product liability lawsuits became *big business* for the lawyers aggressively chasing them.

The pursuit and development of countless new and innovative products for the marketplace was suddenly abandoned because of the recognized risk potential for frivolous lawsuits. The prices of many other types of products carried substantial markups because of the costs associated with risk insurance and litigation. Product liability lawsuits continued to place a financial burden on corporations of all sizes and were reflected in either the insurance premiums corporations are required to pay, or in their own self-insured expenses.

Unlike the quality programs every manufacturer recognized the need to adopt, manufacturing corporations and their executive staffs first learned the substantial benefits and opportunities in store once they began the process of focusing on *Product Liability Prevention.* Up to this point most manufacturers felt that they were doing everything they could to limit their exposure to product liability lawsuits, but once they really studied the focus they began to realize how much their efforts were lacking.

As manufacturers successfully learned to track quality costs, losses due to scrap, rework, warranty, and other areas of failure, they neglected to track other key financial line items such as insurance or liability costs. Manufacturing executives typically overlook this financial line item and end up accepting whatever premium their people can best negotiate. This could be tens of thousands or hundreds of thousands of dollars in annual costs, based on their history of losses and recognized exposure to risk by underwriters. As the litigious nature of society grows, and personal injury awards as well as punitive damages continue to hit new highs, it becomes a real necessity for corporations to focus on product liability prevention and incorporate it into their quality program and effort.

IT STARTS WITH THE QUALITY PROGRAM

An effective product liability prevention effort will never be successful if the manufacturer doesn't have a sound comprehensive quality program in place. You cannot add to something that isn't there. The product liability prevention effort is meant to be an addition to the established quality program, taking the existing comprehensive program to the next step, or next dimension. It cannot take the place of a nonexistent quality program, nor can it be developed from scratch or be a self-standing program. It only works if it is adding steps to procedures that are already in place.

The author also recognizes the semantic argument that the quality system and effort shouldn't be referred to as a *program,* which could imply that it has a specific beginning and end. The word also means *a plan or system under which action may be taken toward a goal.* In the common usage as it relates to quality, the future goal is always being reidentified, so it is never finally reached. So for the sake of simplicity, we're going to use the term *program* to describe the system and effort.

One of the problems commonly found in the manufacturing world is that most manufacturers feel that they have a good quality program in place, even though they are light years away from this goal. It is easy to find small manufacturers that maintain a quality manager or quality supervisor, and possibly a small department of inspectors, and feel that they have a good effort in place even though little is documented. General managers of other small companies have no real quality program formally in place, but because their employees are very concerned about quality and everything produced is 100 percent inspected, they feel they have a comprehensive quality program. In addition some may either have a small quality manual which employees may or may not follow, or they might have a collection of procedures or process instructions posted in various areas throughout the shop.

This is a special concern for those manufacturers who have never received certification or acknowledgement by an outside body that their program meets the criteria for some baseline standard. Examples of certification would be the ISO and QS standards, as well as standards for quality systems that have been created over the years by the major U.S. companies and industries. Therefore, we want to establish some standard for what is considered to be a sound program.

Initiating a Comprehensive Quality Program and Effort

Comprehensive quality programs are usually the outcome of one of two driving forces: the CEO recognizes the need for its initiation due to financial losses, severe customer dissatisfaction, or the recognition of situations being out of control; or the program could be initiated because of a demand from an outside force, for example, major customers require it, certification requirement, or some other governing force. Naturally, it is best if the CEO of the company initiates the effort and is fully convinced of its need and benefits. In this situation the company is always likely to stay committed, and the CEO will be there to offer direction and support when situations become challenging.

This, however, isn't always the case and quite commonly the requirement for such programs is brought on by outside forces. This is not as impressive as having the company take on the initiative themselves, but many times is almost as effective. Being required to initiate such a program isn't always a bad thing. The organization isn't left any option but to do it, and in many situations the outside *force* continues to monitor the program and effort and demands continuous improvement. So even though the program may not have been the company's brainchild, after it is launched it normally follows a route of continuous improvement and becomes ingrained within the organization.

LAUNCHING THE PROGRAM

Choosing the Head of a Quality Program

One of the first moves in launching a comprehensive quality program is to secure a *champion* to drive it. Such a major program and effort isn't going to stay on course without a devoted driver. This individual should have significant experience in the field and profession, especially in the area of developing a program from scratch. This requires a lot more knowledge and experience than taking over an existing program.

Manufacturers who select an in-house person who lacks adequate experience to drive the quality program should also secure the services of an experienced consultant to help guide the team for at least the first year. We're not talking about a *Product Liability Prevention* consultant here, just a good quality consultant. Keep in mind, there is a difference between someone who has experience in developing a comprehensive program from scratch, and one who has experience working with programs already in place. The latter will not be as effective in handling all the logical questions that will surface during the development stage.

The most effective way to initiate a company-wide quality effort is to have the CEO launch it. The CEO needs to show the organization that he or she is firmly behind the effort and wants the program to work. The CEO should express the need for the program, establish the goals for everyone involved, and make it clear what the company wants to achieve. Programs that initiate in the middle-management ranks, or at one division instead of the corporate headquarters, are going to have a hard time succeeding if they succeed at all.

There are hard, challenging, and demanding times in the development of a comprehensive quality program, and various employees, management as well as hourly, are going to fight it. If the executive management didn't initiate the program and doesn't visibly and strongly support it, they may at times challenge certain requirements which will send the wrong message to the employees. This will result in the downfall of the effort, and the employees will use every opportunity to challenge future requirements knowing that executive management may intervene again. So the CEO and executive staff have to remain the most visible supporters of the program.

Mission and Vision Statements

The first things the CEO and the executive staff need to establish and agree on, if they're not already in place, are the *mission* and *vision* statements. These help clarify for the employees the company's primary objectives as it conducts its business.

The mission statement describes what the company is about and what it is striving to achieve. An example is shown below.

Another way of writing a mission statement is shown on page 49.

Mission Statement

It is our mission to manufacture and sell high-quality products at a competitive price, provide our customers with the highest level of customer service, and maintain an image as the industry leader.

**The Mission Statement of our company
is as follows:**

1. To effectively represent and help advance the image and interests of our customers
2. To serve the industry with highly dependable delivery and outstanding service
3. To be recognized as the best in our business

Vision Statement

Our vision is to be the recognized industry leader in new products and innovation and provide our customers with leading edge technologies that will set us apart from any competition.

The vision statement tells the organization where the company is trying to go, or what it is striving to become. An example might be as shown above.

Once these have been established by the executive group and signed off by the CEO, they need to be visible, well promoted throughout the entire company, and published in the quality manual. Everyone needs to know the objectives and future goals of the company. This includes every hourly plant employee, as well as every management person. If asked by a customer, any employee should be able to recite these two statements. The company can't achieve its goals and objectives if the employees don't know what they are.

Creating a Steering Committee and Plan

Because the comprehensive quality program along with the product liability prevention effort involves all of the departments and management, there should be an administrative team that develops and drives it, and they need to be working from a plan.

The quality program and effort should be lead by an administrative body known as the quality steering committee. The steering committee should be comprised of heads of each of the primary departments within the organization, without duplication. As an example, the steering committee might consist of the following department heads: quality, engineering, sales, marketing, customer service, manufacturing, finance, purchasing, human resources, data processing, research and development, and the president or general manager, whoever is the highest position at corporation, division, or location. It is clearly evident from such membership that all of the primary departments are represented. What isn't needed, however, are two people from the same department or interest.

The quality head should serve as the facilitator of the committee, but the outcome needs to be created by consensus. The same is true for the President or CEO. The individual needs to be a member of the committee, but should function as a regular member of the team and not take control. The CEO should ensure that the effort stays on track, meets its commitments and remains productive, but the CEO should not overpower the committee or members will stop constructively participating and just wait for the CEO to call all the shots.

Once the committee has been formed, one of their first objectives will be to create a quality plan. The quality plan will outline all the procedures, processes, training programs, and other activities that the company needs to put into place in order to improve the overall quality effort. The plan should resemble a Gantt Chart, and should be about three years in length. No comprehensive quality program is going to be developed in a year. It will typically take two years just to have most of the basics in place, say 60 percent of the planned programs and efforts, and three to five years before it gets to about the 80 percent level.

CONTENTS OF A COMPREHENSIVE PROGRAM

In order to create a quality plan, the newly created steering committee needs to understand all of the potential elements of a typical total quality program in order to establish their priorities. This would involve the development of procedures as well as other plant programs and efforts to support the newly created quality effort. The following list includes a number of such elements under the appropriate headings:

Administration
- Developing the quality steering Committee's agenda for routine meetings
- Conducting informative presentations to all the management employees on what the quality program and effort consists
- Procedure for developing and maintaining the quality plan
- Procedure showing outline of departmental quality responsibilities
- Procedure for the development and revision of quality procedures

- Procedure for the development and revision of (office) process instructions
- Procedure for establishing personal quality goals and objectives
- Training for shop supervisors and leads on holding effective departmental quality meetings
- Training for shop employees on their role in departmental quality meetings
- Procedure for holding departmental quality meetings
- Procedure for internal quality systems audit
- Putting together the comprehensive quality cost program
- Procedure for quality records retention
- Procedure for outlining a disaster plan

Human Resources
- Procedure for new employee orientation
- Plans for ongoing employee quality training
- Procedure for the documentation of employee quality training
- Procedure for timing and content of performance reviews
- Program for quality improvement recognition and reward

Marketing
- Procedure or plans for conducting external customer satisfaction assessments
- Procedure for warranty control

Sales
- Procedure for addressing project requests
- Procedure for handling requests for estimates
- Procedure for entering a sales order
- Procedure for changing a sales order
- Procedure for inventory planning and management

Product Creation
- Procedure addressing new product development and introduction
- Procedure for the handling of prototypes
- Procedure for addressing design reviews
- Procedure outlining reliability testing of new products/components/processes

- Procedure for addressing graphics and color control
- Procedure to control the development and distribution of blueprints
- Procedure for engineering change requests/notices
- Procedure outlining first piece approvals (internal)
- Procedure for the control of packaging/crating development

Manufacturing Engineering

- Procedure for the development and control of process instructions
- Procedure for the development and control of tools, jigs and templates
- Procedure for the development and control of bill of materials

Purchasing

- Procedure for external first piece approvals
- Procedure for receiving inspection
- Supplier performance evaluation program
- Procedure for supplier and subcontractor selection and qualification
- Control of subcontracted or vendor supplied products/materials

Production

- Procedure for the development and control of manufacturing process instructions
- The display and accessibility of manufacturing process instruction manuals
- Assigning responsibilities for the documentation of processes
- Procedure for daily scrap reporting
- Detailed tracking of internal rework
- Corrective action procedure
- Preventive maintenance program
- Equipment calibration program
- Program and procedure for the routine testing of products
- Final inspection procedures and processes
- Procedures for placing products on-hold
- Procedures for the control of nonconforming materials
- Daily process audits by supervisors

Customer Service

- Procedure for handling customer quality complaints
- Procedures for handling returned goods
- Recall procedure

Putting together a good quality plan may take the steering committee days or weeks. The committee needs to study issues like the ones previously listed, as well as other known issues, and they need to set priorities on which to address first. The initial planning meeting should take place off-site where all the members can concentrate on the objective. This might be a multiday off-site meeting. The quality plan created may look like that shown in Figure 3.1.

Elements of a Quality Plan

Important elements to remember in creating a quality plan are as follows:

- Each line item should be a specific project that is well identified.
- Identify one person as being responsible for driving one line item project.
- Firmly establish the start and finish timelines.
- List milestones.

Identify the Project

Let's expound further on these elements and explain the significance. To begin with, each line item needs to be a specific and understandable project. During a brainstorming session it is very common to get into a deep discussion, initiate what everyone feels is an important plan line item, and six months later not remember what the line item means anymore. Secondly, no line item is likely to be accomplished by just the individual listed; in all probability each line item will require an effort by two to three people. But only one person should be listed as the primary driver or party responsible. When you list all three that will work on it, often nothing happens because each is waiting for the other to act.

Establish a Timeline

Firmly establish the start and finish lines. It is understood if a major two- to three-year program is launched on a specific date, say January, that everything still needs to be done. But you wouldn't have all the

QUALITY PLAN

PROJECT/PROCEDURE DESCRIPTION	JAN	FEB	MAR	APR	MAY	JUN	JUL	AUG	SEP	OCT	NOV	DEC	RESP
1 ADMINISTRATION													
A Develop a procedure for establishing quality goals	ABDE												
B Establish a comprehensive cost of quality program			A B C	D E	F								
C Develop a procedure for quality records retention			A B	D E F									
2 PERSONNEL DEVELOPMENT													
A Develop plans for ongoing employee training			A D E										
B Develop a procedure for employee quality reward and recognition					A B	D E F							
3 MARKETING													
A Develop a procedure or plan for conducting external customer satisfaction assessments									A B	C D E F			
4 SALES													
A Develop a procedure for handling contract review							A B	D E F					
B Develop a procedure for entering a sales order								A B C	D E F				
5 PRODUCT CREATION													
A Develop a procedure addressing new product development and introduction				A B C	D E F								
B Create a design review team, and a product safety team						A B	D E F						
C Develop a procedure outlining reliability testing of new products							A B C	D E F					
6 MANUFACTURING ENGINEERING													
A Develop a procedure for the control of manufacturing processes				A B C		D E F							
B Develop a procedure for equipment calibration								A B C D E F					
7 PURCHASING													
A Develop a procedure for receiving inspection				A B C D E F									
B Develop a procedure for supplier or subcontractor selection and qualification									A B	C D E F			
8 PRODUCTION													
A Develop a procedure for final inspection procedures & processes				A B C	D E F								
B Develop a procedure for the identification and control of materials						A B D E F							
9 CUSTOMER SERVICE													
A Develop a procedure for handling customer quality complaints								A B C	D E F				
B Develop a procedure for handling returned goods										A B C D E F			
BAR COLOR CODE				COMPLETED					TO BE COMPLETED				

QUALITY PLAN MILESTONES

A. Assign project to Committee member
B. Develop rough draft of final plan / procedure / process
C. Develop associated forms
D. Obtain approval of final form / plan
E. Distribute new procedure / process
F. Orientate or train employees

Figure 3.1 Quality Plan Gantt Chart

implementation lines start in January because each individual project wouldn't start at the same time, nor would they finish at the same time. The priorities first need to be established as to which projects to address early, and then the designated driver of that project should commit to a timeline that is agreeable to everyone. This means that the committee shouldn't agree to a 12-month timeline if they only think it should take two to three months to complete a project. And most importantly, they should not allow project timelines to be moved because the driver is too busy doing other things. Commit to a timeline for a line item project, and make it happen.

Determine Milestones

There needs to be milestones within each timeline so the committee knows that the project is developing on schedule. If you just place on the chart a two-month bar for a specific project, the individual responsible for the project can try to make everything happen in the final week and technically always say they're on schedule. When people follow this type of practice they're not likely to get their projects done on time, and the projects are apt to look like something that was crammed together instantly. So a generic list of milestones should be created that have universal application. It should also be mentioned that a timeline doesn't require the use of all the milestones listed, just the ones that relate. So while one project timeline might include milestones A–F, another might only involve milestones A, C, D, and F. At each upcoming steering committee meeting the group should go over the plan and members should update their progress on each individual project. Each of the timelines should then be lightened according to the milestone met.

In the early stages and months of the program's development, the committee will likely meet on a weekly basis in order to stay on track and maintain the momentum. As the program continues and the initial wave of elements are completed, the committee will meet on a biweekly basis, and eventually it will become a monthly meeting which will continue indefinitely.

THE QUALITY SYSTEM

One of the most significant products of the quality effort is the documented system of procedures and processes which will be created and continuously updated. If properly designed and followed, the quality system will be one of the most effective tools in the prevention of quality problems, as well as potential product liability incidents. In its best form, it is the single most comprehensive collection of documented practices and safeguards for ensuring that the corporation is going to produce a safe and reliable product for the marketplace. If needed at a later date, it will also become one of the most effective tools in proving in court through the records maintained that the manufacturing firm did make every effort to assure the production of a safe and reliable product.

There are a multitude of ways taught on how a corporation should go about developing their own quality program. This book minimally describes how the system should be developed but focuses more on what it should include for the sake of preventing unsafe products and designs.

In all the recommendations that exist on proposed quality system content, probably the best list of ingredients is incorporated in the ISO standards.

Understanding the ISO 9000 Standard

The ISO standard was created by the International Organization for Standardization. The organization is the specialized international agency for standardization, at the time of this publication comprising the national standards bodies of 91 countries. The American National Standards Institute (ANSI) is the member body representing the United States. ISO is made up of approximately 180 Technical Committees. Each Technical Committee is responsible for one of many areas of specialization ranging from asbestos to zinc. The purpose of ISO is to promote the development of standardization and related world activities to facilitate the international exchange of goods and services, and to develop cooperation in intellectual, scientific, technological, and economic activity. The results of ISO technical work are published as international standards.

From their initiation until the year 2000 the ISO 9000 series was a set of five individual, but related, international standards on quality management and quality assurance. They are generic, not specific to any particular products. They can be used by manufacturing and service industries alike. These standards were developed to effectively document the quality system elements to be implemented in order to maintain an efficient quality system. The standards were broken down in the following manner:

ISO 9000   The basic guidelines for selection and use.

ISO 9001   The actual document used for implementation and registration. Includes design, development, production, installation and servicing requirements.

ISO 9002   Actual document for implementation and registration. Includes production, installation, and servicing.

ISO 9003   Document for implementing final inspection and testing.

ISO 9004   Quality management and quality systems elements-guidelines.

Corporations around the globe have built and continue to build their quality systems around these standards. Both large and small companies with international businesses perceive the ISO 9000 series as a route to open markets and improved competitiveness. European and other foreign customers expect U.S. companies to have their quality systems registered to the ISO 9000 standard. This generally involves having an accredited independent third party conduct an on-site audit of the company's operations against the requirements of the appropriate standard. Upon successful completion of this audit, the company will receive a registration certificate that identifies the quality system as being in compliance. Your company will also be listed in a register maintained by the accredited third-party registration organization.

The ISO 9001 standard looks for the following 20 elements to be in place:

1. **Management responsibility:** To define, document, and implement a policy for quality.

2. **Quality system:** To establish, document, and maintain a quality system which includes a quality manual, system procedures, and quality planning.

3. **Contract review:** To establish and maintain documented procedures for contract review.

4. **Design control:** To establish and maintain documented procedures to control and verify the design of the product to ensure conformance to specified requirements.

5. **Document and data control:** To establish and maintain documented procedures to control all documents and data (including hard copy and electronic media) including such documents as standards and customer drawings.

6. **Purchasing:** To establish and maintain documented procedures to ensure that purchased product, associated documents, and data conform to requirements. Subcontractors are to be evaluated and selected on their ability to meet subcontract requirements and the type and extent of control exercised by the supplier over subcontractors is to be defined.

7. **Control of customer-supplied product:** To establish and maintain documented procedures for the control of verification, storage, and maintenance of customer-supplied product provided for incorporation into the supplies or for related activities.

8. **Product identification and traceability:** Where appropriate, to establish and maintain documented procedures for identifying the product from receipt and during all stages of production, delivery, and installation.

9. **Process control:** To identify and plan the production, installation, and servicing processes which directly affect quality, and to ensure these processes are carried out under controlled conditions.

10. **Inspection and testing:** To establish and maintain documented procedures for inspection and testing activities, in order to verify that the specified requirements for the product are met.

11. **Control of inspection, measuring, and test equipment:** To establish and maintain documented procedures to control, calibrate, and maintain inspection, measuring, and test equipment (including test software) used by the supplier to demonstrate the conformance of product to the specified requirements.

12. **Inspection and test status:** The inspection and test status of product shall be identified and maintained throughout the production, installation, and servicing of the product to ensure that only product that has passed the required inspections and tests (or released under an authorized concession) is dispatched, used, or installed.

13. **Control of nonconforming product:** To establish and maintain documented procedures to ensure that product that does not conform to specified requirements is prevented from unintended use or installation.

14. **Corrective and preventive action:** To establish and maintain documented procedures for implementing corrective action in the handling of customer complaints, product nonconformities, and the application of controls to ensure corrective action is taken and that it is effective. Preventive action procedures will detect, analyze, and eliminate potential causes of nonconformities.

15. **Handling, storage, packaging, preservation, and delivery:** To establish and maintain documented procedures to prevent damage or deterioration of product.

16. **Control of quality records:** To establish and maintain documented procedures for identification, collection, indexing, access, filing, storage, maintenance, and disposition of quality records. Quality records shall be maintained to demonstrate conformance to specified requirements and the effective operation of the quality system.

17. **Internal quality audits:** To establish and maintain documented procedures for planning and implementing internal quality audits to verify whether quality activities and related results comply with planned arrangements and to determine the effectiveness of the quality system.

18. **Training:** To establish and maintain documented procedures for identifying training needs and provide for the training of all personnel performing activities affecting quality. Appropriate records of training shall be maintained.

19. **Servicing:** Where servicing is a specified requirement, to establish and maintain documented procedures for performing, verifying, and reporting that the servicing meets the specified requirements.

20. **Statistical techniques:** The supplier shall identify the need for statistical techniques required for establishing, controlling, and verifying process capability and product characteristics, and shall establish and maintain documented procedures to implement and control their application.

Starting in 2000 the standard was revised and identified as ISO 9001:2000. The structure of the ISO 9001:2000 brings together the original 20-element requirement structure under four major headings.

TOTAL QUALITY MANAGEMENT

The TQM Focus

As the ISO standard primarily focuses on the technical product and control of the production process, the focus of TQM programs is to ensure total employee involvement in the management process, and in attaining total customer satisfaction. A fault in the TQM perception in the early '90s was that it steered too far away from the technical product and concentrated more on the promotion of teamwork, employee involvement, and customer surveys aimed at measuring satisfaction. Teamwork and customer satisfaction were significant improvements to the original quality control focus, but the dissemination of capacities like quality engineering and reliability assurance, even quality management, were a mistake.

The Structure of ISO 9001:2000

ISO 9001:2000

5.0 Management Responsibility
    5.1 General
    5.2 Customer needs and requirements**
    5.3 Quality policy
    5.4 Quality objectives and planning
    5.5 Quality management system
    5.6 Management review
6.0 Resource Management
    6.1 General
    6.2 Human resources**
        training
    6.3 Other resources
        information**
        infrastructure**
        work environment
7.0 Process Management
    7.1 General**
    7.2 Customer-Related**
        needs and expectations**
        review of needs, etc.**
        capability to meet needs
        customer communications**
    7.3 Design and Development
        design and development
        product/service validation/verification**
        configuration management
        Purchasing
        Production/Service Operations
        identification and traceability
        control of process operations
        handling, storage, etc.
        validation of processes**
    7.6 Control of non-conforming product
    7.7 Post-delivery**

8.0 Measurement, Analysis, and Improvement
    8.1 General
        Measurement
        system performance**
        customer satisfaction**
        internal audits
        process measures
        product measures
        inspection and test records
        control of test, measurement, inspection equipment
    8.3 Analysis of Data
    8.4 Improvement
        corrective action
        preventive action
        improvement processes

ISO 9001:1994

4.1-Management Responsibility
4.2-Quality System
4.5-Document and Data Control
4.16-Quality Records
4.1-Management Responsibility
4.9-Process Control
4.18-Training
4.3-Contract Review
4.4-Design Control
4.6-Purchasing
4.7-Control of Customer-Supplied Product
4.8-Product Identification and Traceability
4.9-Process Control
4.10-Inspection and Testing
4.12-Inspection and Test Records
4.13-Control of Nonconforming Goods
4.14-Corrective and Preventive Action
4.15-Handling, Storage, etc.
4.19-Servicing
4.1-Management Responsibility
4.10-Inspection and Testing
4.11-Control of Inspection, Measuring, Test Equip.
4.17-Internal Quality Audit
4.20-Statistical Techniques

Many manufacturing corporations in the late '80s and early '90s finally got on the quality bandwagon and involved all their employees, but some got carried in the wrong direction. The management and employees should have been involved in assuring quality. It wasn't just the quality control department's responsibility. The manufacturing corporations decided that now that management and the employees were significantly focused on following the quality program, they could eliminate the quality titled positions. Quality managers and directors were laid off or moved into other roles within the organization.

Manufacturing corporations have to focus on total quality, steer toward the ISO standard whether they actually go for certification or not, and get management and the employees involved. This may not be to the extent of self-managed departments, line employees on steering committees, and other radical aspects taught in some versions of TQM, but there needs to be a comprehensive program in place, there needs to be experienced quality people driving it, and the hourly employees need to be an active part in the process. So rather than calling the program a TQM program, it might be better to refer to it as a total quality program.

Writing a Quality Procedure

Although we have identified 45 to 50 key procedures that should be developed, it is not unusual for the entire system once established to consist of up to 75 procedures. Although such systems and procedures appear to represent bureaucracy to a certain degree, it should not be perceived as being *bureaucratic*. Every organization has to establish procedures because the lack of procedures breeds chaos. The key to not becoming bureaucratic is to keep the procedures simple. Quality procedures just need to identify what needs to be done and be followed. Procedures need to follow certain guidelines and formats, but there isn't a specific way that they have to be written. The examples shown in this book are just one method for consideration.

AUDITS AND INSPECTIONS

To assure the quality system is being followed, as well as all the associated processes and practices, requires routine auditing by various parties. In decades past, the quality assurance department performed all such audits and inspections with its own department of employees. During the '90s, and the advent of total quality management, most of these quality assurance departments were dispersed. Today's program depends on its players to ensure its success. The program is written by the various members of management, and has to be audited by these members to ensure compliance.

There are basically two primary areas of focus here, one is the audits to ensure the procedures and processes are being followed, and the other is the inspection of the product itself. Both issues require routine formal checks, as well as documented findings for possible future reference.

Audits

The quality system procedures need to be formally audited once every 6 to 12 months, to assure compliance. There are a number of ways in which this can be handled. One method for handling this is for the quality head to give the responsibility to the primary member of the quality steering committee, and monitor that the function is carried out. For instance, a procedure for controlling blueprint development would be audited to ensure its compliance by the head of product engineering, who would have initially had the key role in its development. An alternative method would be for the steering committee to create an auditing team of cross functional employees, and give them the project of auditing the system. And probably the last method would be for the quality head, or any members of the department, to audit the system. The best method, I find, is for the heads of the various departments to audit their own procedures, which helps ensure continuous buy-in and ownership. When the audits take place, they should be fully documented. There will typically be one of three findings: (1) the procedure was being fully followed; (2) the procedure wasn't totally being followed as written and it was found that there were slight deviations, requiring either disciplinary action, or a need for the procedure to be updated and revised; or (3) the procedure wasn't being followed at all, which would logically require serious reaction.

Product Inspection

As it relates to inspections, these are typically the verifications that the components of the product, or the product itself, was produced in compliance with the standards and specifications that apply. Just like auditing procedures and processes, this too would often involve documented results. Was the final product fully inspected and tested prior to it being shipped? Were there inspections that were made at key intervals of the products assembly? Were there inspections of the raw materials when they were received to ensure they complied with what was specified? There are many possible key stages in a product's development where the product requires an inspection. The important elements are that management supplies good documented direction as to what the inspection needs to involve, and that there is a good record that the inspection took place. Although the stage is referred to as *inspection* it doesn't necessarily mean that it is handled by quality control type inspectors. It can simply mean that the production operator is responsible for performing a detailed inspection at some stage of the process, per a predefined set of instructions, and is hence referred to as an *inspector*. Just like the management in a total quality environment, the individual operators are responsible for producing a good quality product and assuring it themselves, as opposed to having someone else ensure everyone is doing their job.

TRACKING KEY PERFORMANCE INDICATORS

Establishing Quality Costs

Quality costs, or the cost of quality, are primarily the costs that a manufacturer incurs for not producing a product right the first time. These consist of costs related to scrap, rework, returns, warranty costs, and more. In their most comprehensive form, quality costs cover all associated areas of the quality effort, including costs associated with all aspects of prevention and appraisal, as well as internal and external failure costs. This would include quality departmental salaries, costs of training programs to improve quality, inspection costs, special testing and analysis, and other costs and efforts that were either expended to help control or improve on quality, or were the result of poor quality.

These costs are compiled and then compared to the actual sales dollar volume of production. In other words, if the manufacturer produced $1 million worth of product (sales dollar value) in a given month, and in the course of producing that amount of product experienced $40,000 worth of scrap, $30,000 in having to rework various components and product, $10,000 worth of returns from customers in the field, another $10,000 in warranty repairs in the field, and lastly spent another $10,000 on inspection salaries, costs of training, laboratory testing, and so on, these would be the manufacturer's quality costs, or cost of quality. They would amount to 10 percent of sales.

Comparing Quality Costs

It is also important for the manufacturer to gather the costs and compare the costs to output, as opposed to just looking at the figure itself. In the previous example the manufacturer experienced $40,000 worth of scrap, but produced $1 million worth of product. If the manufacturing team reduced this scrap figure to $30,000 in the following month, it would first appear as though a substantial improvement was made, or that scrap was reduced 25 percent. But if in fact the plant only produced $500,000 worth of product that month, the percent of scrap would have gone from 4 percent up to 6 percent, and their performance would have in fact, worsened. So in the analysis of any cost factor, it is important to compare that figure to the overall picture.

The management's objective would be to then gather these costs on a regular basis (at least monthly), chart the costs, do a breakdown by source, identify the root causes, and initiate corrective actions. If the manufacturer doesn't perform a comprehensive breakdown of quality costs, they should at least track costs related to scrap, rework, warranty, and returns. These costs are the dollars lost due to poor quality and serve as part of the report card for how well the company, or any department within the company, is doing. Charting these figures on a monthly basis allows the quality steering committee to identify trends and immediately see whether such trends are getting worse, better, or remaining relatively flat. Naturally the goal is to show continuous improvement.

Other key performance factors might include on-time performance, as it would relate to shipping the product to the customer, as well as incremental factors such as producing the product on time, generating the required blueprints and specifications on time, and ensuring that raw materials arrive on time.

Engineering Change Requests
Another element to track is the number of engineering change requests submitted, or the number submitted due to engineering error as opposed to changes submitted as a result of improvements of material substitutions. The more design or engineering error found in a product, the more potential for catastrophic failure, which could lead to product liability. Other key performance indicators include tracking overall customer satisfaction and ratings points collected through the use of customer satisfaction surveys.

In their most comprehensive form, quality costs track everything from preventive and appraisal costs to internal and external quality failure. If a company elects not to track all of those costs, especially the costs of prevention and appraisal, they at least need to track the losses ranging from scrap, rework, and warranty. They can *gut feel* the amount of prevention and appraisal, but they need to have hard facts regarding dollar losses and which way they are trending.

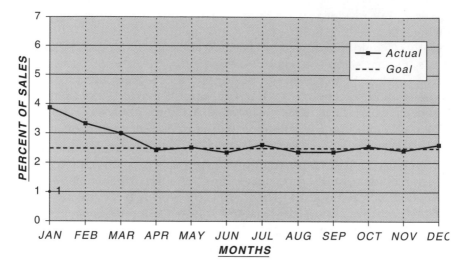

Figure 3.2   Lacking incentives for continuous improvement.

Quality Costs Goals

Another important element in monitoring quality costs is establishing goals. Managers need to have goals set for them, and they need to be evaluated on how well they're achieving those goals. Setting a goal of *zero defects* is admirable but impractical. There will always be a level of defects and losses, so achievable goals and objectives need to be established.

Another common problem occurs when management establishes a flat line goal for the plant or a department within the plant. Say for instance the quality costs were between 2 percent to 4 percent for the previous year, so management sets the flat line goal at 2 percent for the next year. The problem with this scenario is once manufacturing reaches the goal line, they can then coast from that point forward, maintain *status quo,* and not have to worry about trying any harder. They achieved the goal set by management and can't be criticized for not doing any better. Such a trend is shown in Figure 3.2.

The better way to set operating goals is to establish descending monthly goals that are achievable and demonstrate continuous improvement. The managers can be evaluated each month on whether they met or exceeded their goals and are continually challenged. Such a graph is shown in Figure 3.3.

The bottom line to determining and tracking key performance indicators is that the management team will never know the exact

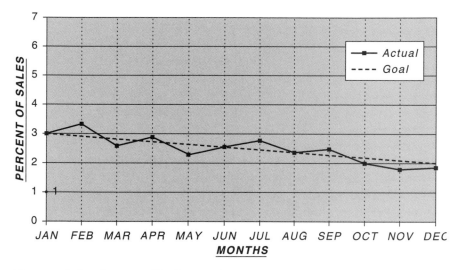

Figure 3.3 A more effective goal.

amount of improvement they were responsible for creating, unless they can assign some value to the element and analytically track it. The quality cost chart is the key performance indication on how well your quality program and effort is doing. It is quite common for any management team to try their hardest to bring about improvement, and from a *gut feel* think they have in fact contributed to an overall improvement in the operation. But without gathering some sort of statistical data, such *gut feels* are usually without merit and lack credibility.

THE THREE PRIMARY FOCUSES OF THE STEERING COMMITTEE MEETING

When the quality steering committee meets, their agenda should be divided into at least three areas of focus (as shown in Figure 3.4): the administrative system, key performance indicators, and other quality issues and opportunities. Where they are in the development of the program will determine how much time will be set aside for each topic. For instance, in the early part of the program when most of the systems and procedures still need to be developed, the lion's share of the meeting will likely be devoted to administration. As time goes on, however, the percentages might change and eventually even out. The key thing is for the quality head to develop agendas for the meetings that will cover activities and issues in all these focus issues, and not just meet on the development of quality procedures or process instructions.

Figure 3.4   The steering committee focus.

TAKING QUALITY TO THE NEXT LEVEL

Whether the company already has a comprehensive system in place, or needs to build one, the next objective is to incorporate the product liability prevention elements into the system and take the entire program to a whole new level. These elements will be explained in each of the upcoming chapters.

A whole new role develops for the quality professional, if that is the individual who is selected to drive this expanded effort. The director of quality could now be titled the Director of Quality and Product Liability Prevention, as an example. As opposed to the quality position losing ground as it did during the TQM onset, it now gains significant responsibility in not only helping the corporation steer clear of potential product liability actions, but also by playing an important role in any future litigation matters.

Reliability Testing

A critical step in the new product design process, especially as it relates to assuring quality and product reliability, is product testing. It is also a key factor in the courtrooms of product liability. Manufacturers need to thoroughly assure their products will live up to customer expectations, as well as withstand probable misuse. Ultimately, the manufacturer needs to be in a position to one day say to the courts if necessary, "We are a concerned and caring company, and made every practical effort to ensure the safety and reliability of our product."

Reliability tests come in at least four phases: component reliability verification, prototype design validation, field beta tests, and routine daily production tests. Each of these tests is critical in the new product development life cycle.

The routine everyday inspection and reliability tests performed on or off the assembly lines help ensure the consistency of the products being produced. These might be performed on 100 percent of the units or a daily statistical sampling. Laboratory or controlled environment reliability tests are conducted to push the product to its extreme in many areas. They might entail extreme temperature tests, mechanical endurance tests, moisture and other forms of climatic tests, dynamics tests, drop tests, and other types of controlled tests to ensure that the product will withstand what it may be made to endure.

Many leading manufacturers and their quality assurance departments create their own reliability testing labs furnished with the necessary equipment. Creating an in-house testing laboratory or test center has significant advantages for the manufacturer, and especially the in-house product liability expert. Many products are designed on speculation and theory, but in a properly equipped test center elements of design can be proven and become a wealth of knowledge for the organization. In some instances, the manufacturer even has the lab certified by agencies such as Underwriters Laboratories, allowing them to perform the same tests needed to attain Underwriter Laboratory (UL) Approval.

ESTABLISHING A POLICY

Reliability tests as well as routine inspection tests play an important part in assuring the quality and dependability of a product. In addition to testing and assuring the reliability of complete products, manufacturers also need to validate the reliability of supplied components. Suppliers of component parts will often flaunt the product's abilities to withstand certain exposures and applications, such as saying, "Our product will not fade in direct sunlight for at least three years," but will actually offer the end user a 12-month warranty against fading. The manufacturer then takes the supplier at his word and uses the product in an application where it is critical that the product definitely not fade within three years, and loses. When such failures take place, the manufacturer tries to go after the supplier for resolution, but the supplier merely references his published warranty which never stated that the product was guaranteed for that time frame or actual type of exposure.

The manufacturer of the end product cannot afford the risks of placing untested products in the marketplace, or gambling on weak assurances. To ensure adequate testing routinely takes place, the quality system administrative group needs to put a policy and procedure in place that outlines the requirements for testing new products or newly introduced materials. The testing should prove that the products or components will live up to expected applications, as well as comply with any standards set by the industry or regulatory agencies.

The organization needs to recognize the extreme parameters of what their products are likely to be exposed to in trying to establish procedures and guidelines for testing products and materials. From a climactic perspective this might involve temperature extremes, exposure to sunlight, high humidity or rain, extreme dryness, or salt spray. From other perspectives it could involve variations in voltage, or handling misuse and abuse or other considerations. The management team needs to determine the required parameters of such testing and incorporate it into related procedures. The quality procedure on page 71 is an example of such a policy.

GE
 	
Goodden
Enterprises
	QUALITY PROCEDURE
	
	RELIABILITY TESTING
	OF NEW
	PRODUCTS/COMPONENTS/PROCESSES
		Number 503
		Effective Date 1/1/20xx
		Revision Date
		Page 1 of 2
		TOTAL
		    QUALITY
		        SYSTEM

1.0 PURPOSE

1.1 To ensure that all new products, components, or special assembly processes are tested for reliability in performance, prior to utilization.

2.0 TEST PARAMETERS

2.1 All materials and processes designed for indoor products must be able to withstand a -10F degree exposure as well as a 120F degree environment for a 24-hour period, before being considered acceptable. The product must be able to function at 120F degrees for 24 hours.

2.2 All products, materials, and processes designed for outdoor application must be able to withstand a temperature range of -40F to 130F for a 48-hour period prior to being considered acceptable.

2.3 Electronic components will be submitted for testing and analysis at the same temperature parameters listed above, prior to their use.

2.4 Materials considered for use in windows will be subjected to accelerated sunlight testing for a 3-year equivalent, without noticeable color fade or material degradation, prior to their use.

2.5 Materials and coatings considered fro outdoor use will be subjected to accelerated sunlight testing for a 5-year equivalent, without showing signs of noticeable color fade or material degradation, prior to their use.

2.6 New adhesives will be dynamics tested at -10F and +120F degrees, prior to their use.

3.0 PROCEDURE

DEPT 3.1 Must submit all new concepts, untried electronic components,
HEAD   as well as coatings and adhesives, to the Test Center for reliability testing, prior to their purchase or use.

DEPT 3.2 Will complete the Evaluation Request form (Process
HEAD   Instruction QA005) and submit it along with samples to the Test Center.

AUDITOR:_____ DATE: _____	**AUDIT**	IN COMPLIANCE OUT OF COMPLIANCE

Continued

Continued

QUALITY PROCEDURE	Effective Date 1/1/20xx	Number 503
RELIABILITY TESTING PROCEDURE	Page 2 of 2	Revision Date

RELI ENG 3.3   Will perform the necessary tests outlined under TEST PARAMETERS.

RELI ENG 3.4   Will furnish the requesting department a final report on the product's test performance.

RELI ENG 3.5   Will maintain a master file of all products tested and the results, for a 10-year period.

President	Director of Quality & Product Reliability
Sales Manager	Controller
Director of Engineering	Director of Customer Service

RELIABILITY TEST RESULTS AND REPORTS

Test Results

A major concern in the field of product liability is the results attained and the reports generated related to testing. If not handled properly such reports could have a devastating effect on the manufacturer, should the product ever be involved in a product liability action. Just like many other areas of document control, the liability expert or corporate review team has to watch the types of reports generated by this function and how they are handled.

Product reliability tests can generate some pretty surprising and unexpected results. A motor is put through an extreme endurance test and suddenly bursts into flames. An electrical product is run under reasonably adverse conditions and catastrophically shorts out. A mechanical apparatus is dynamics tested and suddenly falls apart. The results were totally unexpected, but are now noted in a report. There isn't anything wrong with this; what is important is how the manufacturer reacts once this information is known. If improvements were made to the product and the product was then retested and proven successful, then the manufacturer reacted in a responsible manner. If the manufacturer sees the test results and elects to do nothing regarding design improvements, this reaction could be viewed as negligent at a later date.

Test Reports

Results generated by various reliability tests are needed in the evaluation of potential risks, but the actual reports followed by the company's actions can be as detrimental as they are beneficial. Training on how to write such reports should take place with the parties involved. For instance, when writing a test report the reliability test engineer should state only the facts, what actually happened in the test, and should not add personal opinions or speculative possibilities to the report. This isn't to say that such concerns can't be verbally discussed, but they should not be contained in any written document unless some type of design improvement is going to be made.

Test reports and memos should be void of such words as *defective, unsafe,* or *hazardous* when referring to the results of a test or condition of a product, unless the design at that point is completely revised. If the company identifies in a report or memo a potential problem with a product design, and then elects to do nothing about it for no appreciable reason, the report could surface during future litigation and end up being read in the courtroom.

IN-PROCESS AND FINAL INSPECTION TESTING

Equally as important as laboratory or reliability testing is the element of daily production tests. These could be receiving inspection tests, in-process testing at various stages of production, or final inspection tests which might take place just before the product is packaged or shipped. As with more sophisticated laboratory testing, daily production tests can sometimes yield unexpected results that end up being recorded on some document or daily test report. An electrical product or motorized product suddenly malfunctions during routine testing and starts on fire. The question then arises as to how the manufacturer reacted and what the corrective course of action included. Was just the product itself removed from production, or were investigations launched to determine whether there is a widespread component or design defect? Were actions taken to address the rest of the products produced or being produced?

Another important question that arises when dealing with in-process inspection tests is whether the employers and supervisors know what to do in the event a defective condition suddenly surfaces during the course of normal testing. A common practice would be for the defective unit to be removed from the line. However, the operator or department supervisor needs to notify the quality assurance department of the defective product.

STANDARDS FOR TESTING

It is common for management or new product development teams to establish their own reliability test criteria for each new product conceived. It is even common to see customers dictate to suppliers the type of reliability testing procedures they want to see the manufacturers carry out for products they plan to purchase. When manufacturers look at testing their products, they should first determine whether a recognized test standard already exists, before they develop a custom test program. If the reliability testing of a product comes into question at a later date, the manufacturer will be in a better position to say they followed a recognized standard than to say they tested the product per their own procedure. Manufacturers who aren't aware of the testing standards that exist need to look into MIL Standard tests or search the ASTM standards materials.

Selecting the In-house Product Liability Expert and Creating the Corporate Product Liability Team

5

SELECTING THE IN-HOUSE EXPERT

The key aspects of this book are not only to promote the concept of taking the comprehensive quality program to the next level or dimension which is product liability prevention, but also to promote the creation of the position of in-house product liability expert. This is especially the recommendation for those companies that do not have a legal department, or a legal department that gets involved in the design and manufacture of new products or other day-to-day management and product issues.

The selection of an in-house product liability expert is critical to the ongoing success of this focus and effort. Although all the members of the management team will be forever involved in this effort, it will still require a constant driver to keep the program on track. In addition, this select individual will be directly involved in any future product liability incidents that surface, as well as play a key role in litigation management and to represent the company in trial.

The position of in-house product liability expert is not proposed to be a full-time position, unless the company is overwhelmed with lawsuits, which we will assume is not the case. The expert will likely be selected from the current management staff and will assume these responsibilities in addition to those already held. Of course the author is proposing that the head of quality be the in-house product liability expert for all the reasons which follow.

It is important to state, however, that the in-house product liability expert must be someone who is on the executive staff, as opposed to a *middle-management* individual or engineer. The expert must report to the president, or the highest position within the corporation, and not just to a staff member. If the head of quality is not at this level, it may be a problem. In situations where the highest quality position reports to a staff member, the individual will in all probability have a difficult time impressing other staff management to change the ways of their departments, as well as to incorporate a great number of other improvements.

In some manufacturing corporations, especially those that may only maintain one titled quality person, that person may be a quality manager or even a quality engineer, while the rest of the staff consists of vice presidents or directors of manufacturing, engineering, research and development, and sales, which this individual may have little influence over. So the selected candidate needs to be a member to the company's executive staff and at the same level as the others reporting to the CEO.

Responsibilities of the In-house Product Liability Expert

The in-house product liability expert must have expert knowledge of the technical product. This cannot be a modern day TQM instructor who maintains little to no in-depth technical knowledge of products or processes. Critiquing new product designs, as well as investigating catastrophic product failure in the field, requires an in-depth knowledge of every aspect of the product and its capabilities. A promoter of teamwork and customer satisfaction won't suffice. If this is the case with the quality head, the individual either needs to start learning about the technical product, or someone else needs to head up this focus and the quality head will just be a member of the product liability team.

This is one of the unfortunate situations with many companies that may have gone to an extreme measure with TQM in the late '80s and early '90s, and probably pursued Malcolm Baldrige criteria instead of programs like ISO 9000 or its related counterparts. In extreme cases the advent of TQM meant the disembodiment of the quality assurance departments and the technical product focus quality once held. In its wake the movement may have left one titled person in quality who now functions more in the terms of a human resource (HR) instructor, conducting training sessions and serving as the champion of teamwork.

Quality Reliability Testing Centers

Although I, too, embraced many of the principles of TQM, I married it with the criteria outlined in ISO 9000 and formed what I consider the best overall program and effort. Prior to the introduction of either movement, I made a unique and very rewarding decision to create an in-house quality reliability testing center, which was the first in our industry. I wanted to have the ability to thoroughly test products and ensure they would live up to the conditions exposed to them. It is all too common for companies to design products on engineering and material specs which indicate that the product design and materials incorporated should live up to the conditions that will be subjected to them. It is also quite common for suppliers of materials to either over-rate a product's abilities, or make claims that end up being very subjective. The creation of a product reliability testing center allowed me to recognize what would cause products to fail, and to see firsthand what such failure would involve.

To do this, I furnished the test center with lab equipment and test chambers that would allow us to conduct accelerated weather testing and testing for other concerns. We designed our own custom dynamics testing apparatuses, had numerous electronic monitoring devices, and a large number of other pieces of equipment and special rooms for the complete evaluation of anything we wanted to observe. This test center gave me more technical knowledge of how a product would really perform than the knowledge anyone else in the corporation, including engineering, could possess.

This was a real learning experience for me in quality, and meant that I could sit at the table in a new product development analysis and many times have more factual technical knowledge than anyone else. It is quite typical for everyone involved in technical product design and executive management to have their own opinions of how products will function in extreme or adverse conditions, and for many of these opinions to have little accuracy. I have sat through countless design reviews with product engineers, and executive managers with numerous years of experience, and discussed critical hypothetical aspects of product design and dynamic performance. The meetings would turn into personal debates of who is the smartest. Naturally the highest ranking individual commonly won.

After creating the test center and performing actual tests to either prove or disprove theory, the findings were quite often very surprising and enlightening. In future reviews, as others talked theory and speculation, I could speak for a point of fact and even supply backup data. This began to make me more of a product expert than those who were in the positions to be experts. At times such factual input was personally challenging, especially to ego driven senior management who attempted to impress others with their years of experience and knowledge.

What it taught me, however, was that everyone has an opinion. Opinions aren't worth the time it takes to express them, and nothing takes the place of the real data gained from actual studies and tests. The biggest problem is when companies react and design products from opinions and speculation, and don't take the time to acquire the needed facts. Similarly, as it relates to the nature of this book, management who think they know the law and concerns surrounding product liability can many times be more dangerous than those who outwardly admit they don't have a clue.

Another major advantage to testing products and understanding their failure mechanisms is that when a situation allegedly does happen somewhere around the country, the in-house expert can go to that location, understand what allegedly transpired, and determine its credibility. This is a major first step in debunking a possible liability case.

CHARACTER TRAITS

The in-house expert needs to be someone that the rest of the management team will listen to and respect. The seriousness of this focus will call for trying times, when critical decisions need to be made regarding important issues that may leave the company susceptible to liabilities. This individual needs to be part of that decision-making process, and the opinion of the expert needs to be heeded. If the person is in middle management, staff groups are going to meet and discuss issues not privy to such an individual. More significantly, when management teams are faced with very important issues to address in the area of product liability, such as determining whether to go with certain components or suppliers, or when talks center around whether products need to be redesigned or recalled, the in-house expert needs to be someone who the decision makers are going to listen to and respect.

The individual must also serve as consultant and educator to the rest of the organization. From the point that the in-house expert is made known, it will be common for employees in all departments to periodically have questions centered around some aspect of the product liability field, and they need to feel comfortable with contacting the in-house expert. Engineers may have questions pertaining to the need and design of warning labels or operating manuals, marketing may have questions regarding verbiage in product brochures, sales may have questions regarding customer contractual demands, and reliability engineers may have questions regarding product testing results. In all such scenarios, these individuals must not have any reservations to calling the in-house expert and discussing their concerns.

In addition, the product liability expert will need to conduct in-house seminars for the benefit of all the employees at all levels. He or she must be the kind of person that can give good presentations and lead seminars, and also be the type of person listened to by others. All of this will be crucial if the individual and effort are going to be successful in bringing about change and taking the organization in a new direction.

POSITION DEMANDS

Although the position isn't being proposed as a full-time role, it can demand periodic full-time attention. For instance, if the company is involved in litigation, the plaintiff at some point will submit to the defendant a set of interrogatories along with a request for documents. The defendant company, and its in-house expert, will have 20 days to respond to all the interrogatory questions, as well as to supply all the documents which will be demanded. Complying with such requests can take a lot of time, especially when it involves searching for the numerous documents and records demanded. Usually a product liability incident involves a product that was made years earlier. Because there is a court ordered timeline involved, the expert will need to drop everything else and begin to address the demand.

Some of the demands that come with the position of in-house product liability expert are the requirements to travel at a moments' notice when a situation involving a potential product liability incident is known, and traveling to meet with insurance representatives, attorneys, and experts when required. This can be difficult for the typical executive who maintains a constant schedule of meetings and other special appointments and conferences, but it can be critical in stopping a potential action in its tracks.

These requirements become even more demanding if a case actually goes to trial in another state and requires that the in-house expert be there for a one- or two-week period. The expert will likely testify on behalf of the company, and will therefore be present for the duration of the trial. All of this needs to be considered when accepting or selecting the best individual to fill the position.

TRAINING

Once the in-house product liability expert has been selected, the individual needs to pursue training on the subject of product liability prevention. Studying this book will be extremely helpful in not only supplying a tremendous amount of knowledge on the subject from a wide spectrum, but it will also effectively help guide the individual through all stages of program development.

Nonetheless, the individual needs to receive outside training in the field of product liability and be exposed to all the classroom discussion that would naturally be part of any seminar. Finding seminars on the subject will not be easy, however; this is such a cutting-edge topic, there are very few organizations that offer anything. Computers and the Internet will definitely be helpful in searching for various seminars and conferences.

A few places to contact for possible seminars are the American Society for Quality and their Product Safety & Liability Prevention–Interest Group, the Defense Research Institute in Chicago and their Manufacturer's Risk Prevention Specialized Litigation Group, or the University of Wisconsin—School of Engineering—Division of Continuing Education. All the sources have been involved in seminars on the subject for a number of years. The Defense Research Institute (DRI) is basically the defense attorney association, but many corporate executives, risk managers, and outside professional engineers and forensic investigators also are members. Nonmembers are allowed to attend their conferences and seminars. In addition, one can always search for the author via the Internet and inquire about upcoming seminars or conferences.

Some of the definite advantages in attending product liability related seminars is the ability to hear various attorneys discuss countless aspects of their cases, and to hear some of the horror stories from other attendees. One can learn a tremendous amount from the mistakes of others. No seminar is likely to cover all the ground of this book, but will instead address certain specific elements. This means that the expert will need to continue attending different seminars for at least the first few years, and should continue attending annual conferences like the DRI Annual Product Liability Conference.

CREATING THE CORPORATE PRODUCT LIABILITY TEAM

Once the in-house product liability expert has been selected and is in place, there also needs to be a top level administrative team. Just as no one person can attempt to solely drive a quality program and effort, neither can just one person drive this effort. When the individual and company get involved in a potential product liability incident, or actual litigation, the in-house expert needs to feel comfortable discussing ideas and action plans with a small peer group of others. In addition, there are going to be numerous new internal programs and safeguards that are going to be designed and implemented which would be overwhelming for one individual to spearhead. So there needs to be a small corporate liability team.

The in-house expert should use discretion when selecting the members of this team in order to ensure its success and maintain a long-term relationship. It is recommended that the team consist of three to four members. Anything larger than this will likely get out of control. The selected individuals should bring something unique to the table. Having two members from the same department or area will be of little value. Also, having someone as a member from some nonrelated function would be of no value.

The team's ideal composition will largely depend on how the corporation is set up. A single plant organizational structure will logically be different than a multiplant operation with a corporate headquarters. Although in a multiplant operation with a corporate headquarters, those staff members are likely to be far removed from the manufacturing of the product itself, that isn't important here. In addition to the creation of the corporate team, we will also be creating product safety teams at the plant level. The effort will be carried out and controlled from different levels. In selecting the members of the corporate team, the expert needs to consider individuals who will compliment the effort. A list of good potential candidates and the reasons for choosing them are:

> **Quality Head**   Although the author recommends that this person be the expert, it is recognized that someone else may be selected to drive this program. In that event, the quality head should be recognized as a good candidate for the team because of the improvements that will be made to the quality system, and because a product liability incident is logically the ultimate quality failure of a product.
>
> **Risk Manager**   Naturally if a company has a risk manager, the individual needs to be a member of this team, if the individual hasn't already filled the role as the expert.

Head of R&D or Technology   Once again, it depends on how the company is organized, but this individual will have a lot to offer from a number of perspectives. When a company first learns of a technical failure of its product in the field, this individual logically has the most in-depth technical knowledge of the product's abilities, as well as those of the component parts, especially in the area of electrical or electronic products. If a company is sophisticated enough to have a technology department, it will probably contain laboratories which will be of real value in the analysis of the alleged failure mechanism. In addition, this individual can become a well-trained expert witness in a trial environment.

Head of Engineering   Engineering is commonly the first department ever involved in the product liability prevention effort, although typically from the product perspective as it relates to design, labels, and other product safeguards. This focus will go well beyond that, but product design will always be the most important aspect.

Head of Finance   Although it may seem surprising to some, the head of finance can play an important part as a member of the team. Whether the company carries liability insurance or is self-insured, the head of finance will normally control the expenses and typically serve as the main contact with the insurance carrier. If the company is self-insured, or has a high deductible, the head of finance will naturally want to be part of the team that decides on such expenditures.

One of the first objectives the corporate team should undertake is to help the corporation develop a *Product Liability Policy Statement,* or if the corporation would rather, a *Product Reliability Policy Statement.* Although the corporation may already have a quality policy statement as part of its quality program, it needs to be reviewed in order to determine if it demonstrates the commitment toward safe and reliable product design now being focused on by the company. An example of just such a commitment is shown on page 83. When signed by the CEO and incorporated into the quality system, these measures then become policy and are administered and driven by the corporate team.

Product Liability Policy Statement

(Company) is committed to ensuring that the products we design, engineer, and manufacture will be safe and reliable for our customers and the end user in the application that the product was intended. This policy statement is issued as part of our overall quality program and the objective will be accomplished through the following means:

- All newly designed and manufactured products will be reviewed by the Product Safety & Reliability Review Board to ensure that they are safe and reliable and will function as required in their intended application.
- All newly designed products will be reviewed to ensure that we as a manufacturer, or any outside subcontractor we select, have the ability and provisions in place to produce the product in a consistent manner.
- We will ensure that all new products, components, materials and processes, receive the necessary testing, prior to their use in production.
- We will concentrate our design and engineering process on *designing out* potential risks and hazards, and make adequate provision for warnings and instructions concerning any other *residual* hazards, as well as to warn against any *reasonably foreseeable* misuse of the product.
- We will ensure through routine testing and inspection during the course of manufacturing that the products being produced conform to the standards, specifications, and performance factors that apply.
- We will maintain records that prove that the above safeguards were properly addressed, and retain these records for a reasonable period.

The policy statement will serve as our guideline in ensuring safety and reliability in the products we manufacture, and will be incorporated into the appropriate procedures of our quality system. Compliance to these statements and guidelines will be the responsibility of every employee of our organization.

Assistance in the interpretation and application of these policy statements and guidelines will be given by the corporate product liability team.

Chairman	President

ROUTINE MEETINGS

This three- to four-member team works closely with the product liability expert and begins to put all the elements in place to try and prevent incidents of product liability. Very similar to the start of any quality program, the liability team should meet on a regular basis and distribute minutes of their meetings to the president, CEO, chairman, and anyone else that heads up the corporation.

As this effort gains greater focus throughout the country, and many attorneys and law firms gain training in product liability prevention programs and efforts, corporations and their corporate product liability teams should seriously consider and pursue preventive lawyer consultants to serve as advisors to the teams. These wouldn't be just any attorneys, nor would they just be experienced trial attorneys, but would instead be attorneys that specialize in the field of product liability prevention.

In the routine meetings, which may take place on a monthly basis, this new team should discuss any new incidents or cases that have surfaced, updates on any existing cases, programs that need to be initiated to improve on product safety, and any training or awareness sessions that are planned. Even though several members of the executive staff may not be members of this team, they remain aware of what is happening and being planned and have the opportunity to present any recommendations to the members themselves.

However, because of the serious nature of these meetings, and especially the updates on new and existing cases, these minutes should be stamped *Confidential,* and should not fall into the hands of the rank and file. The minutes shouldn't even be distributed to other members of the staff. Much of what will be reported regarding cases should not become common knowledge within the corporation, or it may become common knowledge outside of the company as well. The less the individual employees know regarding product liability incidents, the less chance of problems should they ever be brought into a trial as witnesses, or deposed. This is sometimes hard for various employees to understand, especially for members of sales who may have brought a specific situation to light in the first place, and now expect updates on where the case stands. Such updates should just be given verbally by a member of the team, and only when asked. Other unrelated situations shouldn't be discussed. The rank and file need to accept the fact that the situation is now in the hands of others who have the responsibility to handle it on behalf of the corporation. The sales department, as well as their customers, don't need to remain involved.

The corporate liability team meeting minutes or summaries should be brief in nature. State the facts as to what the current status is of each case, but not the planned strategies. Remember that any such document or minutes can be sought out at future dates by counsel for a plaintiff during the discovery process. You don't want the minutes to include defense strategies on new or existing cases, nor do you want the members to expound on an internal situation or problem that could put the corporation in a bad light if it was read by others.

For instance, if the team discussed a claim involving a personal injury or fire and tried to decide whether the product in question should be recalled, but decided not to for various reasons, such documented discussions could become a liability to the organization especially if another incident followed afterward and the meeting minutes fell into the hands of plaintiff's attorney. The minutes should only state briefly the current status of each claim, and future programs planned by the team.

It is also important for the organization to institute the recommendations made by the corporate team, or such situations could cripple the team's effectiveness, and could also have other potentially negative repercussions. The team needs to be given the responsibility of putting in place any actions necessary to help prevent the possibilities of future product liability. These proposed actions should not be challenged by anyone other than the president. It is not like a quality program where one seeks *buy-in* by the others. This is a dedicated group that has to decide on behalf of the organization what the company needs to do.

Even with an existing quality system and program in place, corporations will find that this newly focused effort will bring about numerous improvements to the way they do business. The corporation will benefit significantly by the in-house expert and corporate liability team and the new programs that they introduce. Furthermore, when the product liability expert gains additional knowledge and education in product liability law, and how the product is being used on the outside, the individual has a better forum for sharing this new knowledge and enabling the membership to react on the issues accordingly, such as expanding the instructions and needed warnings.

When it comes to product liability law, corporations not only typically lack any specific knowledge on the subject, but more dangerously, some executives may think they know a lot about the subject. When the company begins to react on speculative knowledge they run more risk of creating problems than had they not reacted at all. There is a lot to be learned by the company in all these areas, and through this book and by attending seminars they will begin to do it.

MULTIPLANT CORPORATIONS

In a corporation that has multiple plant operations, the role of the corporate product liability team may have to be complimented by similar teams at the plant level. In this scenario, the corporate team may establish policy and guidelines as well as training and awareness programs, but they will need to depend on additional efforts at the plant level in order to ensure that the entire mission is completed.

In this setting, there may be a corporate team driving the overall effort, and there may be plant teams, or product safety teams, that focus specifically on the development and production of various new products. Similar to the composition of its corporate senior group, this junior organization would also try to comprise its membership of departments such as quality, engineering, possibly manufacturing engineering, the controller, and/or any other representatives of management the plant or corporation decides. By having teams at both the corporate and local levels, the organization stands the best chance of controlling all aspects of product liability.

Effective Design Reviews

The design review is the most important first step in a product's life cycle. It is the least expensive time to propose a change to a product, and the most effective and economical place to catch and address potential reliability and liability concerns. It is a crucial element that many companies feel they have under control, when in fact they don't even come close. In some instances, the whole concept is entirely overlooked, possibly because the management team may feel that they don't have time for what they consider to be a luxury.

A common misperception about the design review is that its entire focus is on risk and hazards analysis. This isn't true. The design review is a technical critique of the product, its components, and the processes required to manufacture the product. Part of this review will also involve a product safety review or hazards analysis, but it is not the sole purpose of the review.

The question commonly comes up as to when a design review of a new product should be held. In fact there are potentially four different design reviews that could take place on a product. They include:

> **Introductory Design Review**   This may be held when the company first receives an order for a concept that was proposed by design, or is a new product that was attained through the bidding process. The objective would be to make everyone involved familiar with the new product or concept. This would also launch the new product introduction

team. Recommendations of how the product should be engineered should be made at this point.

Preliminary Design Review   This would be held once the engineering drawings have been completed, but prior to their release. This may be the only review held, in place of the other two. The objective of this review would be for the representatives of key engineering and production departments to review the proposed drawings and specifications, ensure you have the capabilities to build the product to the specs, identify areas of concern regarding quality, materials and design reliability, needed instructions and labels, and any other aspect that could later come back to haunt you.

Final Design Review   This would be held after the drawings have been released and the first sample unit produced, in order to address any problems that couldn't be identified earlier, and to make any last minute changes to the design and specifications necessary. Production and final assembly would follow this review.

Post Production Design Review   This would be held after the product was produced and possibly shipped. It serves as an overview of the entire product and process, and although it won't have an impact on the specific product that was just produced, it will offer opportunities for improvement on a rerun of the product.

A new product could be the subject of all four reviews, or three of the reviews, or even two. The key is that a design review actually takes place, and the product in question is thoroughly analyzed by the design review team.

DESIGN REVIEW CONSIDERATIONS

In designing and evaluating a newly proposed product idea, the company needs to give thought to the entire spectrum of produceability, useability, and ultimate reliability, as well as potential liability as shown in Figure 6.1. Far too often, engineers design a product to perform a specific function or satisfy a required need with limited other consideration for what it might be subjected to or how it might be used. In addition, they tend to function as the *Jack of all Trades* as it

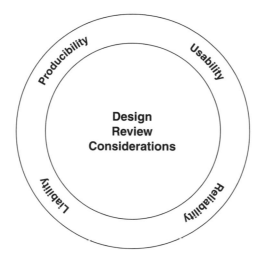

Figure 6.1 The design review spectrum.

relates to various aspects of manufacturing and process capability. The manufacturer needs to depend on the entire management team, in this case the design review team, to effectively analyze the new product from many different angles.

Producibility

To begin with, the manufacturing arm of the design review team needs to consider whether they have the capability to produce the product in compliance to the proposed specifications, as well as have the ability to continue producing the products in a consistent manner. Answering such questions logically requires process capability studies as well as an expert knowledge of all the processes themselves. Management needs to depend on the manufacturing and process engineering functions for this critical determination.

Usability

Then the company needs to determine if the ultimate customer is going to have problems using or servicing the product. Product engineers can design a product, and process engineers can best determine how to assemble the product, but many times everyone gives inadequate consideration to the practicality of what the end user is expected to do in the operation of the product, or especially the serviceability of the product. As an example, after staying overnight at my daughter's new condominium, I woke up the next morning and proceeded to the bathroom to take a shower. The tub/shower faucet was one that I had never seen before. There was a large rotating faucet handle, which started the water pouring out the lower spout, and in the middle of the handle was a small dial that adjusted the water temperature. In all my experience the larger handle not only started the water flowing, but the further you turned it, the hotter the water became. Not this one. The large rotating arm increased the water pressure as you turned it, and the smaller dial in the center of the handle increased the temperature. Well, that wasn't too hard to figure out, but the next part was. The water was pouring out the lower spout, and I wanted it to come out the showerhead. Normally, there would be a pop-up valve on the spout itself that you would pull up, which would then divert the water to the showerhead, but there wasn't one. Nor was there anything else that indicated that it was the switch for the shower. For 20 minutes I stood there trying to figure this out, while everyone else slept. After almost reaching wits end over the absurdity of not being able to figure this thing out, I discovered an almost invisible pull-down ring at the end of the faucet opening that diverted the water to the shower. It was incredible that anyone could have designed such an everyday fixture in such a complicated manner and made it so difficult to figure out. My first instinct was to contact the manufacturer's engineering department and ask them how they could have ever dreamt up such a stupid concept. And secondly, how could no one else on the design review team have challenged the useability of such a faucet?

Serviceability

The other half of useability is serviceability. How serviceable is the product you're designing? I have seen companies assemble metal cabinets designed to contain flourescent lamps, but if the end user ever had to replace one of the lamps, they would almost have to break the lamp in half to get it out of the unit. Of course the manufacturer only assembled the unit, and inserted the lamps at some opportune moment in the assembly process, but never had to attempt to take the lamps out of the finished unit. I have owned central humidifying units that attached to the furnace duct, and each year the internal water panel or metal filter device would need to be replaced. Rather than something that just pulls out the top, or something you can easily get to by simply removing a rear or top panel, this would require the complete disassembly of the entire unit in order to replace the water panel, which would religiously launch me into an hour-long cursing event. Here, too, I could never understand what the design engineers were thinking when they came up with the concept.

There are countless examples, such as trying to get at the spark plugs in today's automobiles, or trying to get at bolts in numerous products in order to loosen them. Manufacturing teams aren't looking at how complicated some products are to use or service. The product functions the way it is expected to function, and everything else is taken for granted. This is one area that quality and other functions need to review and critically analyze. One effective way to address this issue is to have someone totally removed from the technical product brought in to operate or service it, while others observe the process.

Then there is the element of reliability. Products are commonly designed to perform in a reliable manner under optimum conditions, but what considerations are given to adverse or extreme conditions? How reliable will the product be when subjected to extreme climactic or other challenging elements? It is easy to spec out component parts that are said to be rated for certain extremes. But don't let that take the place of testing them yourself.

Lastly is the element of liability. What in-depth analysis has taken place to explore the possible hazardous angles of the design? What are the possibilities of the end user being injured in any way during the use of the product? What are the possibilities of the product failing in such a manner as to result in fire or lead to other types of property damage? If the proposed concept fails any of these criteria, it could result in high defect rates, scrap, rework, warranty problems, returns, and possible recall. That would be bad enough, but then the company could also face the threat of liability. So it becomes apparent there is a lot that depends on the design review.

CREATING THE DESIGN REVIEW TEAM

When a design review is held on a product, the manufacturer needs to ensure the right technical parties are present. Too often, the design or product engineer takes control of the review process, or worse yet, is the sole reviewer. The engineer feels that he or she is expert enough to decide on the best design, or may discuss certain aspects with a few other individuals. Part of this comes from the design engineer assuming ownership of the product, and sole responsibility for the product's success. This is the wrong type of attitude for the manufacturer to allow.

The management team needs to assemble a highly effective design review team that consists of all the right parties. The product that is about to be created will belong to everyone, and everyone will be responsible for its success. Members of the team need to include such parties as product or design engineering, reliability engineering, quality and quality engineering, sales, manufacturing and process engineering, and Manufacturing itself. Naturally, the composition of the team will largely depend on the organizational structure. All of these individuals represent different areas of expertise and offer unique perspectives on the analysis of the design.

The roles and responsibilities for each member of the design review team should be outlined so that all product reliability and process capability bases are covered. It is crucial to remember that the design review is not intended to be just a new product awareness session, but a full-scale technical review and critique of the product, as well as the process for making the product. Therefore, parties capable of providing a technical critique need to be the ones present.

The advantages gained are that all members of the management team now share in the ownership of the product. The team approach is always more successful than an individual approach, and the engineer no longer has to bear the burden for the success of the product. It is now everyone's product, and more importantly, everyone's responsibility.

DEVELOPING THE DESIGN REVIEW PROCEDURE

A significant contribution to the quality system is the design review procedure. In writing the procedure, consideration might be given to starting it out with a policy statement that enforces the necessity for holding design reviews. This shouldn't be a prerogative, but a requirement. The procedure needs to identify the different types of design reviews, recognize the team members as well as the different teams, and lay out the steps to follow (see pages 93–95).

WRITING DESIGN REVIEW MEETING MINUTES

When management teams hold design review meetings, they need to generate meeting minutes. What concerns were discussed? What action plans were decided? What design changes were agreed on? All of these things need to be documented for future reference by the team. When management teams review a design and discuss everything they want to change, materials they want to use, tests they want to conduct, and other considerations, but then fail to establish a complete set of minutes, problems will result. Participants will forget their assignments, changes that were discussed might not be carried out to the degree expected, and other changes might be forgotten altogether.

| GE

Goodden
Enterprises | QUALITY PROCEDURE

DESIGN REVIEWS | Number 500 |
|---|---|---|
| | | Effective Date 1/1/20xx |
| | | Revision Date |
| | | Page 1 of 3 |
| | | TOTAL QUALITY SYSTEM |

1.0 POLICY

1.1 A formal documented design review will take place on all new products intended for production.

2.0 PURPOSE

2.1 To ensure that new products being considered for manufacturing are thoroughly reviewed, taking into consideration elements that include: customer specifications, manufacturing capability, product safety and reliability, and the best methods for manufacture.

3.0 SCOPE

3.1 This applies to all new products being considered, and reruns that involve substantial redesign, regardless of their complexity.

4.0 DEFINITION OF TERMS

4.1 **Introductory Design Review**
A review of a new product we intend to design and manufacture. The review may involve samples, pictures, and/or an artist rendering of the product to be produced and all backup information.

4.2 **Preliminary Design Review**
This review takes place after engineering has been completed on the product but before it has been released for production. The review would allow all departments involved in the manufacturing process to critique the proposed product design and address concerns.

4.3 **Final Design Review**
This review takes place after a prototype or first piece sample of production has been completed. It offers all departments the chance to review any problems that occurred during manufacturing of the first piece or prototype prior to the production order of the first piece or prototype.

AUDITOR:_____	**AUDIT**	IN COMPLIANCE
DATE: _____		OUT OF COMPLIANCE

Continued

Continued

QUALITY PROCEDURE	Effective Date 1/1/20xx	Number 500
DESIGN REVIEWS	Page 2 of 3	Revision Date

4.4 **Post Production Design Review**
This review takes place after the production order is completed. It will offer all departments a chance to review any problems that occurred during production that would justify a revision.

5.0 REVIEW TEAMS MEMBERSHIP

5.1 The *Design Review Team* will consist of sales, customer service, product engineering, manufacturing, purchasing, estimating, quality, and manufacturing engineering.

5.2 The *Product Safety Team* will consist of the R&D, engineering, and quality.

6.0 PROCEDURE FOR INTRODUCTORY DESIGN REVIEW

Sales 6.1 Holds an Introductory design review meeting for all new projects being introduced or quoted.

Review 6.2 Asks the necessary questions to ensure all members are fully
Team aware of what is being proposed, and will begin to make the necessary recommendations related to the engineering of the product.

Eng. 6.3 Documents all discussions and recommendations into meeting minutes for future reference.

7.0 PROCEDURE FOR A PRELIMINARY DESIGN REVIEW

Sales 7.1 Holds a preliminary design review prior to releasing engineering drawings to manufacturing.

Eng. 7.2 Brings copy of the print and the *Design Review Questionnaire*, to help in the analysis of the product.

7.2.1 All questions are read for each department to critique the drawing and recognize potential concerns.

Safety 7.3 In addition to the standard design review and analysis, will
Team review and analyze proposed new design from a product safety perspective and address any potential hazards.

Continued

Continued

QUALITY PROCEDURE	Effective Date 1/1/20xx	Number 500
DESIGN REVIEWS	Page 3 of 3	Revision Date

Eng. 7.4 Documents all discussions and items to be addressed that were identified during the review, and publish meeting minutes.

QA 7.5 Distributes the Design Review Verification form for all to sign after the review has been completed, if all the parties approve.

8.0 PROCEDURE FOR FINAL DESIGN REVIEWS

Eng 8.1 Holds a final design review after building a prototype or first piece and prior to running the production order.

Review 8.2 Reviews manufacturing problems found during development of the first piece.

Safety 8.3 Reviews and analyzes the final product from a product safety
Team perspective and addresses any potential hazards.

Eng 8.4 Documents all discussions and items to be addressed that were identified during the review.

QA 8.5 Distributes the Design Review Verification form for all to sign after the review has been completed, if all the parties approve.

9.0 PROCEDURE FOR POST-PRODUCTION DESIGN REVIEWS

Eng 9.1 Holds post-production design reviews at the completion of a production run, to discuss possible revisions and improvements.

    9.1.1 Post-production design reviews are required for new products.

    9.1.2 Post-production design reviews for reruns as deemed necessary.

Eng 9.2 Brings copies of the prints and all Engineering Change Request forms that were issued during the production of the product.

Review 9.3 Discusses problems that may have occurred during production,
Team or with the customers in the field.

QA 9.4 Documents all discussions and corrective actions items to be addressed prior to the product ever being produced in the future.

THE IMPACT OF POOR DESIGN REVIEWS

The president of a major manufacturing company specializing in office equipment gave an excellent analogy of the significance of a design review when he addressed the ASQ's Quality Forum a few years back. He was reflecting back to 1985 when his company expeditiously introduced their copy machines to the U.S. marketplace, only to find out shortly afterward that the unit contained a defect. He expounded on the incident, stating:

⌐

Had the defect been caught in the design review stage, it would have cost $35 to correct.

Had they caught it after the design review, but before part procurement, it would have cost $177 to correct.

Had they caught it after part procurement, but before assembly, it would have cost $368 to correct.

If they had caught the defect after production, but before they shipped the product, it would have cost $17,000 to correct.

But the defect wasn't caught until the products reached the US marketplace, and it cost them $590,000 to correct a $35 defect. This amounted to 16,500 times the original expense!

◢

This clearly demonstrates the type of disaster that can happen when we don't take the time to adequately critique and test our newly proposed products. Think of how much more devastating this situation could have become had the defect resulted in personal injury or fire.

Another graphic illustration of how effective design reviews can be is shown in Figure 6.2 where two competing car manufacturers track the amount of engineering changes generated during the start-up of a new car assembly. In the comparison you can see that Car Company A's engineering department receives the highest quantity of engineering changes during the design review stage, and from that point on the quantity begins to fall. At Car Company B, they peak out at the material procurement/prototype stage and reach another high right after assembly start. This would signify that many of the errors or problems are not being detected up front, but later on when they are more costly to correct.

The graph shown in Figure 6.3 shows how an aerospace company tracked their engineering changes, but instead of being concerned with all the changes submitted, they focused on those which represented *engineering errors*. As you can see by the graph, the actual amount of

MEASURING THE EFFECTIVENESS OF DESIGN REVIEWS

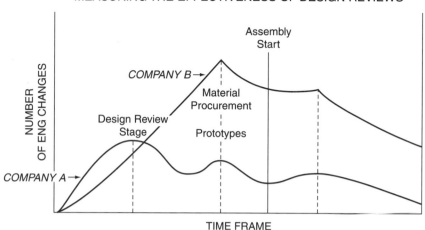

Figure 6.2 Graphing the effectiveness of design reviews.

TRENDING ENGINEERING ERRORS

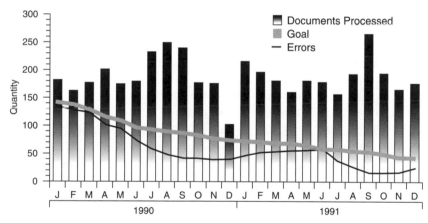

Figure 6.3 Tracking engineering errors.

engineering changes submitted each month didn't vary much, or show any kind of trend. But those that represented engineering errors showed a favorable downward trend. The other requested engineering changes represented such things as product improvement and value engineering ideas, materials changes possibly due to availability and/or better pricing, and process improvements. These are welcome changes and no attempt is made to discourage them.

GAINING THE NEW PERSPECTIVE

Once the design review team has learned to hold effective design reviews, the next effort is to get the product safety team to hold effective safety reviews or hazards analysis. This specialized second team would be a smaller group then the design review team, but depending on the company's size may involve some of the same players. The ultimate composition for the product safety team would be individuals who play a neutral role within the organization, but maintain a high level of technical product knowledge. Such individuals might be found in R&D, reliability, standards areas, and quality assurance. The product safety team needs to focus on all the aspects of the product, as they relate to the possibilities of injuries and/or catastrophic failure:

In order for the Product Safety Team to be effective in the analysis of new product designs, training in the science of hazards analysis is required. There are a number of different types of recognized methods for analyzing hazards, including the following:

Preliminary Hazards Analysis (PHA*)*** This is an inductive method used to identify, for all phases of life of a specified system or subsystem, the hazards component, hazardous situations and hazardous events which could lead to an accident. The method identifies the accident possibilities and qualitatively evaluates the degree of possible injury or damage to health. Proposals for safety measures and the result of their application are then given.

Failure Mode and Effects Analysis (FMEA) FMEA is an inductive method where the main purpose is to evaluate the frequency and consequences of component failure. When operating procedures or operator error are significant, other methods can be more suitable.

Method Organized for a Systemic Analysis of Risks (MOSAR Method) MOSAR is a complete approach in 10 steps. The system to be analyzed (machinery, process, installation, and so on) is considered as a number of subsystems which interact. A table is used to identify the hazards, the hazardous situations, and the hazardous events.

Fault Tree Analysis (FTA) FTA is a deductive method carried out from an event considered as unwanted and enables the user of this method to find the whole set of critical paths that lead to the unwanted event.

DELPHI Technique   A large circle of experts is questioned in several steps, whereby the result of the previous step together with additional information is communicated to all participants.

The team needs to understand these different hazards analysis techniques. The team also needs to understand the standards that exist for warnings and instructions, which are described in chapter 7. If the team doesn't perform a formal hazards analysis of a product being reviewed where they score points for each type of hazard and identify the risk level, they should at least perform a review based on a product safety questionnaire they create which pertains to their company's product lines.

Such a questionnaire might consist of two parts. The first would be a general list of possible hazards for the team to be looking for, such as:

Crushing hazards

Shearing hazards

Cutting hazards

Entanglement hazards

Drawing-in or trapping hazards

Impact hazards

Puncture hazards

Abrasion hazards

Exposed live part—electrical hazards

Electrostatic exposure

Thermo hazards (exposed high temperature parts)

Noise hazards (exposed to high sound frequencies)

Exposure to gases or fumes hazards

Fire or explosion hazards

Unexpected start-up hazards

The second part would involve a critical analysis of the product where the team would ask and discuss questions such as the following:

- From all perspectives, is this a reasonably safe product for the intended end user?
- What tasks would the end user have to perform with the product that could contain hazards?
- What could an end user do with the product that would be considered *reasonably foreseeable misuse?*
- Are safety devices absent from the design?

- How could the product possibly lend itself to property damage?
- What kind of warning labels or instructions should we be thinking about including with this product?
- How does it relate to *state of the art* in the industry?
- Will this be expected to comply with any codes or regulations?
- What could be some extreme applications for this product, climatic or environmental?
- What types of unique tests should we immediately undertake to ensure that the product or its materials will prove to be reliable?
- What similarities does this product have with others that may have historically led to problems in the field?

Once the team creates their own checklists based on their specific product lines, the lists will be a few pages in length, and the review will probably take two to three hours to complete. The manufacturer wants to be in a position to show that they addressed every reasonable concern.

There are many things to take into consideration when performing a hazards analysis on a product, whether it be a formal analysis or an abbreviated version. Take this actual case into consideration:

⌐

The company manufactures range hoods for above the stove in the kitchen. In a product liabilities case, two young brothers were fighting in the kitchen when one suddenly pushed the other into the sharp edge of the range hood, causing a massive head injury.

The attorney acknowledged that his client was involved in horseplay at the time of the accident, but stated that the mother could have been walking around in the kitchen, lost her balance and hit her own head on the sharp projecting corner of the range hood, and suffered the same massive head injury. It isn't the actions that are to be blamed, but the hazard the range hood poses. In cross-examination of the manufacturer's design, engineers counsel for the plaintiff asked, "Would it have cost any more for you to have manufactured a rounded edge on the range hood, versus the sharp pointed edge shown on the product in question?" The designer replied, "No." The attorney asked, "Would a rounded edge on the product have affected the performance of the range hood in any manner?" Once again the designer answered, "No." Counsel for the plaintiff won the case based on defective design, *and* reasonably foreseeable risk of harm.

⌐

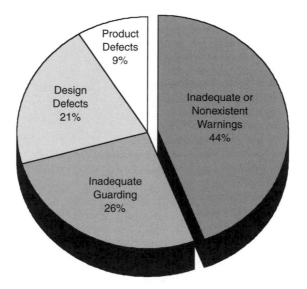

Figure 6.4 A breakdown of product liability causes.

CAUSES OF PRODUCT LIABILITY LAWSUITS

Design defects, however, aren't normally the primary cause of a product liability lawsuit. A major insurance company conducted a study of 27 random product liability cases which ended up with settlements between $100,000 to over $2 million, and found the largest cause of manufacturer's negligence centered around *inadequate or nonexistent warnings* (see Figure 6.4).

In many situations, the greatest amount of engineering effort goes into the actual design of the new product, and the responsibility for addressing such things as warnings and operating instructions is given to a lesser ranked individual. The company isn't as interested in how good the instructions and warnings are, they just need to have something to supply with the product. The primary interest is to get the product into the marketplace and begin to generate sales. As shown in Figure 6.4, *inadequate warnings and instructions* are the primary cause for product liability lawsuits.

DOCUMENTING THE PRODUCT SAFETY REVIEW

Similar to design reviews, a record of the product safety review or hazards analysis needs to be maintained for future reference as well. At some later date, these minutes may also serve as a notable piece of evidence to factually show that the company's management team made every effort to thoroughly evaluate the safety and reliability of the product.

The primary concern for the manufacturer is ensuring that this document is beneficial to the organization and doesn't become a liability. This could be the case if certain reliability concerns are noted in the minutes, with no mention of corrective action or resolve. The safety team states in the minutes that they feel the edges of the product are too sharp and could result in cutting the hands of the end user, but there is no mention of any proposed corrective action. Five years later the product is in court, and no one from the manufacturer can remember what was done regarding the statement or concern. Or if other safety or reliability improvements are proposed but are rejected for what will be viewed as irresponsible reasons, the document could become a liability. For example, the minutes reflect a discussion centering around the concern that the electrical wiring of a product could contribute to a shock injury or electrically short out, but it is decided that placing a guard on the product would cost too much money. These types of documents now become *dangerous documents* for anyone to discover at a later date. There are going to be times when a sensitive issue is discussed, and your team will decide for good reason that they don't need to make any changes to the product because the threat of hazard is too remote. Rather than saying all of this in a set of minutes, these discussions could be handled in one of two ways: (1) either make the decision and not write anything, or (2) state the concern addressed and note that the team didn't feel there was any hazard. A good rule of thumb that I have shared with management teams everywhere is, *Never write anything on paper that you wouldn't mind someday reading in a courtroom.*

IN CONCLUSION

Management teams need to understand the significance of design reviews and conduct them in the manner described. They should generate comprehensive meeting minutes with closed loop action plans. The next step in this critical analysis is to create product safety teams and hold product safety reviews. They not only need to incorporate these efforts into their daily routine, but they also need to incorporate the requirements into their quality system. We live in a very litigious world, and new products cannot be rushed into the marketplace without a thorough critiquing from every technical perspective.

Warnings and Instructions

7

Product engineers and other members of manufacturing management can become so familiar with their own product lines, the inherent dangers and elements of caution, that they feel such information is common knowledge among the end users as well. The more products the company creates, the more the warnings and instructions become somewhat standardized and the more potential there is for oversight. Adding to this critical oversight is that many products that were once used by trained members of certain trades or industries are now used by individuals with a fraction of the knowledge or training. Look at computers. Who were the likely users 10 or 15 years ago, and who are the users now?

This level of expertise also becomes a problem when it comes to writing product instructions. Most companies would determine that the logical individual to write an instruction sheet or manual for a product would be one of the engineers or technicians with the most technical knowledge of how the product works. This isn't always true. Who is likely to be the user of the product? Would it be someone with as much knowledge and expertise, or would it be someone with little to no technical knowledge or expertise regarding the use of the product?

Companies need to remember that most newspapers are written on a sixth-grade level, not because the writers only went as far as the sixth grade, but because that is where they find their average reader. If they wanted to, newspapers could write at a college level. After all, that is the level of education of most of the writers. But then only about 15 percent of their readers would understand everything they have written. This could be the same issue facing many manufacturing companies as they write operating manuals and instructions for their end users.

Look back at the computer industry as another example. Software programs often come with manuals that are as thick as *War and Peace*. When the average novice user tries to figure out how to use the computer or run a program, they don't know where to look in the manual and become lost instantly. When they read the sections of the operating manuals, they don't understand the terminology and become confused. So they talk to someone else who has the same program and ask how certain things are accomplished. If there isn't someone else to ask, they either crawl through the operation and learn through trial and error, or they mess up the computer and programs. Or they take the easy way out and find the technical service number in the operating manual and call the manufacturer if the product is still under warranty.

The bottom line is that engineers and technical specialists are not always the best people for writing instruction manuals. The company should at least consider having someone else be the final reviewer. Someone who is less familiar with the product or is less apt to write in a technical manner could be a better choice. Someone who can translate technical into nontechnical or someone who is a good writer, but isn't as literate in the technical product, would be a good choice. At the very least, once the instruction is written, bring in the switchboard operator or someone from HR and see how successfully they can operate the product purely by following the proposed instructions.

PROBLEMS WITH PRODUCT EVOLUTION

The problem with product development and design evolution is the same in many industries. Engineers and manufacturers put out better versions and different variations of the same types of product lines, from circular saws to lawnmowers. Too often they take a lot of their knowledge for granted, not only as it relates to the development of the basic instructions, but also for the basic warnings.

⌐

If the manufacturer has greater knowledge than the average consumer would likely possess regarding pertinent safety information for safe use of the product, the manufacturer has a duty to pass that knowledge on to the consumer through a warning. Generally, a duty to warn exists where there is unequal knowledge, actual or constructive, and defendant, possessed of such knowledge, knows or should know that harm might or could occur if no warning is given. (Miller v. Dvornik, 149 Ill. App.3d 883, 501 N.E. 2d 160 1986)

⌐

For the person who hasn't owned one of these products, would they automatically know many of the basic do's and don'ts that might be common knowledge to others? Probably not. The story is told about a champion professional golfer who bought his first bass boat so he could take up the sport of fishing on his weekends off. With great pride he sat in the new boat in his garage, started the motor, and listened to it run for half an hour. Suddenly it burst into flames which rocketed up to the ceiling. The golfer instantly jumped out of the boat, grabbed the front of the trailer, and pulled the boat out of the garage to keep the house from burning down. Was it known to this professional that the boat had to be in water before starting the engine? Obviously not. Was he considered to be an ignorant individual? Hardly. Might such basic knowledge be something an outboard motor or boat manufacturer might take for granted? Probably so. Manufacturers need to make sure they don't drop their guard with instructions and warnings or take anything for granted.

Furthermore, manufacturers need to understand how to separate warnings from instructions. The following describes the difference as cited in one legal case.

Γ

Warnings and instructions are not necessarily the same. The former call attention to danger; the latter prescribe procedures for efficient use of the product and for avoiding danger. A manufacturer might provide one and still be liable for failing to provide the other, as where instructions fail to alert the user to the danger they seek to avert, or where a warning alerts the user to peril but does not enable him to avoid it. (Boyl v. California Chemical Co, 221 F. Supp. 669, 676 n. 6)

⅃

First, the manufacturer should address the instructions needed for the operation and servicing of the product. Second, the manufacturer needs to identify the critical elements the end user should be warned of in the handling and operation of the product, as well as where such warnings should be placed.

LEGAL GUIDELINES

Congress, with the Uniform Safety Act of 1987, endorsed the phrase, *what a reasonably prudent person might do,* as a standard for determining a manufacturer's liability as it pertained to potential negligence. This is also how a court would decide when the operator or user was negligent for performing a certain action. A manufacturer normally won't be held liable for failing to warn about a danger that would be considered open and obvious, such as warning the owner of a power mower of the dangers associated with sticking their hand in by the blade.

Ⅼ

Neither seller nor manufacturer of lawn mower had a duty to warn plaintiff of danger of inserting her hand near mower blade, and plaintiff could not recover on theory that inadequate warnings of such danger were provided, since the blade posed an open and obvious danger as a matter of law to one placing a hand into the running mower, particularly after the user has lifted the guard chute from its protective location. (Ragsdale v. K-Mart Corp 468 N.E. 2d 524 Ind. Ct. App. 1984)

Many courts subscribe to the presumption that, had an adequate warning been given, the user would have read and heeded such a warning. This is referred to as the *read and heed assumption.* If the plaintiff is successful in this attack on the defendant with the court and jury, the plaintiff is able to bypass causation (or having to prove any other defective condition in a product) by identifying that the actual defect was the lack of adequate warning. The origin of this presumption may be found in Comment (j) of section 402A of the Second Restatement of Torts which states:

Ⅼ

Where warning is given, the seller may reasonably assume that it will be read and heeded; and a product bearing such a warning, which is safe for use if it is followed, is not in a defective condition, nor is it unreasonably dangerous.

Therefore, if a defendant can take refuge in supplying what is viewed as adequate warning, then the plaintiff should be entitled to an opposite presumption.

CONSIDERING THE END USER

It becomes easy for the manufacturer to lose touch with reality and to overlook the level of common knowledge the average user of their products may possess. It is a nuisance for the manufacturer and engineers to have to focus on this subject and the random possibilities. Yet, when the company enters into serious product liability litigation involving personal injury, and the manufacturer is accused of inadequate warning, a major emphasis in this area is initiated in order to prevent potential future incidents. However, with the appointment of the product liability expert and the creation of the corporate product liability team, it will become more routine for this issue to be addressed.

Determining the elements of caution and potential danger requires thought and consideration. Middle ground has to be sought between the electrical generator with no warnings and the step ladder with 110 warning labels attached to it. This can be an evolutionary process as the company gains more knowledge and experience in the field.

For instance, the manufacturer of a portable metal framed electrical display with a higher potential for producing electrical shocks than an average product started out with no warning labels or instructions. As years passed, the manufacturer began to experience infrequent minor accidents where the users received severe shocks from the product. The accidents were the result of negligence on the part of the user, but required in-depth investigation before being revealed. In the first phase of warning, the manufacturer placed a warning label on the product as shown in Figure 7.1.

As the years went by, the manufacturer experienced a decline in incidents, and periodically when a situation arose that was the result of the user attempting to make adjustments to the product, the manufacturer was in the proper position to point out the warning which advised against such activity. But in a few situations, no repair was

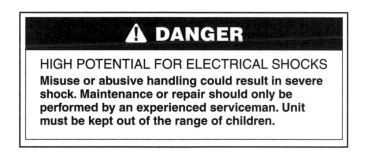

Figure 7.1   A warning with standard wording.

attempted. Somehow the product became subjected to a physical motion or disturbance that altered its assembly, and thereby created an unsafe electrical condition. When the user simply made contact with the product, to aesthetically adjust it while it was lit up on display, the user received a severe shock. In the investigation of the incident, the expert could not explain how the defective condition had been created, and was unable to allege user negligence for simply handling and adjusting the powered-up display.

In trying to determine how they (the manufacturer) could prevent future episodes, they decided to expand on the wording on the warning label. It was now changed as shown in Figure 7.2. Years later, when once again a similar situation surfaced where an end user supposedly received a severe shock from merely adjusting the display as it hung on the wall, the expert met with the user's legal counsel and pointed out the red warning label on the product with the new wording advising against any physical contact. The attorney never pursued the case. As years passed and the industry evolved into newer and safer electronic concepts, replacing the earlier electrical designs, the manufacturer was able to change the product to such a degree that it no longer posed a potential for such danger.

In this example, the function that the product performed basically outweighed the potential risk, and with the proper warnings the manufacturer stood a good chance of defending the product. The attorney for the plaintiff could have tried to pursue the case alleging that the product was *unreasonably dangerous for the marketplace,* but it obviously was too challenging and expensive to pursue.

⚠ DANGER

HIGH POTENTIAL FOR ELECTRICAL SHOCKS
Misuse or abusive handling could result in severe shock. Maintenance or repair should only be performed by an experienced serviceman. Do not make physical contact with any part of this display, without first disconnecting it from its power source. Unit must be kept out of the range of children.

Figure 7.2 An example of unique wording.

UTILITY VERSUS RISK

In attempting to balance a product's utility against its potential risk, a company may find it helpful to use the seven factors developed by Professor John Wade:[1]

1. The usefulness and desirability of the product—its utility to the user and the public as a whole

2. The safety aspects of the product—the likelihood that it will cause injury, and the probable seriousness of the injury

3. The availability of a substitute product which would meet the same need and not be as unsafe

4. The manufacturer's ability to eliminate the unsafe character of the product without impairing its usefulness or making it too expensive to maintain its utility

5. The user's ability to avoid danger by the exercise of care in the use of the product

6. The user's anticipated awareness of the dangers inherent in the product and their avoidability, because of general public knowledge of the obvious condition of the product, or of the existence of suitable warnings or instructions

7. The feasibility, on the part of the manufacturer, of spreading the loss by setting the price of the product or carrying liability insurance

In a hypothetical situation, a manufacturing company created a set of decorative electrical lights that initially were designed for indoor or outdoor use. But through testing it was found that the lights posed a serious threat if used outside while it was raining. The manufacturer decided to place a label on the product warning against allowing the product to get wet. If the product was marketed as an indoor or outdoor product and clearly presented as such, the courts may rule against the manufacturer regardless of the stated warning, in recognition of how the product was being marketed for use.

A similar argument could be made of the cellular carphone. The purpose of the carphone is for the owner to be able to place and receive calls while on the road, thereby avoiding the need to pull off the road to use a pay phone. The potential dangers of a driver talking

---

[1]Professor John Wade. *On the Nature of Strict Tort Liability for Products.* 44 Miss. L.J. 825.

on a carphone while they should be concentrating on their driving led some carphone makers to stipulate in their instruction manuals that the phone was not intended for use while driving. To place or receive a call, the driver is expected to pull off the road and stop. Although the carphone makers may try to use this documented warning in their defense, it is yet to be seen how the courts may respond if such a case is presented where talking on the carphone is cited as the cause of the accident.

When a product is marketed within a special trade or profession, and the potential dangers are considered common knowledge within that trade or profession, the manufacturer may have no duty to warn, even though the dangers may not be known to an ordinary person. But the manufacturer of a piece of equipment used in industry may still have a duty to warn through the use of instructions about the potential dangers inherent in the machine, even though the end users may be considered experienced.

DEVELOPING WARNING LABELS

When developing warnings or warning labels, one must determine the best way to present the information in a manner that will be noticed and understood by the end user. Guidelines for developing warning labels are contained in the American National Standards Institute (ANSI) Standards Z535.4. The ANSI Z535.4 Standard is the standard that provides specific guidelines for the design of product safety signs and labels. Prior to approval of this standard in 1991, product manufacturers did not have a uniform national standard for designing product warnings. Most manufacturers either developed their own warning designs, borrowed the OSHA designs for environmental and facility safety signs, or purchased generic warnings from inventory-based safety sign companies. The result was a proliferation of product safety sign designs, colors, and messages.

The ANSI Z535.4 Standard was specifically developed to correct this problem. It establishes definitions for a product safety sign's layout, content, and color. Its overall objective is to achieve a national uniform system for the recognition of product-related personal injury hazards. The ANSI Z535.4 committee (made up of representatives from a wide range of industries) took over 12 years to develop this standard. Its passage and subsequent revisions represent nothing less than a breakthrough for manufacturers. Now there is a single cohesive standard for the majority of product warnings, including those for use on industrial equipment.

This standard is important to you, the manufacturer, for two reasons. First, as the number of manufacturers complying with the Z535.4 standards grows, people will more easily recognize personal injury hazards before they happen. This should result in a lower number of product-related injuries and deaths. Second, the ANSI Z535.4 Standard gives manufacturers an officially recognized state-of-the-art benchmark for their product warnings. Prior to the ANSI Z535.4 Standard, any warning could easily be challenged in court as *inadequate*. In recent years, lawsuits based on *inadequate warnings* have replaced design defect cases to become the leading form of product liability lawsuit in the United States. Compliance with the ANSI Z535.4 Standard helps strengthen a company's product liability defense.

According to the ANSI Z535.4 Standard, a product safety sign must alert persons to: (1) the type of hazard, (2) the degree of hazard seriousness, (3) the consequence of involvement with the hazard, and (4) how to avoid the hazard.

Components of the Label

Signal Word

There are four key components that make up an ANSI Z535.4 product safety sign or label. The first component is the signal word. The signal word is the large word appearing in capital letters on a colored background at the top of a product safety sign. The ANSI Z535.4 Standard defines three choices for the signal word: DANGER, WARNING or CAUTION, as shown in Figure 7.3. Each signal word (and its corresponding background color) communicates a different level of hazard seriousness.

⚠ DANGER ⚠WARNING ⚠ CAUTION

Figure 7.3   Signal words.

DANGER indicates an imminently hazardous situation which, if not avoided, will result in death or serious injury. This signal word is to be limited to the most extreme situations.

WARNING indicates a potentially hazardous situation which, if not avoided, could result in death or serious injury.

CAUTION indicates a potentially hazardous situation which, if not avoided, may result in minor or moderate injury. It may also be used to alert against unsafe practices.

There are two key decisions to make when choosing the appropriate signal word for your product's hazard:

1. How severe will the injury be if the safety sign is ignored? If it is serious injury or death, then your choice for signal word is either DANGER or WARNING, as shown in Figure 7.4. If the injury is minor or moderate, CAUTION should be used.

2. What is the likelihood that the injury will occur if the safety sign's message is ignored? Is it a *will* or a *could* situation? If you have decided that serious injury or death is the result of interaction with the hazard, and it *will* occur if the safety sign is ignored, then your choice for the signal word is DANGER. If the likelihood is that the injury or death *could* happen, then your signal word choice should be WARNING.

Figure 7.4 The use of DANGER or WARNING.

Severe injury makes DANGER or WARNING the proper options for the signal word. If the hazard is imminent and a person *will* have their fingers amputated if they disobey the instruction, DANGER would be the proper choice. If the hazard is not imminent and a person *could* have their fingers amputated if they disobey the instruction, WARNING would be the proper signal word choice.

It is not a good choice to overwarn about your hazards by inappropriately using the signal word DANGER when WARNING or CAUTION would be the right choice. Overwarning dilutes the meaning of those safety signs which correctly require DANGER for their signal word as in Figure 7.5. A mistake to avoid is to underwarn about your hazard by inappropriately using the signal word CAUTION when DANGER or WARNING would have been the correct choice. Remember, if the injury is severe, like in the finger amputation example, the signal word choice should be either DANGER or WARNING, not CAUTION.

Color

The signal word panel's colored background combines with the signal word to alert the user to the level of hazard seriousness. Each signal word has a specific colored background associated with its use. DANGER appears in white letters on a red background, WARNING appears in black letters on an orange background, and CAUTION appears in black letters on a yellow background.

The use of a pictorial or symbol is optional but it is highly recommended that you incorporate them into your warnings. As shown in

Figure 7.5 Making DANGER the correct choice.

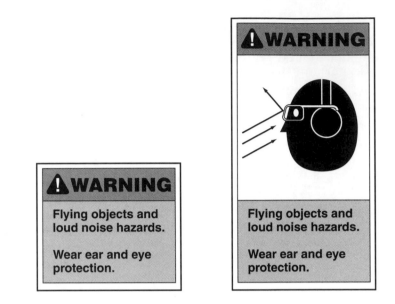

Figure 7.6 Pictorials and symbols.

Figure 7.6 the pictorial safety sign stands out and communicates the safety message efficiently. The safety sign with only words does not convey the hazard information as quickly or precisely. Long word messages also tend to be ignored. And most importantly, for those users who are illiterate or do not speak English, safety signs with only words are practically meaningless. This factor is all the more significant as the population of the United States continues to become more diverse. The ability of pictorials to communicate across language barriers, combined with the attention-getting speed with which they convey hazard information, makes them indispensable to any new warnings program.

Word Messages
The product safety sign's word message works together with the pictorial to communicate the type of hazard, the consequence of interaction with the hazard, and how to avoid the hazard.

Placement
With regards to the placement of the warning label, the standard states that it should be distinctive on the product, be located in the immediate vicinity of the hazard readily visible so the viewer can recognize the hazard and take appropriate action, and be designed with the expected life of the product and the foreseeable environment in mind.

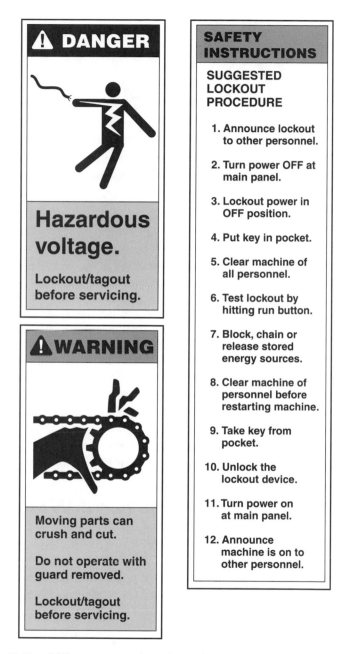

Figure 7.7 Different examples of word messages.

Figure 7.8 International signs.

It should be recognized that the ANSI Standards have been established as a recommended guideline for designing labels, but do not have the force of law. These standards are much like the Underwriters Laboratories Standard for construction, which is the recommended standard for state of the art safety, but there is no requirement for conformance. However, it is in the manufacturer's best interests to demonstrate compliance to the standards, just as in a UL comparison, or it will become a plaintiff's advantage to make a point of the noncompliance. Labels that comply with the ANSI Standard can be purchased through companies like Hazard Communication Systems.

International Signs
International safety labels as shown in Figure 7.8 are designed to meet global marketplace requirements and European compliance directives.

THE CONTINUING DUTY TO WARN
In addition to the responsibilities a manufacturer has regarding the initial duty to warn, if the manufacturer becomes aware of an unsafe condition existing in the product even after the sale, the product manufacturer may bear a continuing duty to warn responsibility. It is recognized that at the time of manufacture, or the time of sale, that the manufacturer can only be held liable for information or knowledge that is known at that time.

As the manufacturer gains more knowledge of the product and its potential hazards, some courts have imposed that the manufacturer has a responsibility to share or communicate that knowledge with the purchasers or users of the product. Such knowledge may be gained through additional testing or industry studies which lead to an improvement in the state of the art, or the knowledge could be gained by accident reports received by the manufacturer.

Just as in the initial responsibilities regarding the duty to warn, the continuing duty to warn would still be based on what would be considered *reasonable*. Factors in the determination of what would appear reasonable and practical are: (1) the nature and severity of the hazard, (2) the burden that it would impose on the manufacturer to locate the end users, (3) the attention that one could expect from any type of reasonable notice, and (4) the nature of the product and amount that may have been produced and circulated. This becomes even more complicated when the original product was sold to various distributors and the records stop as to where the products went from there, or in situations of equipment and machinery where the products may have been resold from company to company.

In some states, the courts have declined rulings regarding the manufacturer's continuing duty to warn (for example, Massachusetts), and in others the duration required remains unclear.

⌐

It is beyond reason and good judgement to hold a manufacturer responsible for a duty of annually warning of safety hazards on household items . . . when the product is 6 to 35 years old and outdated by some 20 newer models equipped with every imaginable safety innovation in the state of the art. It would place an unreasonable duty upon these manufacturers if they were required to trace the ownership of each unit sold and warn annually of new safety improvements over a 35-year period. (Kozlowski v. John E. Smith's Sons Co., 87 Wis. 882, 275 N.W. 2d 915, 923–34 1979).

⌐

If a manufacturer does recognize the duty to warn based on newly attained information, the manufacturer can carry out this responsibility through several fashions. The first and foremost is to contact the end user directly and supply them with the warnings, instructions, or safeguards necessary. A second way is through direct mass mailings which communicate the newly learned hazards and give specific instructions. A third way could be through the use of notices in specific industry or direct focus publications. It needs to be mentioned that this is all in addition to the responsibilities that a manufacturer may have regarding the laws and regulations imposed by the Consumer Product Safety Commission.

On the other hand, most jurisdictions do not impose on manufacturers a post-sale duty to warn product purchasers or users of safety improvements or other state of the art developments since the product was produced. In distinguishing between a previous design versus a newly improved and safer product design, the Court in *Lynch v. McStome and Lincoln Plaza Associates* stated:

🛛

Certainly the law does not contemplate placing the onerous duty on manufacturers to subsequently warn all foreseeable users of products based on increased design or manufacturing expertise that was not present at the time the product left its control.

🛓

Determining the boundaries for the continuing duty to warn responsibility is not a clear-cut project. The best definition of responsibility is found in Section 10 of the Restatement (Third) which advocated a post-sale duty limited to the following circumstances:

(a) One engaged in the business of selling or otherwise distributing products is subject to liability for harm to persons or property caused by the seller's failure to provide a warning after the time of sale or distribution of a product when a reasonable person in the seller's position would provide such a warning.

(b) A reasonable person in the seller's position would provide a warning after the time of sale when:

   (1) The seller knows or reasonably should know that the product poses a substantial risk of harm to persons or property; and

   (2) Those to whom a warning might be provided can be identified and may reasonably be assumed to be unaware of the risk of harm; and

   (3) A warning can be effectively communicated to and acted on by those to whom a warning might be provided; and

   (4) The risk of harm is sufficiently great to justify the burden of providing a warning.

In the end, many courts may leave the final decision of whether a manufacturer had a post-sale duty to warn up to the juries.

ILL-CONCEIVED WARNINGS

Lastly, some product creators and copywriters realize the need for including warnings on products, but use little common sense or discretion in what they develop. The following are a few examples:

A warning on a major department store hair dryer:

> Do not use while sleeping.

A warning accompanying a clothes iron:

> Do not iron clothes on body.

A warning on a box of children's cough medicine:

> Do not drive a car or operate machinery.

Then there are the problems with not adequately understanding the language, as shown on a Korean kitchen knife:

> **⚠ WARNING**
> Keep out of children.

or Chinese Christmas lights:

> For indoor and outdoor use only!

And lastly, on a child's Superman costume:

> Wearing this outfit does not enable you to fly.

Records Retention
and Document Control

Records are a critical part of any comprehensive management and quality system. Records are needed as reference tools to verify conformance to specification, serve as historic record of transactions, supply data for analytical studies, and validate agreements, just to name a few considerations.

Records retention and specific aspects of document control can also play major roles in a product liability lawsuit. As manufacturers begin to focus on product liability prevention, one of the key questions that instantly arises is, "What records should we be keeping, and for how long?" Manufacturers that aren't part of tightly controlled trade industries with well-established guidelines, such as medical equipment, pharmaceutical, food, aerospace, nuclear, or government suppliers, fear there might be legal time frames for records retention that they're not following, so they become concerned.

As companies seek advice from various attorneys on what their practices should be regarding the keeping of documents, they might be surprised as well as confused by the recommendations. One group of attorneys may recommend that manufacturers retain their documents and records for as long as possible in the event they may be needed in future litigation. The other group will tell them to throw everything away as soon as possible because they fear the records will actually hurt future defense efforts. This second group largely fears the discovery of "dangerous documents," or what is known as the "smoking gun," documents that show the manufacturer at some point in time was cognizant of a defective condition and didn't handle the situation in a proper manner.

Actually, for many companies that don't fall into those previous categories, there is no *legal* time frame that they must maintain records, other than those that pertain to taxes. Those manufacturers should maintain each type of record for as long as they may need it, and then they should dispose of it. What if they are asked for a specific record five years later in a court case, and they can't provide it any longer, won't they appear to be negligent? The answer is no. If the manufacturer explains that the record in question is only maintained for a three-year period per their records retention program, the fact that it has been discarded does not imply negligence.

What becomes a real problem is the manufacturer who never throws anything away. This is a problem that affects far too many companies. Some sales, customer service, and manufacturing people keep every letter and in-house memo for as long as they're employed, maybe 20 some years in cases. Files eventually go from the office drawer or cabinet to storage boxes in basements, attics, or off-site areas. Some engineering and quality departments never throw anything out—memos, reports, test documents, change orders. These are the things that create the largest legal problems, as well as the most time-consuming problems when a company enters into a product liability lawsuit. Eventually, such documents could be requested by the courts requiring everyone involved to have to spend countless hours collecting and pouring through them.

Even for companies that develop record retention programs with established guidelines, the problem becomes the lack of enforcement. Management is least concerned and focused on the issue until they begin to run out of storage room and border on possible fire hazards. Then a sweeping effort is made to have teams of people spend days going through the storage areas, throwing out whatever boxes and files are well beyond the time frames stated in their own policies. That doesn't include the files kept in individual offices.

Inconsistencies in practice can also pose other legal problems. If customer service and sales never throw documents away, even though their procedures tell them to do so, and other test reports and critical quality records are thrown away exactly as prescribed, it could create the impression that the company is selectively getting rid of certain documents that might pose a greatest risk, while indefinitely hanging on to others. This isn't to imply that the answer is to initiate a major effort to throw away everything. Companies just need to decide reasonable retention periods and then abide by those decisions.

It is especially crucial that a company not begin the process of disposing of records if they have entered into any form of litigation on the product. There are a number of reasons for this. First, certain records may be crucial for the defense in reconstructing important events and/or rebuking various claims or assertions against the manufacturer. From the opposite perspective, the destruction of related documents at the onset of litigation could lead to the perception that the manufacturer was intentionally trying to hide information from the courts. This could then lead to serious consequences such as severe sanctions, fines, and in some cases criminal prosecution for specific individuals involved. They could be charged with tampering with evidence, or the obstruction of justice for discarding documents known to be relevant to an ongoing or anticipated legal proceeding.

CREATING A RECORD RETENTION PROCEDURE

The first step in a meaningful effort to control record retention is to create the needed policy or procedure. The procedure needs to identify the following information:

1. Specifically state which records are being referred to for retention.
2. Designate the department or employee position that is responsible for maintaining the record.
3. State the time frame that the record must be kept.
4. State who is responsible for disposing of the record at the end of the time frame, along with possibly the logging of the disposal and the method of disposal (for example, trash vs. shredding).

As part of the development of such a procedure, the management team will need to establish the time frames for each type of document generated. This isn't always easy, and deciding the retention periods can seem like picking numbers out of the air. Table 8.1 may serve as a good starting point for various types of documents.

DOCUMENT CONTROL
OR CONTROLLING CONTENT

In addition to managing the proper retention of records, there is another element that often ends up being more important in a product liability case, and that is what the records actually say. Nothing is more disastrous for the manufacturer's defense in a product liability case than the plaintiff's discovery of internal documents, or e-mail messages, that prove the manufacturer had prior knowledge of product or design defects and failed to react in a responsible manner. Such documents have put the final nail into many manufacturers' coffins.

⌐ **Table 8.1** Sample retention periods	
Record Type	**Retain**
Audit records	3 years
Blueprints (obsolete)	10 years
Blueprint revision records	7 years
Correspondence (general)	1 year
Correspondence (general, customers, and suppliers)	1 year
Customer product complaints	3 years
Customer (supplied) product specifications	10 years
Design reliability verification lab test reports	10 years
Design review meeting minutes	3 years
Insurance policies (expired)	5 years
Internal reports	3 years
Inventory records	7 years
Invoices	7 years
New product introduction minutes	3 years
Procedures (obsolete)	5 years
Process instructions (obsolete)	5 years
Production inspection and audit reports	3 years
Product test reports (daily)	3 years
Purchase orders	7 years
Receiving records	1 year
Sales records	7 years
Scrap records	1 year
Shipping and distribution records	3 years
Supplier performance evaluations	1 year
Supplier rejected material reports	1 year

Documents are crucial for explaining the development and entire life cycle of a product. They can serve as evidence that the manufacturer made every effort to assure a well-thought out safe and reliable product. Various records can identify problems experienced in the development and testing of a new product, along with the actions taken to correct the problems. Such documentation can be effective in proving that the manufacturer operated in a very concerned and responsible manner.

If not handled properly, documents can also prove just the opposite. They can tell the story of concerns that were expressed over the safety and reliability of a product, and the lack of any action on the part of management. They can tell how known defects were identified and disregarded by management possibly due to cost considerations, the drive to get the product into the marketplace, production pressures, or a number of other actions that will be regarded as being negligent and self-serving.

One of the first problems faced in document control is the misconception by management, even top executives within a corporation, that their letters and memos are confidential and are protected from the viewing of outsiders. Nothing could be further from the truth. When a company enters into a product liability lawsuit, and counsel for the plaintiff demands to see every memo, report, correspondence, and letter written that discusses the product, the manufacturer will be under court order to provide them. This would even include a highly confidential letter from the CEO to the chairman of the board regarding marketing plans for the product.

From the other end of the spectrum, plant management might speculate that their lesser important daily memos or e-mail messages are insignificant, and could be discarded if such a legal search and demand took place. This is also a false perception, and in fact if such memos were discarded at the time of litigation, managers involved could face serious liabilities and consequences.

RECOGNIZING *DANGEROUS DOCUMENTS*

The first step in the control of documents is to get the management team to recognize the different types of *dangerous documents* and how they are typically generated. In everyday production, management teams are exposed to problems and issues that they have to address, some of which might represent ongoing feuds. They might feel the constant problems are brought on by the incompetence of others, so their correspondence is meant to demonstrate such frustrations with the rest of the management group. (I hesitate to say *team* because in such open conflicts the individuals involved don't really represent the definition of a team.)

The example in Figure 8.1 shows a type of everyday correspondence one might easily experience in a manufacturing environment. This memo not only demonstrates certain hostilities between members of management. but the writer also chose to possibly exaggerate the severity of the problem. Such technical problems will develop with products, and the management team needs to understand how to best

---

MEMORANDUM

Date: 09/07/20XX

To: Director of Engineering

CC: Director of R&D

Sales Manager

General Manager

From: Quality Director

Subject: Design of Model XL 350

After receiving a number of complaints from the field regarding these units overheating and shutting down, and even beginning to smoke at times, I investigated the situation myself and found that your department specified an inadequate sized thermo protector. You specified a TP-270 protector, when in fact it should have been a TP-170 protector.

I have now stopped production of the Model XL 350 until the change is made. We are likely to have a substantial return rate on the units which is going to cost us thousands. By last count we probably have over 20,000 units in the fields.

We can only hope that none of these results in a fire!

Figure 8.1   A dangerous document.

address them. A better way to communicate the same concern is shown in Figure 8.2

In the incident involving the Model XL 350, once the director of engineering and quality get together, they can say anything they want in order to address the issue. They can even voice concerns regarding the possibility of the units starting on fire. At that point it will be a verbal conversation, and no one can expect you to remember what was said in a conversation. But such issues shouldn't be put on paper, unless you are prepared to show that all the product was recalled and rebuilt.

MEMORANDUM

Date: 09/07/20XX

To: Director of Engineering

CC: Sales Manager

General Manager

From: Quality Director

Subject: Design of Model XL 350

We need to meet as soon as possible to discuss the engineering design of the Model XL 350.

In the interim, I have found it necessary to stop production of the unit.

Please give me a call and let me know what would be a convenient time.

Figure 8.2 A well-phrased document.

The incident described can easily be recognized for the problems it can create, but there are other types of dangerous documents, ones that aren't so obvious. The example in Figure 8.3 illustrates another problem document. This memo may not seem like it could be a problem, but it could easily be. If the unit were to be involved in a fire, and it was proven or speculated that the cause of the fire had to deal with the plastic used in construction, such an internal memo could demonstrate to the court that the manufacturer was more interested in making money than in the safety of the end user.

Another example of a document that could easily lead to problems, is shown in Figure 8.4. This memo might not seem like a problem, but once again it displays that the company was more interested in cutting corners and getting the product into the marketplace in order to start generating quick sales. Although companies are always likely to want to fast-track the production of new products, expressing such interests on documents can lead to serious problems and accusations down the road.

INTEROFFICE MEMO

Date: 09/07/20XX

To: Director of Engineering

CC: Inferno Product Engineer

From: VP Sales

Subject: The Inferno Space Heater

I have reviewed our estimated cost of our new Inferno Space Heater, and find that once we add our standard markup, we won't be competitive.

One of the recent changes you made was to go from acrylic plastic to flame retardant polycarbonate, for twice the price!

I realize that we are concerned about safety and everything, but if I can't sell it, the improved safety won't matter. We need to change the material back to the original acrylic plastic and get our price back in line.

Figure 8.3   Another dangerous document.

OTHER TYPES OF DANGEROUS DOCUMENTS

Dangerous documents come in other forms beside memos and letters. Take for instance an engineering change request form, where the initiator is requesting a specific change because of recent findings. For instance, in an electronic product it is found after long-term testing that the internal ballast was improperly sized for the application and is beginning to overheat. The engineering change request initiator fills out the form with the following information:

⌐

Engineering Change Request

Nature of change: Change ballast from a model 175 to a 225.
Reason for change: Ballasts are undersized and overheating after long-term operation. Possibility for premature failure, and even fire.

INTEROFFICE MEMO

Date: 09/07/20XX

To: Director of Engineering, Estimating, Production
            Control, Plant Manager

From: President

Subject: The Mega-Power Generator

We have been given an excellent opportunity to be the
manufacturers of this new generator. It will require that we get
into production within 4 weeks instead of our normal 12-week
leadtime. We need to keep the engineering and product costs at
a minimum. All we need are the basics.

I am expecting all of you to quickly figure out how we will
achieve this, but I have a lot of faith in your abilities.

Sales of this product are expected to really take off which will
provide a lot of work for us over the next year or more. Let's
swing into gear as quickly as possible.

Figure 8.4   Another example of a dangerous document.

*When change is to take effect: This will be a running change. Change
will take place as soon as the 225 ballasts can be obtained.*

⅃

There are a number of critical issues regarding this request. First and
foremost is the fact that the initiator referenced the fire hazard. This
may have been done for effect, in order to help eliminate the possibilities of anyone challenging the need for the change, but it now
adds a very dangerous element to the request. Secondly, the proposal
is to make this a running change, as opposed to stopping production
and reworking inventory, much less any product that might already
be in the field. Such a document might only be seen by two individuals and might be taken as being quite routine. The issue and problem
might be openly discussed among various members of management,
but few if any might know that the document sits in the file in its present form waiting to be discovered. In a product liability lawsuit the

manufacturer can fully expect counsel for the plaintiff to request all drawings and revision changes made from a period long before the subject product was built to long afterward. When this change request is pulled from the file as part of a court ordered *Request for documents,* what is the management team to do, dispose of it? Not unless you want to face possible criminal charges for destruction of evidence.

OTHER TIPS FOR DOCUMENT CONTROL

There are a number of personal tendencies which contribute to the creation of dangerous or problem documents. One such common tendency is for individuals to generate their written opinions on technical issues which are outside their field of expertise. "I may not be an expert on the subject, but I think . . .," and then they go on to speculate on the possibilities of potential flammability, personal injury, or other conditions of liability. Normally these people want to ensure they are heard and have the opportunity to offer their opinion on what they consider to be important issues facing management. In addition to documenting their often worthless opinion, they compound the problem by ensuring the memo is sent to everyone they consider important. Now you're not only faced with the fact that a dangerous document was created, but the memo is in numerous files waiting to be found. Although they aren't experts on the subject, the fact that they expressed an opinion on what might be a delicate or potentially hazardous condition or situation creates problems. At a later date, should the product actually be involved in an accident or injury, and in discovery this memo surfaces, the court will be of the opinion that the company had prior knowledge of the hazardous condition and failed to respond in a responsible manner. The originator of the document might say, "I had no idea that such a thing would really happen, I was just guessing at the time." Would the court believe such a story? Not likely.

Another problem shown in the preceding examples is the tendency for people to exaggerate conditions. Sometimes this is done in order to command attention or help further their cause. When such exaggerations discuss or identify potential hazards, it could easily become a dangerous document to have around.

Electronic Documents: E-mail

Modern communication technologies have lead to the reduction of many printed documents and correspondence in favor of e-mail messages and electronically created files. In the year 2000 it is estimated there were 40 million e-mail users sending 60 billion messages. Because of the simplicity of the communication medium, the lack of a hard copy, and the perceived quick elimination of the record, many users fail to recognize the dangers.

The fact is, corporate computer systems are constantly backed up, and the message you think you deleted is probably still in your computer or backed up on the main system waiting to be discovered. When a user sends someone an e-mail message, the original message is not sent. Instead, the user's computer stores the original document and produces a copy it sends to a file server. The file server, in turn, stores the copy and produces another copy to send on. Depending on the computer network structure, the e-mail message may go through two or more servers, with each storing a copy and making new copies to forward to the intended recipient. Each time the message is *handled* by another server or personal computer, another copy is made.

Attorneys for plaintiffs in product liability cases know such records of communication exist and can demand access to the corporate tapes. Computer experts hired by these attorneys can be brought into the corporation to search for communications that could be advantageous to their case. The computer message has become the *digital smoking gun* in today's high tech world.

Corporate representatives with knowledge of the computer systems may be called under F. R. Civ. P. 30(b) for depositions to identify how data is maintained and to determine what hardware and software is necessary to proceed with merits discovery.

EMPLOYEE EDUCATION

To help prevent such problems as defined requires the education of the workforce. People do all the things mentioned purely because they don't know any better, or recognize any potential problems. Remember that employees are likely to think that internal memos are considered confidential and could never get into the hands of someone on the outside.

The corporate product liability team needs to spearhead training and awareness programs for all the employees, and part of that training would deal with the topic of dangerous documents. Once the employees learn these key precautions, it is amazing how they react from that day forward. Employees will call attention to dangerous documents the instant they see them and correct others for generating them.

Contractual Agreements

The company purchase order is a vital contract between the organization and its suppliers and subcontractors. In many cases, it is also the only legal contract bonding the two companies. How the purchase orders are originated, what they need to include as specification, what contractual agreements need to be spelled out or included, and what needs to be sent along with them should be reviewed by the product liability review team and incorporated into procedures.

It is surprising how many companies don't pay attention to the fine print of their own purchase order until they become involved in a product liability action. Some companies expect to be indemnified by their suppliers in the event of a product liability lawsuit but never say as much on their purchase order. Other companies expect subrogation in the event of an insurance claim but fail to state the requirement. Regardless of customer goodwill, the corporation's insurance company will pay the bill in the event of a product liability action. Unless there is a contractual agreement for the supplier to indemnify their customers, the insurance company is not likely to honor a customer goodwill request. Both suppliers and customers need to pay special attention to what the other is stipulating.

CUSTOMER CONTRACTS

Manufacturers need to be cognizant of the exact wording of contractual agreements and product specifications handed them by the customer, as part of any initial qualification program or as the result of an order being placed. In some instances, the customer may be many times larger than the supplier/manufacturer, which could mean an in-house legal department or at least a well-written protective contract. It could even mean that, in addition to requiring indemnification, the customer may require subrogation for any legal fees incurred at the start of an incident. The supplier/manufacturer may not realize this until months later. In addition to the logical indemnification clauses, many other product-related specifications and special handling requirements may be stipulated in pages of customer fine print that go unnoticed in the excitement of receiving the order.

When new customers are brought into an organization and orders received, sales needs to forward the fine print documents and product specifications to the in-house expert or the corporate product liability team for review, if there is no legal department. Although the supplier/manufacturer isn't likely to challenge such stipulations, it is important that they remain aware of what is demanded or will be expected of them, in the event of an incident.

SUPPLIERS AND SUBCONTRACTORS

Another element that most companies and purchasing departments don't consider is whether their suppliers and subcontractors, small or large, have liability insurance. Most manufacturing companies will secure bids from at least three suppliers for each component part to be purchased, with their primary concern being price, leadtime, and quality. But the purchasing company often fails to ask the potential supplier whether they carry liability insurance. It normally isn't part of their selection and qualification criteria. Combine that with the fact that their purchase orders probably don't include indemnification clauses, and you have the right recipe for disaster. If the supplier's or subcontractor's product creates catastrophic failure in the field, result-ing in death, injuries, or property damage, and the subcontractor closes his doors, the primary company suffers the liability loss. It is too late at this point to find out that the supplier never had product liability insurance because they thought it would be too expensive.

The corporate product liability team needs to assure that all sup-pliers and subcontractors have product liability insurance prior to being selected. They should also ensure that the levels are adequate for your line of business, with a minimum of $1 million. You should also require that your company be listed as an *Additional Insured* on the supplier's policy, which not only insures indemnification but also makes you aware if they drop the policy. The company needs to then put out an *Approved Supplier/Subcontractor* listing that incorporates this qualification criteria along with the other elements already used.

CONTRACT REVIEWS, A CRITICAL ASPECT OF PREVENTION

The following material was summarized by Attorney Helena Haapio, principle of Lexpert in Helsinki, Finland. Ms. Haapio is a recognized expert in the field of international industrial contract law. She also serves as an arbitrator.

⌐

In international sales, thousands of routine business documents develop into contracts every day. Business people involved in export transactions seldom recognize that they are creating binding contracts or dealing with foreign laws. They may follow procedures and work instructions that no corporate counsel knew existed or ever had a chance to look at. This may lead to lost opportunities and unintentional liabilities. Great benefits can be gained through integrating the theory and practice of preventive law with quality and risk management. An integrated approach leads to streamlined procedures, consistency of approach and an improved awareness, analysis, and management of risks. Certain features of quality systems, such as contract reviews, can facilitate integration and secure that everybody is doing it right the first time and every time.

Winston Churchill once stated, "War is too important to be left to the generals." International sales contracts and contracting procedures are too varied and too important to be left solely to lawyers. This section illustrates how quality systems can be used to improve the legal quality of export documents focusing specifically on how contract reviews performed within a quality system framework can and should be used as a preventive tool by lawyers and non-lawyers alike.

The quality management and quality assurance vocabulary standard in ISO defines contract review as systematic activities carried out by the supplier before signing the contract to ensure that requirements for quality are adequately defined, free from ambiguity, documented, and can be realized by the supplier.

According to Clause 7.2.2 of the new ISO 9001:2000 standard, the organization shall review the identified customer requirements together with additional requirements determined by the organization. The review shall be conducted prior to the commitment to supply a product to a customer (for example, submission of a tender, acceptance of a contract or order) and shall ensure that: (a) product requirements are defined; (b) where the customer provides no documented statement of requirement, the customer requirements are confirmed before acceptance; (c) contract or order requirements differing from those previously expressed (for example, in a tender or quotation) are resolved; (d) the organization has the ability to meet defined requirements. The results of the review and subsequent follow-up actions shall be recorded. It further goes on to state: Where product requirements are changed, the organization shall ensure that relevant documentation is amended. The organization shall ensure that relevant personnel are made aware of the changed requirements.

As referred to in the relevant ISO standards, contract review relates to sales and aims to ensure that the supplier understands and is capable of meeting the customer's requirements. Contract review is the responsibility of the supplier in a sales transaction. Purchasing documents, on the other hand, such as contracts between the supplier and its subcontractors, are governed by ISO 9001: 2000 Clause 7.4 (Purchasing). In Clause 7.2, contract review activities are not provided for under that name. However, in accordance with ISO 9001:2000 Clause 7.4.2, the supplier shall review and approve purchasing documents for adequacy of the specified requirements prior to release. For the subcontractor, the same situation is a sales situation (the supplier being the subsupplier's customer) and the subsupplier's quality system would refer to the relevant contract review procedures. Clearly, such provisions create sufficient cause for all parties to consider carrying contract reviews out jointly.

Two definitions which aid in the interpretation of the intended scope of a contract review are included in Section 3 of the ISO standard:

- *Tender*—Offer made by a supplier in response to an invitation to satisfy a contract award to provide product
- *Contract*—Agreed requirements between a supplier and customer transmitted by any means

While these definitions do not fully comply with a contract lawyer's view, their addition to the quality systems vocabulary was useful. It took into account a fact of everyday life: informal (*camouflaged*) contracts and verbal orders.

Contract review has been understood by many to be a post-contract activity related to formal written contracts only. This may still be the case with some organizations, and according to surveys conducted by quality auditors. Contract review is an area that is often poorly handled.

Quite often, supply contracts for machinery are made through a chain of documents, none of which bears the heading *contract*. To believe that a contract is always a piece of paper, formally acknowledging that it is a contract, is a mistake and far from the myth. Such an erroneous belief is dangerous. From a pragmatic lawyer's point of view, there are three kinds of contracts: (1) specifically negotiated contracts; (2) standard form contracts formed through offer and acceptance, quotation, tender or bid, followed by a purchase order or followed by order acknowledgement or confirmation (the fine print and risk of a *battle of forms* is often present in this category of contracts); and (3) *informal deals* which are contracts made informally, for example through telephone conversations or a simple exchange of letters.

Case studies and business practice experience show that standard form contracts and informal deals are the most frequent cases and are often misunderstood by business people as *noncontractual* events. An understanding of the scope of delivery, price, and schedule may be reached in general terms, while other contractual matters dealing with issues such as safety, failure, liability, and insurance may be perceived as cumbersome. When this happens, contractual review may be forgotten and contracts will not be used as planning tools to proactively guide the success of a transaction. Unfortunately, the opportunities offered by contracts to effectively control one's business future and risk exposure will be lost as well.

Whether and when a contract is formed is often difficult to recognize. In addition, it may be difficult to determine what was agreed. In international sales and purchases, the answer may be completely different from what either party (or both) originally intended.

Let us assume a straightforward export sale of a $50,000 production machine is made by a Norwegian company to a customer in the United States. The individuals involved in the deal know one another and the sale is made informally through telephone conversations. Based on a one-page purchase order acknowledged by only a few lines by the supplier, the delivery is made and the machinery is put into production. In a few weeks time, a failure occurs, causing damage to property, plus a loss of production and profit, totaling $200,000.

A less-experienced exporter might assume that since nothing was specifically noted regarding liability for loss or damage, there is no liability. However, an experienced exporter knows better; silence or lack of specific mention in documents does not share or limit liability. This simplified situation describes a typical gap in communication which leads to a gap in documentation, erroneous assumptions and beliefs, and ultimately, disappointment and major legal and financial problems.

In this example, as in many international sales of machinery or other goods, the gap-filling law is the Convention on Contracts for International Sale of Goods (CISG). The CISG is now in force in many countries, including Argentina, Australia, Austria, Canada, Chile, China, Cuba, Denmark, Finland, France, Germany, Mexico, New Zealand, Norway, Poland, Russia, Singapore, Spain, Sweden, Switzerland, and the United

States. With so many participating nations, the CISG is having increased influence on international commercial transactions. Some assert that the CISG provides businesspeople and lawyers with a simpler and more secure legal basis for international trade. Others say quite the opposite. Despite this debate, CISG is the uniform international sales law of countries that account for over two-thirds of all world trade today. The effects of this law on the rights, obligations, liabilities, and remedies in international sales or purchases are not very well known or understood.

If the parties in the example had used vague specifications and did not specifically resolve issues related to the performance of fitness of the machinery for its intended purpose, the gap-filling provisions of the CISG would be triggered. Under Article 35 of the CISG, unless the parties have agreed otherwise, the seller must deliver goods which "are fit for any particular purpose expressly or impliedly made known to the seller at the time of the conclusion of the contract, except where the circumstances show that the buyer did not rely, or that it was unreasonable for him to rely, on the seller's skill and judgement." This is just one of many examples proving that the requirements implied by law are not a very clear basis for successful transactions in a modern technically complex world.

If we were to assume that the parties in our example did not agree upon liabilities and remedies, and assuming further that the failure was due to the seller's breach of an express or implied obligation, according to Article 74 of the CISG, subject to foreseeability, "damages for breach of contract by one party consist of a sum equal to the loss, including loss of profit, suffered by the other party as a consequence of the breach." No ceiling or maximum liability is specified for the protection of the seller, who may not only end up losing profit (and a customer), but also paying damages that are many times greater than the original purchase price.

How does a supplier ensure that it has the capability to meet the requirements, if the requirements are not clearly expressed, but only implied by a law that neither party was aware of when they entered into the deal? Ignorance is not bliss. If the contract is not specific and crucial issues remain unaddressed, it is not clear who will be held responsible for what, and the parties will face unforeseen complications and negative surprise. It is not unusual for internal disputes to arise within an organization. The supplier's risk managers, quality engineers, customer satisfaction personnel, and lawyers may all *know* the correct answer, but disagree about it. Moreover, the answers given by gap-filling laws may come as a shock to all parties.

Our simplified example also illustrates *contractual gambling.* Contractual gambling refers to situations where neither player knows whether and how much it may gain or lose. However, one thing is certain: both parties may lose and probably the only people who will benefit are the litigating lawyers. Certainly, had the parties known how to avoid the result, they would have done so.

How does one avoid problems such as those presented in our hypothetical? Could the problem or risk have been managed earlier? How can recurrence of the same or similar problems be avoided? A contract review could answer these questions and lay the groundwork for a proactive plan of action. A productive use of contract reviews can ensure the discovery of hidden problems. Moreover, contract reviews can secure a proactive course of action, where contracts can be used as tools for planning as well as for project, quality, and risk management.

A contract for the supply of machinery typically contains technical, commercial, and legal information. All three parts are essential elements of the whole. It is crucial that all three areas are mutually shared, understood, and accurately documented. If the specifications and contractual documents are carefully prepared, even those not directly involved in the negotiations can verify what was agreed. It is important for the purchasing function, project management, and others to know about the commitments of the selling function, and vice versa. Those involved should know early on what their legal and bargaining position is in the event of machinery failure or other problems.

In industrial machinery supply contracting, certain territories are known to be liability minefields. Ambiguous specifications, site investigation clauses, warranties, liquidated damages, indemnities, disclaimers, and overlooked choice of law or jurisdiction provisions are typical examples. These types of problematic areas should be recognized at an early stage. Documented procedures for contract review can make appropriate personnel aware of possible dangers related to such clauses to ensure early action is taken. From a risk management and preventive law point of view, contract reviews can provide reminders to key personnel of do's and don'ts, such as inadvertently created warranties and the necessity of either modifying or eliminating *red flag* words in promotional materials and contracting documents.

Case histories show that contract reviews can be successfully used to go to the root causes of problems, including those pertaining to safety and liability risks. A contract review carried out with appropriate care can further diminish the possibility of misunderstandings, disappointed expectations, and negative surprise. When appropriate checklists and guides are created and used, essential questions are not forgotten.

The machinery supplier must thoroughly understand its customer's needs. In a quality management system, contract review is the process by which customer requirements are determined. The overall purpose of the contract review is to accurately determine what the requirements are and to make certain the supplier can meet them. Ideally, the needs and requirements are accurately reflected in the contract. From a preventive law and risk management point of view, it is crucial that the supplier and the purchaser arrive at contract requirements which are adequately defined and documented, and the supplier must examine its capabilities and resources before it commits itself to its customer.

Contracts determine what is to be provided to external customers, as well as the where, when, and how it will be provided. One basic function of contracts is to facilitate successful business exchanges and the fair allocation of risks between the contracting parties. Thus a contract is an entity of technical, commercial, and legal information. Like technical specifications and commercial price and payment terms, other conditions of the contract are also instrumental elements of the whole. It is essential that those elements are all addressed, agreed upon, and documented accurately. Meeting contractual requirements includes complying not only with technical specifications, but also with delivery and other terms and after-sales commitments, where included.

Contract reviews are carried out as part of the day-to-day operations of many organizations within the framework of existing quality systems. Comprehensive contract reviews offer enormous integration opportunities. Experience has shown, however, that not all companies' standard operating procedures recognize or encourage the full utilization of solid contracts and effective contract reviews.

Manuals, documented procedures, work instructions, and forms are typical quality system documents. They can be reviewed and updated to effectively support the exploitation of the opportunities offered by contracts and contract reviews. These materials can also be used as risk management and preventive law tools. Checklists, forms, and work instructions can be prepared for management and line personnel to guide them safely through the contracting process by making clear where responsibility for various issues lies, what documents and matters are to be reviewed at what stage, and how exhaustive the review should be. In this way, contractual opportunities and potential problems can be detected early enough to take proactive action. Instructions are further needed for amendments to contracts and also for records of contract reviews.

Areas to be covered by the checklists, forms, and work instructions and the degree of detail will vary depending on the line of business, the economics, the uses and conditions of use of the machinery, the complexity of the transaction, and the standards and safety requirements involved. Depending on company policy, instructions may be included for warranties, with appropriate reminders and recommended courses of action in respect of liability for defects, implied terms, and other matters based on gap-filling laws. A list of *must address* issues may also be provided, as well as questions to ask to ensure that the scope is clearly defined and the requirements are adequately documented. Contract review checklists can include recommendations as to applicable forms and general conditions (the fine print) and *must have* provisions, such as those securing acceptable exposure to risk and limits of liability in accordance with the applicable law and company policy.

Contracts, even *camouflaged* contracts, must be recognized and reviewed as much for what they *do not say* as for what they do say. Problems and liabilities often arise not from a breach of a specific contractual provision, but from breach of an *implied* obligation or liability.

Through contract reviews, efficient use of order confirmations and a consistent approach to the *battle of forms* can be secured. Training is essential in order to gain maximum benefit from the revised contract review activities and documents. This may present a challenge because of prevailing attitudes, such as *contracts are lawyers' (or someone else's) responsibility.* Participating in creating checklists and developing procedures can help, and training can be designed in the spirit of *this can make our jobs easier* or *this will help protect us from future trouble.* Participants must take ownership and understand why contracts and contract reviews are important.

Sales or purchasing people, engineers, quality or risk management, and lawyers should not do their safety audits or contract reviews separately. They should carry them out in team discussion. Team efforts can educate the various players and increase productivity. In the long run, everyone, including the lawyers, benefit from systematic preventive measures because they are much more productive and motivating than continual fire-fighting.

In the current ISO 9000:2000 series of standards, contract review is clearly a precontract activity, looking to future events. Contract review includes not only contracts, but tenders (offers, quotations, and bids), orders, and even verbal communications. The goals of preventive law, contractual risk management, and contract reviews are very much the same. In each case, reaching the goals requires involving management and employees in the process. Success and responsibility are in the hands of management and employees, not just the legal, quality, or safety professionals.

In recent process improvement projects, contract reviews have proven to be a valuable checkpoint and an unexploited resource. There appears to be plenty of room for improvement through integration. Contracts, contract reviews, and related checklists can serve as risk management and preventive law tools. Further, they can be used as internal and external communication aides for the contracting partner organizations and others involved in the process. These tools can become communication aides that guide parties toward conscious and careful planning of crucial issues involved in the undertaking, rather than leaving such matters at tacit agreement, unilateral assumptions, or ignorance of the issues. When planning and negotiating international supply transactions, it is in the interest of everyone involved to avoid the complications and negative consequences of overlooked critical issues.

Solid contract conditions and models can themselves serve as a checklist for matters that should be agreed. In this way, when the parties review the contract proposal together at the beginning of the project, essential questions are not forgotten. The contract also serves as a project management tool and checklist at the implementation stage. When it is carefully prepared, it is easy to verify what has been agreed.

Making use of preventive law tools can be a great contribution toward risk management and loss prevention. Moreover, one need not be a lawyer to benefit from the preventive law approach. The best contract review checklists and optimal contracts are cocreated by a team of future users, with comments by respective experts from the legal, quality, and risk management points of view. The process contains a valuable training element as well.

The awareness analysis and management of contractual and liability risks and the *legal quality* of contractual documents can be integrated into a quality system by means of appropriate instructions, checklists, and contract reviews. This does not require major investment and is a significant step toward continuous improvement in the day-to-day operations of an organization. Quality, safety, risk management, and legal professionals who work together proactively can greatly improve existing contract review procedures to ensure early detection and prevention of problems. Business-to-business contract makers can then reach predictable outcomes and minimize negative surprises.

◾

OFFERING SERVICE CONTRACTS

The following information comes directly from the Federal Trade Commission books on warranties.

A service contract is an optional agreement for product service that customers sometimes buy. It provides additional protection beyond what the warranty offers on the product. Service contracts are similar to warranties in that both concern service for a product. However, there are differences between warranties and service contracts.

Warranties come with a product and are included in the purchase price. In the language of the Act, warranties are "part of the basis of the bargain." Service contracts, on the other hand, are agreements that are separate from the contract or sale of the product. They are separate either because they are made some time after the sale of the product, or because they cost the customer a fee beyond the purchase price of the product. The Act includes very broad provisions governing service contracts that are explained in the following sections.

STATEMENT OF TERMS AND CONDITIONS

If you offer a service contract, the Act requires you to list conspicuously all terms and conditions in simple and readily understood language. However, unlike warranties, service contracts are *not* required to be titled *full* or *limited*, or to contain the special standard disclosures. In fact, using warranty disclosures in service contracts could confuse customers about whether the agreement is a warranty or a service contract.

The company that makes the service contract is responsible for ensuring that the terms and conditions are disclosed as required by law. This is not the responsibility of the seller of the service contract, unless the seller and the maker are the same company.

DISCLAIMER OR LIMITATION OF IMPLIED WARRANTIES

Sellers of consumer products who make service contracts on their products are prohibited under the Act from disclaiming or limiting implied warranties. (Remember also that sellers who extend written warranties on consumer products cannot disclaim implied warranties, regardless of whether they make service contracts on their products.) However, sellers of consumer products that merely sell service contracts as agents of service contract companies *and* do not themselves extend written warranties can disclaim implied warranties on the products they sell.

Warranties and Misrepresentation

10

🔳

Warranties are a key issue for manufacturers as a part of their quality programs, and they are especially a key issue in the legal world. There are a number of legal guidelines a manufacturer needs to know before writing warranties for their products, or they run the risk of serious potential problems. This chapter describes the different types of warranties and laws that pertain to them. It also describes the legal problems and lawsuits that arise from warranties, false advertising and marketing programs, and related statements in various correspondence. This is an area that many companies think is insignificant, but will find that it can be one of the leading causes of lawsuits.

UNDERSTANDING WARRANTIES

The following information is taken directly from the Federal Trade Commissions (FTC) booklets on warranties.

Generally, a warranty is your promise, as a manufacturer or seller, to stand behind your product. It is a statement about the integrity of your product and about your commitment to correct problems when your product fails. The law recognizes two basic kinds of warranties—implied warranties and express warranties.

Implied Warranties

Implied warranties are unspoken, unwritten promises, created by state law, that go from you, as a seller or merchant, to your customers. Implied warranties are based upon the common law principle of *fair*

145

value for money spent. There are two types of implied warranties that occur in consumer product transactions. They are the *implied warranty of merchantability* and the *implied warranty of fitness for a particular purpose*.

The *implied warranty of merchantability* is a merchant's basic promise that the goods sold will do what they are supposed to do and that there is nothing significantly wrong with them. In other words, it is an implied promise that the goods are fit to be sold. The law says that merchants make this promise automatically every time they sell a product they are in business to sell. For example, if you, as an appliance retailer, sell an oven, you are promising that the oven is in proper condition for sale because it will do what ovens are supposed to do— bake food at controlled temperatures selected by the buyer. If the oven does not heat, or if it heats without proper temperature control, then the oven is not fit for sale as an oven, and your implied warranty of merchantability would be breached. In such a case, the law requires you to provide a remedy so that the buyer gets a working oven.

The *implied warranty of fitness for a particular purpose* is a promise that the law says you, as a seller, make when your customer relies on your advice that a product can be used for some specific purpose. For example, suppose you are an appliance retailer and a customer asks for a clothes washer that can handle 15 pounds of laundry at a time. If you recommend a particular model, and the customer buys that model on the strength of your recommendation, the law says that you have made a warranty of fitness for a particular purpose. If the model you recommended proves unable to handle 15-pound loads, even though it may effectively wash 10-pound loads, your warranty of fitness for a particular purpose is breached.

Implied warranties are promises about the condition of products at the time they are sold, but they do not assure that a product will last for any specific length of time. (The normal durability of a product is, of course, one aspect of a product's merchantability or its fitness for a particular purpose.) Nor does the law say that everything that can possibly go wrong with a product falls within the scope of implied warranties. For example, implied warranties do not cover problems such as those caused by abuse, misuse, ordinary wear, failure to follow directions, or improper maintenance.

Generally, there is no specified duration for implied warranties under state laws. However, the state statutes of limitations for breach of either an express or an implied warranty are generally four years from date of purchase. This means that buyers have four years in which to discover and seek a remedy for problems that were present in the product at the time it was sold. It does not mean that the product must last for four years. It means only that the product must be of normal durability, considering its nature and price.

A special note is in order regarding implied warranties on *used* merchandise. An implied warranty of merchantability on a *used product* is a promise that it can be used as expected, given its type and price range. As with new merchandise, implied warranties on used merchandise apply only when the seller is a merchant who deals in such goods, not when a sale is made by a private individual.

If you do not offer a written warranty, the law in most states allows you to disclaim implied warranties. However, selling without implied warranties may well indicate to potential customers that the product is risky—low quality, damaged, or discontinued—and therefore, should be available at a lower price.

In order to disclaim implied warranties, you must inform consumers in a conspicuous manner, and generally in writing, that you will not be responsible if the product malfunctions or is defective. It must be clear to consumers that the entire product risk falls on them. You must specifically indicate that you do not warrant *merchantability,* or you must use a phrase such as *with all faults* or *as is.* A few states have special laws on how you must phrase an *as is* disclosure. (For specific information on how your state treats *as is* disclosures, consult your attorney.)

Some states do not allow you to sell consumer products *as is.* At this time, these states are Alabama, Connecticut, Kansas, Maine, Maryland, Massachusetts, Minnesota, Mississippi, New Hampshire, Vermont, Washington, West Virginia, and the District of Columbia. In those states, sellers have implied warranty obligations that cannot be avoided. Federal law prohibits you from disclaiming implied warranties on any consumer product if you offer a written warranty for that product or sell a service contract on it.

You should be aware that even if you sell a product *as is* and it proves to be defective or dangerous and causes personal injury to someone, you still may be liable under the principles of product liability. Selling the product *as is* does not eliminate this liability.

EXPRESS WARRANTIES

Express warranties, unlike implied warranties, are not *read into* your sales contracts by state law; rather, you explicitly offer these warranties to your customers in the course of a sales transaction. They are promises and statements that you voluntarily make about your product or about your commitment to remedy the defects and malfunctions that some customers may experience.

Express warranties can take a variety of forms, ranging from advertising claims to formal certificates. An express warranty can be made either orally or in writing. While oral warranties are important, only written warranties on consumer products are covered by the Magnuson-Moss Warranty Act.

UNDERSTANDING THE MAGNUSON-MOSS WARRANTY ACT

The Magnuson-Moss Warranty Act is the federal law that governs consumer product warranties. Passed by Congress in 1975, the Act requires manufacturers and sellers of consumer products to provide consumers with detailed information about warranty coverage. In addition, it affects both the rights of consumers and the obligations of warrantors under written warranties.

To understand the Act, it is useful to be aware of Congress' intentions in passing it. First, Congress wanted to ensure that consumers could get complete information about warranty terms and conditions. By providing consumers with a way of learning what warranty coverage is offered on a product before they buy, the Act gives consumers a way to know what to expect if something goes wrong, and thus helps to increase customer satisfaction.

Second, Congress wanted to ensure that consumers could compare warranty coverage before buying. By comparing, consumers can choose a product with the best combination of price, features, and warranty coverage to meet their individual needs.

Third, Congress intended to promote competition on the basis of warranty coverage. By assuring that consumers can get warranty information, the Act encourages sales promotion on the basis of warranty coverage and competition among companies to meet consumer preferences through various levels of warranty coverage.

Finally, Congress wanted to strengthen existing incentives for companies to perform their warranty obligations in a timely and thorough manner and to resolve any disputes with a minimum of delay and expense to consumers. Thus, the Act makes it easier for consumers to pursue a remedy for breach of warranty in the courts, but it also creates a framework for companies to set up procedures for resolving disputes inexpensively and informally, without litigation.

What the Magnuson-Moss Act Does Not Require

In order to understand how the Act affects you as a businessperson, it is important first to understand what the Act does not require.

First, the Act does not require any business to provide a written warranty. The Act allows businesses to determine whether to warrant their products in writing. However, once a business decides to offer a written warranty on a consumer product, it must comply with the Act.

Second, the Act does not apply to oral warranties. Only written warranties are covered.

Third, the Act does not apply to warranties on services. Only warranties on goods are covered. However, if your warranty covers both the parts provided for a repair and the workmanship in making that repair, the Act does apply to you.

Finally, the Act does not apply to warranties on products sold for resale or for commercial purposes. The Act covers only warranties on consumer products. This means that only warranties on tangible property normally used for personal, family, or household purposes are covered. (This includes property attached to or installed on real property.) Note that applicability of the Act to a particular product does *not*, however, depend upon how an individual buyer will use it.

The following section of this manual summarizes what the Magnuson-Moss Warranty Act requires warrantors to do, what it prohibits them from doing, and how it affects warranty disputes.

What the Magnuson-Moss Act Requires

In passing the Magnuson-Moss Warranty Act, Congress specified a number of requirements that warrantors must meet. Congress also directed the FTC (Federal Trade Commission) to adopt rules to cover other requirements. The FTC adopted three Rules under the Act: the *Rule on Disclosure of Written Consumer Product Warranty Terms and Conditions* (the Disclosure Rule), the *Rule on Pre-Sale Availability of*

Written Warranty Terms (the Pre-Sale Availability Rule), and the *Rule on Informal Dispute Settlement Procedures* (the Dispute Resolution Rule). In addition, the FTC has issued an interpretive rule that clarifies certain terms and explains some of the provisions of the Act. This section summarizes all the requirements under the Act and the Rules.

The Act and the Rules establish three basic requirements that may apply to you, either as a warrantor or a seller:

1. As a warrantor, you must designate, or title, your written warranty as either *full* or *limited*.

2. As a warrantor, you must state certain specified information about the coverage of your warranty in a single, clear, and easy-to-read document.

3. As a warrantor or a seller, you must ensure that warranties are available where your warranted consumer products are sold so that consumers can read them before buying.

The titling requirement, established by the Act, applies to all written warranties on consumer products costing more than $10. However, the disclosure and pre sale availability requirements, established by FTC Rules, apply to all written warranties on consumer products costing more than $15.

WHAT THE MAGNUSON-MOSS ACT DOES NOT ALLOW

There are three prohibitions under the Magnuson-Moss Act. They involve implied warranties, so-called *tie-in sales* provisions, and deceptive or misleading warranty terms.

Disclaimer or Modification of Implied Warranties

The Act prohibits anyone who offers a written warranty from disclaiming or modifying implied warranties. This means that no matter how broad or narrow your written warranty is, your customers always will receive the basic protection of the implied warranty of merchantability.

There is one permissible modification of implied warranties, however. If you offer a *limited* written warranty, the law allows you to include a provision that restricts the duration of implied warranties to the duration of your limited warranty. For example, if you offer a two-year limited warranty, you can limit implied warranties to two years.

However, if you offer a *full* written warranty, you cannot limit the duration of implied warranties.

If you sell a consumer product with a written warranty from the product manufacturer, but you do not warrant the product in writing, you can disclaim your implied warranties. (These are the implied warranties under which the seller, not the manufacturer, would otherwise be responsible.) But, regardless of whether you warrant the products you sell, as a seller, you must give your customers copies of any written warranties from product manufacturers.

Tie-In Sales Provisions

Generally, tie-in sales provisions are not allowed. Such a provision would require a purchaser of the warranted product to buy an item or service from a particular company to use with the warranted product in order to be eligible to receive a remedy under the warranty. The following are examples of prohibited tie-in sales provisions.

⌐

In order to keep your new Plenum Brand Vacuum Cleaner warranty in effect, you must use genuine Plenum Brand Filter Bags. Failure to have scheduled maintenance performed, at your expense, by the Great American Maintenance Company, voids this warranty.

⅃

While you cannot use a tie-in sales provision, your warranty need not cover use of replacement parts, repairs, or maintenance that is inappropriate for your product. The following is an example of a permissible provision that excludes coverage of such things.

⌐

While necessary maintenance or repairs on your AudioMundo Stereo System can be performed by any company, we recommend that you use only authorized AudioMundo dealers. Improper or incorrectly performed maintenance or repair voids this warranty.

⅃

Although tie-in sales provisions generally are not allowed, you can include such a provision in your warranty if you can demonstrate to the satisfaction of the FTC that your product will not work properly without a specified item or service. If you believe that this is the case, you should contact the warranty staff of the FTC's Bureau of Consumer Protection for information on how to apply for a waiver of the tie-in sales prohibition.

Deceptive Warranty Terms

Obviously, warranties must not contain deceptive or misleading terms. You cannot offer a warranty that appears to provide coverage but, in fact, provides none. For example, a warranty covering only *moving parts* on an electronic product that has no moving parts would be deceptive and unlawful. Similarly, a warranty that promised service that the warrantor had no intention of providing or could not provide would be deceptive and unlawful.

HOW THE MAGNUSON-MOSS ACT MAY AFFECT WARRANTY DISPUTES

Two other features of the Magnuson-Moss Warranty Act are also important to warrantors. First, the Act makes it easier for consumers to take an unresolved warranty problem to court. Second, it encourages companies to use a less formal, and therefore less costly, alternative to legal proceedings. Such alternatives, known as dispute resolution mechanisms, often can be used to settle warranty complaints before they reach litigation.

Consumer Lawsuits

The Act makes it easier for purchasers to sue for breach of warranty by making breach of warranty a violation of federal law, and by allowing consumers to recover court costs and reasonable attorneys' fees. This means that if you lose a lawsuit for breach of either a written or an implied warranty, you may have to pay the customer's costs for bringing the suit, including lawyer's fees.

Because of the stringent federal jurisdictional requirements under the Act, most Magnuson-Moss lawsuits are brought in state court. However, major cases involving many consumers can be brought in federal court as class action suits under the Act.

Although the consumer lawsuit provisions may have little effect on your warranty or your business, they are important to remember if you are involved in warranty disputes.

Alternatives to Consumer Lawsuits

Although the Act makes consumer lawsuits for breach of warranty easier to bring, its goal is not to promote more warranty litigation. On the contrary, the Act encourages companies to use informal dispute resolution mechanisms to settle warranty disputes with their customers. Basically, an informal dispute resolution mechanism is a system that works to resolve warranty problems that are at a stalemate. Such a mechanism may be run by an impartial third party, such as the Better Business Bureau, or by company employees whose only job is to administer the informal dispute resolution system. The impartial third party uses conciliation, mediation, or arbitration to settle warranty disputes.

The Act allows warranties to include a provision that requires customers to try to resolve warranty disputes by means of the informal dispute resolution mechanism before going to court. (This provision applies only to cases based upon the Magnuson-Moss Act.) If you include such a requirement in your warranty, your dispute resolution mechanism *must* meet the requirements stated in the FTC's *Rule on Informal Dispute Settlement Procedures* (the Dispute Resolution Rule). Briefly, the Rule requires that a mechanism must:

- Be adequately funded and staffed to resolve all disputes quickly.
- Be available free of charge to consumers.
- Be able to settle disputes independently, without influence from the parties involved.
- Follow written procedures.
- Inform both parties when it receives notice of a dispute.
- Gather, investigate, and organize all information necessary to decide each dispute fairly and quickly.
- Provide each party an opportunity to present its side, to submit supporting materials, and to rebut points made by the other party. (The mechanism may allow oral presentations, but only if both parties agree.)
- Inform both parties of the decision and the reasons supporting it within 40 days of receiving notice of a dispute.
- Issue decisions that are not binding; either party must be free to take the dispute to court if dissatisfied with the decision. (However, companies may, and often do, agree to be bound by the decision.)
- Keep complete records on all disputes.
- Be audited annually for compliance with the Rule.

It is clear from these standards that informal dispute resolution mechanisms under the Dispute Resolution Rule are not *informal* in the sense of being unstructured. Rather, they are informal because they do not involve the technical rules of evidence, procedure, and precedents that a court of law must use.

Currently, the FTC's staff is evaluating the Dispute Resolution Rule to determine if informal dispute resolution mechanisms can be made simpler and easier to use. To obtain more information about this review, contact the FTC's warranty staff.

As stated previously, you do not have to comply with the Dispute Resolution Rule if you do not require consumers to use a mechanism before bringing suit under the Magnuson-Moss Act. You may want to consider establishing a mechanism that will make settling warranty disputes easier, even though it may not meet the standards of the Dispute Resolution Rule.

TITLING WRITTEN WARRANTIES AS *FULL* OR *LIMITED*

The Magnuson-Moss Warranty Act requires that every written warranty on a consumer product that costs more than $10 have a title that says the warranty is either *full* or *limited*. (The Act calls these titles *designations*.) The title is intended to provide consumers, at a glance, with a key to some of the important terms and conditions of a warranty. The title *full warranty* is a shorthand message to consumers that the coverage meets the Act's standards for comprehensive warranty coverage. Similarly, the title *limited warranty* alerts consumers that the coverage does not meet at least one of the Act's standards, and that the coverage is less than *full* under the Act.

What the Terms *Full* and *Limited* Mean

Determining whether your warranty is a *full* or a *limited* warranty is not difficult. If each of the following five statements is true about your warranty's terms and conditions, it is a *full* warranty:

1. You do not limit the duration of implied warranties.

2. You provide warranty service to anyone who owns the product during the warranty period; that is, you do not limit coverage to first purchasers.

3. You provide warranty service free of charge, including such costs as returning the product or removing and reinstalling the product when necessary.

4. You provide, at the consumer's choice, either a replacement or a full refund if, after a reasonable number of tries, you are unable to repair the product.

5. You do not require consumers to perform any duty as a precondition for receiving service, except notifying you that

service is needed, unless you can demonstrate that the duty is reasonable.

If any of these statements is not true, then your warranty is *limited.* You are not required to make your entire warranty full or limited. If the preceding statements are true about the coverage on only some parts of your product, or if the statements are true about the coverage during only one part of the warranty period, then your warranty is a multiple warranty that is part full and part limited.

Examples of Full Warranties, Limited Warranties, and Multiple Warranties

When you decide on your warranty's terms and conditions, consider eliminating unnecessary restrictions. Rather than adopting warranty terms just because they are common in your industry, let your experience guide you. For example, a limit on the duration of implied warranties may be the only provision that would prevent your written warranty from being full as shown in Figure 10.1. If your experience indicates that you do not really need this restriction, you may wish to consult your attorney and eliminate it.

Also, remember that the distinctions between a *full* and a *limited* warranty are specified by law, and that the legal meanings of the words *full* and *limited* in written consumer product warranties are far more narrow and specific than they are in ordinary usage. Avoid confusing the legal and ordinary meanings.

STATING TERMS AND CONDITIONS OF YOUR WRITTEN WARRANTY

The FTC's *Rule on Disclosure of Written Consumer Product Warranty Terms and Conditions* (the Disclosure Rule) requires a written warranty on a consumer product that costs more than $15 to be clear, easy to read, and contain certain specified items of information about its coverage. To help you comply with the law and to make your warranty clear and easy to read, you may wish to refer to *Writing Readable Warranties,* an FTC manual that is available from the Government Printing Office.

The information you must disclose in your warranty is explained in the remainder of this chapter. This information includes basic information about aspects of warranty coverage common to all written warranties, and specific information that is required only when your warranty contains certain optional terms and conditions.

Counterpoint Carpet Corporation
Full Five-Year Warranty

What is covered?

This warranty covers any defects in materials or workmanship, including installation, with the exceptions stated below.

How long does coverage last?

This warranty runs for five years from the date your carpet is installed.

What is not covered?

This warranty does not cover fading or discoloration caused by exposure to sunlight or chemicals such as ammonia, laundry detergent, or household bleach. (For information on how to prevent fading or discoloration, consult our manual *Care Tips from Counterpoint Carpet,* available free from your Counterpoint dealer.)

What will Counterpoint do?

Counterpoint will repair any carpet that proves to be defective in materials or workmanship. In the event repair is not possible, Counterpoint will either replace your carpet with new carpet of similar composition and price, or refund the full purchase price of your carpet, whichever you prefer.

How do you get service?

Contact any Counterpoint dealer, listed in the Yellow Pages under *Carpet,* or contact Counterpoint at 800-555-5555. A service representative will come to your home and take any necessary action to correct problems covered by this warranty.

How does state law apply?

This warranty gives you specific legal rights, and you may also have other rights which vary from state to state.

Figure 10.1   Example of a *full warranty.*

BASIC INFORMATION REQUIRED
FOR ALL WARRANTIES

Under the FTC's Disclosure Rule, there are five basic aspects of coverage that your warranty must describe. It is useful to think of these as five questions which your warranty must answer:

1. *What does the warranty cover/not cover?* Answering this question is quite simple when the warranty covers every type of malfunction or defect that may appear in all parts of the product. However, if not all parts or not all types of defects are covered, as in the Counterpoint Carpet example in Figure 10.1, you should clearly describe the scope of coverage.

2. *What is the period of coverage?* If coverage begins at some point in time other than the purchase date, your warranty must state the time or event that begins the coverage. In the Counterpoint Carpet example, warranty coverage begins when the product is installed, which may be different from when the product is purchased.

   Also, you must make it clear when coverage ends if some particular event would terminate it. In the limited warranty Magnifisound Corporation in Figure 10.2, coverage lasts until the first purchaser transfers the product to someone else.

3. *What will you do to correct problems?* This requires an explanation of the remedy you offer under the warranty. This could be repair or replacement of the product, a refund of the purchase price, or a credit toward subsequent purchases.

   If necessary for clarity, you must also explain what you will not do. This requires a description of the types of expenses, if any, that you will not cover. These might include, for example, labor charges, consequential damages (the costs of repairing or replacing other property that is damaged when the warranted product fails, such as food spoilage when a refrigerator breaks down), or incidental damages (the costs a consumer incurs in order to obtain warranty service, such as towing charges, telephone charges, time lost from work, transportation costs, and the cost of renting a product temporarily to replace the warranted product).

4. *How can the customer get warranty service?* Your warranty must tell customers who they can go to for warranty service and how to reach those persons or companies. This means that the warranty needs to include the name and address of your company, and any person or office customers should contact. If they can call you locally or toll-free, you can give the telephone number instead of the address. If you want customers to contact your local or regional service centers first, explain how this should be done.

5. *How will state law affect your customer's rights under the warranty?* Your warranty must answer this question because

Magnifisound Corporation Limited Warranty

What does this warranty cover? This warranty covers any defects or malfunctions in your new Magnifisound hearing aid.

How long does the coverage last? This warranty lasts as long as you own your Magnifisound aid. Coverage terminates if you sell or otherwise transfer the aid.

What will Magnifisound do? Magnifisound will replace any defective or malfunctioning part at no charge. You must pay any labor charges.

What does this warranty not cover? Batteries, or any problem that is caused by abuse, misuse, or an act of God (such as a flood) are not covered. Also, consequential and incidental damages are not recoverable under this warranty. Some states do not allow the exclusion or limitation of incidental or consequential damages, so the above limitation or exclusion may not apply to you.

How do you get service? In order to be eligible for service under this warranty you *must* return the warranty registration card attached within 30 days of purchasing the aid. If something goes wrong with your aid, send it postage paid with a brief written description of the problem to:

Magnifisound Corporation
Box 10000
Auditory, Ohio

We will inspect your aid and contact you within 72 hours to give the results of our inspection and an estimate of the labor charges required to fix the aid. If you authorize repairs, we will return the repaired aid to you COD within 72 hours. You must pay any labor charges upon receipt of the repaired aid.

If you inform us that you wish us to provide necessary parts to you but you wish to have repairs performed elsewhere, we will return the aid and replacement parts to you within 72 hours.

There is no charge for inspection.

How does state law apply? This warranty gives you specific legal rights, and you may also have other rights which vary from state to state.

Figure 10.2 Example of a *limited warranty*.

Full Two-Year Warranty on the
Black Star 2001 Clothes Washer

What is covered? Any defect in your 2001 Clothes Washer.

For how long? Two years after the date you bought your 2001 Clothes Washer.

What will Black Star do? Repair, or if repair is not possible, either replace your 2001 Clothes Washer, or refund the purchase price, whichever you prefer.

Limited Warranty on Parts for the Third
through Fifth Years

What is covered? Any defect in your 2001 Clothes Washer.

For how long? From the start of the third year after you bought your 2001 Clothes Washer until the end of the fifth year.

What will Black Star do? Provide free new or rebuilt replacement parts, but not labor to install the parts. Any servicer you choose can do service during this period.

How do you get service? Contact any Black Star Dealer or any Authorized Black Star Service Center. See the Yellow Pages under *Appliance Repair* for the name of a Black Star Servicer near you, or call 800-111-1111.

Your rights under state law. This warranty gives you specific legal rights, and you may also have other rights which vary from state to state.

Figure 10.2 *Continued.*

implied warranty rights and certain other warranty rights vary from state to state. Rather than require a detailed explanation about this on a state-by-state basis, the FTC adopted the following *boilerplate* disclosure to address this issue. It must be included in every consumer product warranty:

⌐

This warranty gives you specific legal rights, and you may also have other rights which vary from state to state.

⌐

Treadwell Tire Full Warranty During First 20 Percent of Usable Tread Life

If a defect in materials or workmanship appears in your Treadwell Tire before 20 percent of the tread is worn away, Treadwell Corporation will provide, at your choice, either free replacement of the same model number Treadwell Tire or a complete refund of the original purchase price.

Limited Warranty During Remaining 80 Percent of Usable Tread Life

If a defect in materials or workmanship appears in your Treadwell Tire after 20 percent of the tread is worn away and before the remainder of the tread is worn away, Treadwell Corporation will provide you with a credit good for the purchase of any Treadwell Tire of the same model number. The credit will drop by 10 percent of the original purchase price for each additional 10 percent of the tread that is worn away when the defect appears.

How to get service

Just bring the defective tire to any Treadwell Dealer. The address of the dealer near you is listed on the other side of this document

How state law relates to this warranty

This warranty gives you specific legal rights, and you may also have other rights which vary from state to state.

Figure 10.3 Example of a *full and limited warranty.*

Specific Information Required When Your Warranty Contains Certain Optional Terms and Conditions

Generally, if you wish to impose on your customers any obligations other than notifying you that they need service, you must state these obligations in your warranty. Also, if you wish to establish any other conditions, limitations, or terms that you intend to enforce, you must state them in your warranty; you cannot have hidden requirements. An example of such a condition or limitation would be a provision voiding the warranty if the serial number on the product is defaced.

There are also a number of other disclosures you must make in your warranty if it contains certain optional terms and conditions. These requirements are explained in the following paragraphs.

If your warranty contains *a provision that restricts the duration of implied warranties,* the Disclosure Rule requires you to include a statement that state law may override such restrictions. This is required because some states prohibit any restrictions on implied warranties. The requirement applies only to *limited* warranties, because only in limited warranties can you restrict the duration of implied warranties. To tell consumers that state law may not permit such a restriction, the Disclosure Rule requires you to use the following language:

⌐

Some states do not allow limitations on how long an implied warranty lasts, so the above limitation may not apply to you.

⌐

If your warranty contains *a provision intended to restrict or eliminate your potential liability for consequential or incidental damages,* you must include a statement that state law may not allow such a provision. To inform consumers that state law may not permit such a restriction, the Disclosure Rule requires that you use the following sentence:

⌐

Some states do not allow the exclusion or limitation of incidental or consequential damages, so the above limitation or exclusion may not apply to you.

⌐

If your warranty contains *a provision that restricts who has rights under the warranty,* you must include a statement explaining specifically who is covered. For example, if your limited warranty is valid only for the first purchaser, your warranty must state that. Note that this applies only to *limited* warranties. A full warranty must cover anyone who owns the product during the period of coverage, as discussed in *Titling Written Warranties as* Full *or* Limited on page 154.

If your warranty contains *a provision that requires your customers to use a dispute resolution mechanism before suing under the federal Magnuson-Moss Warranty Act for breach of warranty,* as shown in Figure 10.4 you must include:

- A statement informing consumers that they can sue under state law without first using the mechanism, but that before suing under the Magnuson-Moss Act, they must first try to resolve the dispute through the mechanism

- Information and materials about the dispute mechanism, including the name and address or a toll-free telephone number, or a form for filing a claim

Of course, if you include a dispute resolution requirement in your warranty, the informal dispute resolution mechanism must comply with the FTC's Dispute Resolution Rule.

The example in the box on page 163 shows how to make the required disclosures about an informal dispute resolution mechanism that you require customers to use before taking a dispute to court.

ADVERTISING WARRANTIES

The Magnuson-Moss Warranty Act does not cover the advertising of warranties. However, warranty advertising falls within the scope of the FTC Act, which generally prohibits *unfair or deceptive acts or practices in or affecting commerce*. Therefore, it is a violation of the FTC Act to advertise a warranty deceptively.

To help companies understand what the law requires, the FTC has issued guidelines called *The Guides for Advertising Warranties and Guarantees*. However, the Guides do not cover every aspect of warranty advertising, and cannot substitute for consultation with your lawyer on warranty advertising matters.

The Guides cover three principal topics: how to advertise a warranty that is covered by the Pre-Sale Availability Rule; how to advertise a satisfaction guarantee; and how to advertise a lifetime guarantee or warranty.

How to Advertise Warranties Covered by the Pre-Sale Availability Rule

In general, the Guides advise that if a print or broadcast ad for a consumer product mentions a warranty, and the advertised product is covered by the Pre-Sale Availability Rule (that is, the product is sold in stores for more than $15), the ad should inform consumers that a copy of the warranty is available to read prior to sale at the place where the product is sold. Print or broadcast advertisements that mention a warranty on any consumer product that can be purchased through the mail or by telephone should inform consumers how to get a copy of the warranty.

For advertisements of consumer products costing $15 or less, the Guides do not call for the pre-sale availability disclosure. Instead,

Bauhaus Mobile Homes Limited Warranty

What this warranty covers

This warranty covers substantial defects in materials and workmanship in your new Bauhaus Mobile Home, including the heating, air conditioning, plumbing and electrical systems, and all original appliances installed in your Bauhaus Mobile Home.

What this warranty does not cover

This warranty does not cover any problems which result from improper transportation or set-up of the home, abuse, accidents, or acts of God, such as hurricanes or floods.

How long the warranty lasts

The coverage of this warranty lasts for two years after the date of installation of your new Bauhaus Mobile Home.

How to get service

If something goes wrong, contact the Bauhaus dealer from whom you purchased your home. Arrange a mutually convenient time for the dealer's service representative to come to your home and, if possible, correct the problem. In most cases your dealer will be able to correct the problem, but if he is not able to do so, you should contact Bauhaus Mobile Homes directly in writing at the following address:

Bauhaus Mobile Homes
Customer Relations Dept.
10101 Factory Blvd.
Manufacturing City, CA

Bauhaus will send a representative to your home to inspect the problem and to correct it if possible. All service under this warranty will be performed at your home site.

What to do if you are not satisfied with service

We believe you will be fully satisfied by the service you receive from your Bauhaus dealer and from Bauhaus. However, because our aim is your complete and lasting satisfaction, Bauhaus adds another feature to your warranty's protection. In the unlikely event

Continued

Figure 10.4 Warranty containing a dispute resolution.

that you feel our response to a warranty service request is not satisfactory, Bauhaus offers you an opportunity to air your complaint
to an impartial dispute-handling organization. The paragraph
below explains how this works. If you believe your dealer and
Bauhaus have not performed as stated in this warranty, you may
submit a request for further consideration to the National Recon-
ciliation Board of Home Owners and Producers (NRBHOP). You
should make any such request by mailing the attached *Request for
Dispute Resolution* form to NRBHOP, or by sending a letter specifically demanding such dispute resolution and identifying yourself,
Bauhaus, the defect, and the remedy you seek to this address:

NRBHOP
Box 8613
Redress, OK

Upon receiving your Request for Dispute Resolution, NRBHOP will
notify Bauhaus and ask for a response to your complaint. If
Bauhaus disagrees with your complaint, NRBHOP will arrange for
informal dispute settlement between you and Bauhaus. See the
section of your Owner's Manual entitled *The NRBHOP Program* for
more detailed information about how the informal dispute settlement process works.

You may not file suit against Bauhaus under the Magnuson-Moss
Warranty Act until your claim has been submitted to NRBHOP for
informal dispute settlement and a decision has been reached, or you
have waited 40 days for a decision following your submission of a
Request for Dispute Resolution, whichever comes first. However,
you may be entitled to file suit under state laws without waiting.

How state law applies

This warranty gives you specific legal rights, and you may also
have other rights which vary from state to state.

Figure 10.4 *Continued.*

the Guides advise that the FTC's legal decisions and policy statements are the sole sources of guidance on how to avoid unfairness or
deception in advertising warranties. Consult your attorney for assistance in researching and applying the FTC's case decisions and policy statements.

How to Advertise a Satisfaction Guarantee

The Guides advise that, regardless of the price of the product, advertising terms such as *satisfaction guaranteed* or *money back guarantee* should be used only if the advertiser is willing to provide full refunds to customers when, for any reason, they return the merchandise.

The Guides further advise that an ad mentioning a satisfaction guarantee or similar offer should inform consumers of any material conditions or limitations on the offer. For example, a restriction on the offer to a specific time period, such as 30 days, is a material condition that should be disclosed.

How to Advertise a Lifetime Warranty or Guarantee

Lifetime warranties or guarantees can be a source of confusion for consumers. This is because it is often difficult to tell just whose life measures the period of coverage. *Lifetime* can be used in at least three ways. For example, a warrantor of an auto muffler may intend his lifetime warranty's duration to be for the life of the car on which the muffler is installed. In this case, the muffler warranty would be transferable to subsequent owners of the car and would remain in effect throughout the car's useful life.

Or the warrantor of the muffler might intend a lifetime warranty to last as long as the original purchaser of the muffler owns the car on which the muffler is installed. Although commonly used, this is an inaccurate application of the term *lifetime*.

Finally, *lifetime* can be used to describe a warranty that lasts as long as the original purchaser of the product lives. This is probably the least common usage of the term.

The Guides advise that to avoid confusing consumers about the duration of a lifetime warranty or guarantee, ads should tell consumers which *life* measures the warranty's duration in that way, consumers will know which meaning of the term *lifetime* you intend.

In Conclusion

Warranties are a key concern for manufacturers, not only from a legal perspective, but from an everyday marketing and customer service perspective. Many times, manufacturers have a printed warranty form that was created years earlier (author unknown), and they hand that out to whoever requests it. The product liability expert or corporate team needs to review and update current warranties to comply with the guidelines stated in this chapter. Subsequently, it needs to be communicated to the entire management team that these individuals control any future changes to the form content, and must review or be cognizant of any custom warranties offered to special customers.

The warranty form should be dated or include a revision number, so the employees can tell if they are using the most current form. It is also a good practice to include the warranty form in the product package. Customers will then know what is covered and what isn't and will place fewer calls to the customer service department.

Product Recalls

Almost every manufacturer's worst nightmare would be to have to conduct a major product recall. The costs incurred could be devastating. Exceeding that nightmare would be to have the product defect result in product liability lawsuits. Situations like this could take the company out of business.

One reason a product recall can be economically devastating is that many manufacturers enter into the event totally unprepared. The manufacturer may not have ever had to conduct a product recall and therefore has never given much thought as to how such a process should be carried out. Being unprepared in the event of a product recall not only leads to inefficient efforts, but can lead to multiplying the cost factor many times over. Just as in disaster planning, a manufacturer needs to have a well-laid out plan.

A CASE STUDY

I can remember years ago when a company I was working for was suddenly faced with having to conduct a major recall. We were high volume manufacturers of an assortment of large illuminated products. One of the products was a 5' long, wall hung lightbox that we produced for a major international company. In addition to its other promotional attributes, the lightbox incorporated an L.E.D. clock. The clock component was supplied to us by a small supplier, and we assembled it into the center of our product.

167

Shortly after producing nearly 4000 of these products and shipping them all over the continental United States and Hawaii, it was brought to our attention that the L.E.D. clock had the potential for starting on fire. As it turned out, the supplier of the clock, a small company 800 miles away, had inserted the wrong electronic component into 110 of the units. The part was a potentiometer that was loaded into the circuit board and looked the same as the correct part, but it had the wrong electronic value. The part itself had a microscopic model number printed on it, which could be read by someone with very good eyesight or with a magnifying glass. After the clock would operate for about four weeks, it had the potential to suddenly overheat and popp, which created a flame that started the entire product on fire. We were made aware of the defective condition after three of the units started on fire. The units were luckily caught by nearby attendants and extinguished before causing any significant damage.

We quickly called an emergency staff meeting to discuss the situation and develop our action plan. Naturally everyone at this point was in a heightened state of excitement and concern, which didn't help much. We had never been face-to-face with having to carry out a major recall before, and there were no procedures in place to guide us. All we knew was that there were close to 4000 of these units in 363 cities. There were a number of other issues complicating the matter, but the bottom line was that the units couldn't be returned, nor could we ask the end users to perform any mechanical tasks. The problem was ours to correct, and it had to be done as quickly as possible.

After discussing all the possibilities, it was decided by the president that we would create six teams of our employees that would travel the country and inspect and replace the defective clocks. The company that supplied the clocks was too small to handle such a mission, but assured that they would financially handle the costs involved. We realized that at any moment they could claim bankruptcy. Creating six teams of inspectors and flying or driving them around the country to find these units would take 4 to 6 months (we calculated) and would cost a considerable amount of money. It would also be quite paralyzing to our company to have these people gone for this period of time.

This appeared to be the only possible course of action, since we couldn't arrange to have the units shipped back, nor could we ask the end users to disassemble and inspect the units they had. As I walked back from the meeting, I remembered that at one of the recent quality assurance trade shows I came across two booths of companies that advertised huge networks of inspectors across the country that could perform on-site inspections of raw materials that were going to be shipped to your manufacturing plant. The inspectors actually lived in every major city throughout the country and were contract employees for these firms. Rather than have them inspect raw materials from some supplier, I wondered whether they could travel to these local addresses and inspect our products. Within minutes, I had contacted one of these companies, discussed the situation, faxed them pictures of what we were talking about, and was able to put a very practical action plan in place.

Within a few days my quality engineer and I were able to put a command center in place at our company, while the inspection agency did the same 1100 miles away. They identified that it would take 165 of their inspectors to cover all the 363 cities where the products had been shipped. We supplied them with instruction sheets and parts to go out and conduct the inspections. Amazingly, we were able to completely inspect and replace all the defective units within a two-week time frame, for a fraction of the cost we would have incurred had we sent out our own teams, and in one-tenth the time frame. With the supplier covering the costs, which were substantially less than originally expected, we came out in great shape.

The most surprising element was the impact it had on our relationship with our major customer. Sales fully expected the incident would permanently damage this relationship, even though the defect couldn't have been caught with our best inspection and test practices in place. As it turned out, the customer was so impressed with our ability to address such a major challenge so rapidly that it greatly improved the relationship and we received larger orders than in the past.

After that, I authored a procedure on how future recalls would be handled so we would always be prepared to immediately swing into action. Every company must take time to develop a procedure on product recall before it actually happens. Consider the types of products you produce, the nature of problems you could logically experience, and decide the practical ways you could address such situations. If you plan for such a disaster with an open mind, and have the time to determine the logical options, you will be better prepared for such an event should it ever materialize.

EXAMPLE OF A RECALL PROCEDURE

When putting together a Recall Procedure, there are many elements to take into consideration. What do you consider a *recall*, versus a mere return goods issue or minor field fix? Would it be of value to establish classifications or categories for the different types of recalls? Especially in large manufacturing corporations, would it be better to establish cost parameters on what is *officially* considered to be a recall, versus smaller incidents that don't require so much attention? An example of a recall procedure can be found on page 171.

IMPORTANT LEGAL CONSIDERATIONS REGARDING RECALL LETTERS

When manufacturers recognize the need to recall a product, especially those manufacturers not governed under consumer products, they should take into consideration a number of key concerns when developing the actual recall letter or notice. First and foremost, in situations where the defective condition creates a potential hazard, don't downplay the actual hazard in the official notice.

It is troubling for any manufacturer to send out a letter that identifies that a product has the serious potential of starting on fire, contributing to an accident, or creating personal injury. What will your customers think? What damage will such a notice do to your company and product's reputation in the marketplace? What effect would such a notice have on future sales, even after the defect has been corrected? All of these issues can be of major concern, especially to departments like marketing and sales. But you can't allow these concerns to overshadow your responsibilities as a manufacturer and expose your company to much greater liability risks and legal consequences.

When a manufacturer gains the knowledge that their product is defective and potentially hazardous, but fails to fully communicate that to their end users during their effort to recall the product, recall problems and liabilities can result. To begin with, most manufacturers will learn that when they first initiate a product recall, the marketplace isn't very cooperative. Many times, regardless of the severity of the defect or potential hazards, end users fail to follow the manufacturer's directions and take the product in for repair or replacement. If the manufacturer downplays the safety hazard, and the defective product actually contributes to an incident followed by a product liability case, the manufacturer will be found seriously at fault for not fully communicating the true hazard, which counsel for the plaintiff will claim lead to the incident. In the product liability trial, such a lack of responsible action could lead to major punitive damages against the manufacturer.

GE	QUALITY PROCEDURE	Number 904
		Effective Date 2/1/00
		Revision Date
		Page 1 of 2
Goodden Enterprises	**RECALL PROCEDURE**	TOTAL QUALITY SYSTEM

1.0 PURPOSE

1.1 To identify the steps to follow in the event that a product recall would need to be initiated.

2.0 SCOPE

2.1 This procedure pertains to the following situations: an entire production run of product needs to be returned and costs could exceed $3000; a large number of product needs to be inspected and/or returned, and expected costs are anticipated to run in excess of $3000; or the condition that exists falls into the classifications of Levels I or II listed below.

2.2 This procedure will not pertain to easily controllable situations that involve the return of product from the field, or field repair, where the costs are under $3000 and the effort can easily be handled by account management.

3.0 CLASSIFICATIONS

Level I Classification—This is where a defective condition is likely to result in a fire, serious injury, or other type of possible catastrophic event.

Level II Classification—This is where a defective condition is not likely to result in a fire, serious injury, or other type of catastrophic event, but is possible.

Level III Classification—This is where fire, injury, or any other type of catastrophic event is not an issue, but a strong likelihood of product failure is imminent if condition is not corrected.

Level IV Classification—This would pertain to instances where product failure is possible, but its likelihood is either minimal or unknown. This classification would also address all other conditions or situations not defined in the other three classifications.

AUDITOR:_____	**AUDIT**	___ IN COMPLIANCE
DATE: _____		___ OUT OF COMPLIANCE

Continued

Continued

QUALITY PROCEDURE	Effective Date 2/1/00	Number 904
RECALL PROCEDURE	Page 2 of 2	Revision Date

4.0 TYPE OF RECALL

Product Return—This is where we have identified a defective condition within a specific product line and are requiring that the customer either return all products of that design, or specifically identified products from that production run or make.

Field Fix—This is where we have identified a defective condition within a specific product line and are arranging for the product(s) to be corrected in the field.

Customer Notification—This is where we have identified that there could be a potential problem with specifically identified products in the field, and decide to handle the problem through correspondence with the customer or end user.

5.0 PROCEDURE

Empoyee   5.1   Upon gaining the knowledge that a product line is suspect of being defective, informs the director of quality.

Dir Quality   5.2   If it is recognized that a probable recall will need to take place, meets with the president, vice president of sales, director of customer service, and account manager to determine the necessary course of action.

Dir Quality   5.3   Directs or coordinates activities with those departments/parties involved.

VP Sales/ Acct Mgr   5.4   Informs the customer of the situation, and the plan of how we intend to address the product.

_____   _____
President   VP-Sales

_____   _____
Director of Quality   Director—Customer Service

Let's create a hypothetical situation where the manufacturer of a commercial coffeemaker used in various restaurants is made aware that the unit appears to have the possibility of starting on fire. Three units were involved in fires over a five-week period, although the exact causes of the fires is still in dispute. In one incident it is unclear as to whether the coffeemaker was actually the cause of the fire, or just a victim of the fire which may have originated elsewhere. Fire damage was extensive to the restaurant, and although investigators for the restaurant's insurance carrier point to the coffeemaker as the cause, the manufacturer's experts cast considerable doubt.

Within days a second incident surfaces. In a close examination of the charred remains of this unit, the manufacturer recognizes that a specific electrical connector used within the coffeemaker may have shorted out and lead to the unit burning, but the findings aren't conclusive. Various quality reliability and product engineering personnel take sides over the reliability of the connector, identifying that it might have the possibility of leading to electrical shorts.

A week later a third incident surfaces which, although not conclusive, also seems to indicate that the lesser quality connector may have shorted out. With this in mind, the manufacturer decides it would be best at this point to recall the units. Although sales voices concern over what such a recall could do to future sales, especially in light of the internal dispute that exists, attorneys for the manufacturer advise management to go forward with the recall and help write the recall letter/notice as shown in Figure 11.1.

Although the (fictitious) manufacturer properly handled the situation in this scenario, consider what may have happened. Let's say the manufacturer elected not to recall the units and instead challenged the results. As the days and weeks passed, two more fires were brought to their attention, which they challenged as well. Then suddenly, a fire broke out in a small remote restaurant with living quarters above. The fire resulted in one person being killed and two others seriously burned. In the trial that followed it was brought to light that there had been a number of other incidents, but the manufacturer failed to recall the units or warn the end users of hazards.

In fact, it is stated that the manufacturer continued to deny any responsibility, even though a number of outside investigators stated that the coffeemaker was the cause of the other fires. The manufacturer obviously was obsessed with continued sales and profits. In the end the jury found in favor of the plaintiffs, found the manufacturer severely negligent in their actions, and hit the manufacturer even

---

**Recall Notice Important Safety Information
For Owners and Users of the *Super Coffee*
Coffeemaker Manufactured
by Brewmasters Between Oct–Dec 1998**

Attention Owners and Users:

Brewmasters has been advised that a potential for fire may exist in their *Super Coffee* coffeemakers manufactured between October–December of 1998, which is identified on the label on the bottom of the machine. This notice does not involve other coffeemakers made by Brewmasters, or other Super Coffee models made on any other month or year other than that specified.

If you have a *Super Coffee* coffeemaker manufactured by Brewmasters during these select months of 1998, it is important that you immediately unplug your coffeemaker even if it has been operating properly. Then please complete and return the enclosed postcard to Brewmasters. Brewmasters will ship you a free replacement coffeemaker and arrange for the return of your current unit. Please *do not* operate your Super Coffee coffeemaker as you await this replacement.

If you have any questions or concerns regarding this notice or the information being supplied, please contact our Customer Service department at 800-555-1212 for assistance.

We apologize for any inconvenience this may cause you and will make every effort to expedite your replacement.

Brewmasters

Figure 11.1 Example of a recall notice.

harder with substantial punitive damages. Afterward, the devastated manufacturer elected to finally recall the units, but now faced lawsuits from the other reported incidents.

GOVERNMENT GUIDELINES ON CONSUMER PRODUCT RECALLS

The decision to initiate a recall is voluntary for many companies, especially those involved in the manufacture of commercial products.

Companies involved in the manufacture of consumer products are required to follow certain reporting practices. The following material is taken directly from the *Recall Handbook* published by the U.S. Consumer Product Safety Commission, Office of Compliance, Recalls and Compliance Division.

The U.S. Consumer Product Safety Commission (CPSC) is an independent regulatory agency responsible for protecting the public from unreasonable risks of injury and death associated with consumer products. Established by Congress in the Consumer Product Safety Act (CPSA), 15 U.S.C. §§ 2051–2084, the CPSC has jurisdiction over approximately 15,000 different types of products used in and around the home, in schools, and in recreation (consumer products).

REPORTING REQUIREMENTS

A. Section 15 Reports

Section 15(b) of the Consumer Product Safety Act establishes reporting requirements for manufacturers, importers, distributors, and retailers of consumer products. Each must notify the Commission immediately if it obtains information which reasonably supports the conclusion that a product distributed in commerce: (1) fails to meet a consumer product safety standard or banning regulation, (2) contains a defect which could create a substantial product hazard to consumers, (3) creates an unreasonable risk of serious injury or death, or (4) fails to comply with a voluntary standard upon which the Commission has relied under the CPSA. Companies that distribute products that violate regulations issued under the other laws that the Commission administers—the Flammable Fabrics Act, 15 U.S.C. § 1193–1204; the Federal Hazardous Substances Act, 15 U.S.C. § 1261–1278; the Poison Prevention Packaging Act, 15 U.S.C. § 1471–1476; and the Refrigerator Safety Act; 15 U.S.C. §1211–1214—must also report, if the violations may also constitute product defects that could create a substantial risk of injury to the public or may create an unreasonable risk of serious injury or death. The Commission has issued an interpretive regulation, 16 C.F.R. Part 1115, that further explains a reporting company's obligations.

WHAT AND WHERE TO REPORT

A company should file its report with the Division of Recalls and Compliance. The report may be filed by mail, telephone (301-504-0608, ext. 15), or electronically through the CPSC web site (www.cpsc.gov)

or fax (301-504-0359). A company should assign the responsibility of reporting to someone with knowledge of the product and of the reporting requirements of section 15. He or she should have the authority to report to CPSC or to quickly raise the reporting issue to someone who does.

Reporting firms should be prepared to provide the information described below. However, no company should delay a report because some of this information is not yet available. The following information should be transmitted:

- Description of the product
- Name and address of the company, and whether it is a manufacturer, distributor, importer or retailer
- Nature and extent of the possible product defect or unreasonable risk of serious injury or death
- Nature and extent of injury or possible injury associated with the product
- Name, address, and telephone number of the person informing the Commission
- If available, the other information specified in Section 1115.13(d) of the Commission's regulations interpreting the reporting requirements
- A timetable for providing information not immediately available

Retailers and distributors may satisfy their reporting obligations in the manner described above. Alternatively, a retailer or distributor may send a letter to the manufacturer or importer of a product describing the risk of injury or death or the defect associated with the product or its failure to comply with an applicable regulation and forward a copy of that letter to the Division of Recalls and Compliance. A distributor or retailer receiving product hazard information from a manufacturer or importer or other source must report to CPSC unless the firm knows the Commission has been adequately informed of the defect, failure to comply, or risk.

WHEN TO REPORT

Section 15 requires firms to report *immediately.* This means that a firm should notify the Commission within 24 hours of obtaining information described in section A (*Section 15 Reports*) above. 16 C.F.R. § 1115.12 provides guidelines for determining whether a product defect exists, whether a product creates an unreasonable risk of serious injury or death, and whether a report is necessary or appropriate. Section II of this handbook does the same.

A company *must* report to the Commission within 24 hours of obtaining reportable information. The Commission encourages companies to report *potential* substantial product hazards even while their own investigations are continuing. However, if a company is uncertain whether information is reportable, the firm may spend a reasonable time investigating the matter. That investigation should not exceed ten working days unless the firm can demonstrate that a longer time is reasonable in the circumstances. Absent such circumstances, the Commission will presume that, at the end of ten working days, the firm has received and considered all information which would have been available to it had a reasonable, expeditious, and diligent investigation been undertaken.

The Commission considers a company to have obtained knowledge of product safety related information when that information is received by an employee or official of the firm who may reasonably be expected to be capable of appreciating the significance of that information. Once that occurs, under ordinary circumstances, five working days is the maximum reasonable time for that information to reach the chief executive officer or the official assigned responsibility for complying with the reporting requirements.

The Commission evaluates whether or when a firm should have reported. This evaluation will be based, in part, on what the company actually knew about the hazard posed by the product or *on what a reasonable person, acting under the circumstances, should have known about the hazard while exercising due care.* Thus, a firm is deemed to know what it would have known had it exercised due care in analyzing reports of injury or consumer complaints, or in evaluating warranty returns, reports of experts, in-house engineering analyses, or other information.

CONFIDENTIALITY OF REPORTS

The Commission often receives requests for information reported under section 15(b). Section 6(b)(5) of the CPSA, 15 U.S.C. § 2055(b)(5), prohibits the release of such information unless a remedial action plan has been accepted in writing, a complaint has been issued, or the reporting firm consents to the release. In addition, a firm claiming that information it has submitted is trade secret or confidential commercial or financial information must mark the information as *confidential* in accordance with section 6(a)(3) of the CPSA, 15 U.S.C. § 2055(a)(3).

That should be done when the information is submitted to the Commission. The firm will receive an additional opportunity to claim confidentiality when it receives subsequent notice from the Commission's Freedom of Information Office that the information may be disclosed to the public in response to a request. If section 6(b)(5) does not apply, the CPSC staff will not treat information as exempt from disclosure to the public under section 6(a) of the CPSA, 15 U.S.C. § 2055(a), and the Freedom of Information Act, absent a specific claim for confidential treatment.

SECTION 37 REPORTS

Section 37 of the CPSA (Consumer Product Safety Act) requires manufacturers of consumer products to report information about settled or adjudicated lawsuits. Manufacturers must report if:

- A particular model of the product is the subject of at least three civil actions filed in federal or state court;
- Each suit alleges the involvement of that particular model in death or grievous bodily injury—mutilation or disfigurement, dismemberment or amputation, the loss of important bodily functions or debilitating internal disorder, injuries likely to require extended hospitalization, severe burns, severe electric shock, or other injuries of similar severity; and
- During one of the following two-year periods specified in the law, each of the three actions results in either a final settlement involving the manufacturer or in a court judgment in favor of the plaintiff:
  January 1, 1991—December 31, 1992
  January 1, 1993—December 31, 1994
  January 1, 1995—December 31, 1996
  January 1, 1997—December 31, 1998
  January 1, 1999—December 31, 2000
  (subsequent periods follow this pattern); and
- The manufacturer is involved in the defense of or has notice of each action prior to the entry of the final order, and is involved in discharging any obligation owed to the plaintiff as a result of the settlement or judgment.

What to Report

A report under section 37 must contain:

- The name and address of the manufacturer of the product.
- The model and model number or designation of the product.

- A statement as to whether the civil action alleged death or grievous bodily injury, and in the case of the latter, the nature of the injury. For reporting purposes, the plaintiff's allegations as to the nature of the injury are sufficient to require a report, even if the manufacturer disagrees with the allegations.
- A statement as to whether the case resulted in a final settlement or a judgment. However, a manufacturer need not provide the amount of a settlement.
- In the case of a judgment in favor of the plaintiff, the name and case number of the case, and the court in which it was filed.

A manufacturer may also provide additional information, if it chooses. Such information might include a statement as to whether the manufacturer intends to appeal an adverse judgment, a specific denial that the information it submits reasonably supports the conclusion that its product caused death or grievous bodily injury, and an explanation why the manufacturer has not previously reported the risk associated with the product under section 15.

When and Where to Report

A manufacturer must report within 30 days after a judgment or final settlement in the last of three lawsuits. The same is true of any additional lawsuits involving the same model that are settled or adjudicated in favor of the plaintiff during the same two-year period.

Companies must file Section 37 reports in writing to the Director, Recalls and Compliance Division, Office of Compliance, U.S. Consumer Product Safety Commission, Washington, D.C. 20207.

Confidentiality of Reports

Unlike section 15(b) reports, the Commission may not disclose to the general public information reported under section 37 in any circumstances. By law, reporting under section 37 is not an admission of the existence of an unreasonable risk of injury, a defect, a substantial product hazard, an imminent hazard, or any other liability under any statute or common law.

SECTION 102

Section 102 of the Child Safety Protection Act requires that companies report certain choking incidents to the Commission. Each manufacturer, distributor, retailer, and importer of a marble, a ball with a diameter of 1.75" or less (small ball), or latex balloon, or a toy or game that contains such a marble, ball, balloon, or other small part must report information that reasonably supports the conclusion:

1. That a child (regardless of age) choked on such a marble, small ball, balloon, or small part; and

2. That, as a result of the incident, the child died, suffered serious injury, ceased breathing for any length of time, or was treated by a medical professional.

What to Report

The report should include the name and address of the child who choked and the person who notified the firm of the incident, a detailed identification of the product, a description of the incident and any resulting injuries or medical treatment, information about any changes made to the product involved or its labeling or warnings to address the risk of choking, and the details of any public notice or other corrective action planned. Firms should refer to 16 C.F. R. Part 1117 for more detailed information about this reporting requirement.

When and Where to Report

Section 102 reports must be filed within 24 hours of obtaining the information. A company may file a Section 102 report with the Division of Recalls and Compliance by mail, telephone (301-504-0608, ext. 15), or fax (301-504-0359). Telephone reports must be followed with a written confirmation.

Confidentiality of Reports

Section 102 reports receive the same confidentiality treatment as information submitted under section 15 of the CPSA.

IDENTIFYING A DEFECT

The Commission's reporting requirements provide information that assists the Commission in evaluating whether some form of remedial action is appropriate. However, in the absence of a regulation that addresses a specific risk of injury, the product in question must contain a defect that creates a substantial risk of injury to the public to warrant such remedial action. The handbook next discusses the considerations that go into determining whether a product defect exists and, if so, whether the risk presented by that defect is substantial.

A defect could be the result of a manufacturing or production error; or it could result from the design of, or the materials used in, the product. A defect could also occur in a product's contents, construction, finish, packaging, warnings, and/or instructions (see 16 C.F.R. § 1115.4).

Not all products that present a risk of injury are defective. A kitchen knife is one such example. The blade has to be sharp to allow the consumer to cut or slice food. The knife's cutting ability is not a product defect, even though some consumers may cut themselves while using the knife.

In determining whether a risk of injury associated with a product could make the product defective, the Commission considers the following:

A. *What is the utility of the product? What is it supposed to do?*

B. *What is the nature of the injury that the product might cause?*

C. *What is the need for the product?*

D. *What is the population exposed to the product and the risk of injury?*

E. *What is the Commission's experience with the product?*

F. *Finally, what other information sheds light on the product and patterns of consumer use?*

If the information available to a company does not reasonably support the conclusion that a defect exists, the firm need not report to the Commission under the defect reporting provision of Section 15(b)(2). However, since a product may be defective even when it is designed, manufactured, and marketed exactly as intended, a company in doubt as to whether a defect exists should still report. Additionally, a firm must report if it has information indicating the product creates an unreasonable risk of serious injury or death. See 15 U.S.C. 2064(b)(3) and 16 C.F.R. § 1115.6.

If the information obtained by a company supports a conclusion that a product has a defect, the company must then consider whether the defect may be serious enough that it could create a substantial product hazard. Generally, a product could create a substantial hazard when consumers are exposed to a significant number of units or if the possible injury is serious or is likely to occur. However, because a company ordinarily does not know the extent of public exposure or the likelihood or severity of potential injury when a product defect first comes to its attention, the company should report to the Commission even if it is in doubt as to whether a substantial product hazard exists.

Section 15 lists criteria for determining when a product creates a substantial product hazard. Any one of the following factors could indicate the existence of a substantial product hazard:

- *Pattern of defect.* The defect may stem from the design, composition, content, construction, finish, or packaging of a product, or from warnings and/or instructions accompanying the product. The conditions under which the defect manifests itself must also be considered in determining whether the pattern creates a substantial product hazard.

- *Number of defective products distributed in commerce.* A single defective product could be the basis for a substantial product hazard determination if an injury is likely or could be serious. By contrast, defective products posing no risk of serious injury and having little chance of causing even minor injury ordinarily would not be considered to present a substantial product hazard.

- *Severity of risk.* A risk is considered severe if the injury that might occur is serious, and/or if the injury is likely to occur.

- *Likelihood of injury.* The likelihood is determined by considering the number of injuries that have occurred, *or that could occur,* the intended or reasonably foreseeable use or misuse of the product, and the population group (such as children, the elderly, or the disabled) exposed to the product.

A substantial product hazard also exists when a product does not comply with an applicable consumer product safety rule, and the failure to comply creates a substantial risk of injury to consumers.

CPSC EVALUATION OF SECTION 15 REPORTS

When a company reports to the Commission, the staff of the Division of Recalls and Compliance undertakes the same product hazard analysis as that requested of firms. First, the staff considers whether the product contains a defect. If the staff believes there is a defect, it then assesses the substantiality of the risk presented to the public, using the criteria listed in section 15 (that is, pattern of defect, number of defective products distributed in commerce, severity of the risk, likelihood of injury, and other appropriate data). In determining preliminarily whether the product in question creates a substantial product hazard, the staff applies hazard priority standards to classify the severity of the problem.

The hazard priority system allows the Commission staff to rank defective products uniformly. For example, a Class A hazard rating is reserved for product defects that present a strong likelihood of death or grievous injury or illness to the consumer. Should the staff make a preliminary determination that a product creates a substantial product hazard, the hazard priority system also provides a guide for selecting the level and intensity of corrective action.

> *Class A Hazard*—Exists when a risk of death or grievous injury or illness is likely or very likely, or serious injury or illness is very likely. Class A hazards warrant the highest level of attention. They call for a company to take immediate, comprehensive, and imaginative corrective action measures to identify and notify consumers, retailers, and distributors having the defective product and to remedy the defect through repair or replacement of the product, refunds, or other measures.

> *Class B Hazard*—Exists when a risk of death or grievous injury or illness is not likely to occur, but is possible, or when serious injury or illness is likely, or moderate injury or illness is very likely.

> *Class C Hazard*—Exists when a risk of serious injury or illness is not likely, but is possible, or when moderate injury or illness is not necessarily likely, but is possible.

Regardless of whether a product defect is classified as a Class A, B, or C priority hazard, the common element is that each of these defects creates a substantial product hazard that requires corrective action to reduce that risk of injury.

The priority given to a specific product defect provides a guideline for determining how best to communicate with owners and users of the defective product and to get them to respond appropriately. While some companies have exemplary track records in communicating with consumers independently, it is still to a company's advantage to work with the Commission staff, using both the company's and the Commission's skills and resources to conduct an effective product recall.

FAST TRACK PRODUCT RECALL PROGRAM

A firm that files a Section 15(b) report may wish to use an alternative procedure that the Commission has established to expedite recalls. The program is called the *Fast Track Product Recall Program*. If a company reports a potential product defect and, within 20 working days of the filing of the report, implements with CPSC a consumer-level voluntary recall that is satisfactory to the staff, the staff will not make a preliminary determination that the product contains a defect which creates a substantial product hazard.

This program allows the staff and company to work together on a corrective action plan almost immediately, rather than spending the time and other resources necessary to investigate the reported defect further to determine whether it rises to the level of a substantial product hazard.

To participate in this program, companies must:

- Provide all of the information required for a full report (16 C.F.R. § 1115.13(d))
- Request to participate in the program
- Submit a proposed corrective action plan with sufficient time for the Commission staff to analyze any proposed repair, replacement, or refund offer and to evaluate all notice material before the implementation (announcement) of the CAP which is to occur within 20 working days of the report

ELEMENTS OF A RECALL

A company that undertakes a recall should develop a comprehensive plan that reaches throughout the entire distribution chain to consumers who have the product. The company must design each communication to motivate people to respond to the recall and take the action requested by the company.

Once the staff and a company agree on a remedy to correct a product defect, the staff works with the company to put together an effective plan for public notification and implementation of the recall. The information that should be included in a corrective action plan (CAP) is set forth at 16 C.F.R. § 1115.20(a). A plan must include the company's agreement that the Commission may publicize the terms of the plan to the extent necessary to inform the public of the nature of the alleged substantial product hazard and the actions being undertaken to correct that hazard.

The objectives of a recall are:

A. To locate all defective products as quickly as possible.

B. To remove defective products from the distribution chain and from the possession of consumers.

C. To communicate accurate and understandable information in a timely manner to the public about the product defect, the hazard, and the corrective action. Companies should design all informational material to motivate retailers and media to get the word out and consumers to act on the recall.

In determining what forms of notice to use, the paramount consideration should be the level of hazard that the recalled product presents. Class A hazards warrant the highest level of company and Commission attention. Other considerations include where and how the product was marketed, its user population, the estimated useful life of the product, and how the product is most likely to be maintained and repaired.

A company conducting a recall must take particular care to coordinate the notice portion of the recall so that all participating parties, including retailers, have sufficient advance notice so that they can carry out the actions agreed upon. Notice also needs to be balanced—the purpose of some elements, such as news releases, press conferences, and video news releases—is to get the media to publicize information about the recall widely. Other elements, such as advertisements and posters, assure that the information is available to the public throughout the course of the recall and attempts to reach consumers who did not hear the original announcement.

COMMUNICATING RECALL INFORMATION

The Commission encourages companies to be creative in developing ways to reach owners of recalled products and motivate them to respond. The following are examples of types of notice that may be appropriate. This list is meant as a guide only, and is by no means all-inclusive. As new or innovative methods of notice and means of communication become available, such as use of the Internet, the staff encourages their use.

- A joint news release from CPSC and the company
- Targeted distribution of the news release
- A dedicated toll-free number and/or fax number for consumers to call to respond to the recall notice
- Information on company worldwide web sites
- A video news release to complement the written news release
- A national news conference and/or television or radio announcements

- Direct notice to consumers known to have the product—identified through registration cards, sales records, catalog orders, or other means
- Notices to distributors, dealers, sales representatives, retailers, service personnel, installers, and other persons who may have handled or been involved with the product
- Purchase of mailing lists of populations likely to use the product
- Paid notices via television and/or radio
- Paid notices in national newspapers and/or magazines to reach targeted users of the product
- Paid notices through local or regional media
- Incentives such as money, gifts, premiums, or coupons to encourage consumers to return the product
- Point-of-purchase posters
- Notices in product catalogs, newsletters, and other marketing materials
- Posters for display at locations where users are likely to visit, such as stores, medical clinics, pediatricians' offices, day care centers, repair shops, equipment rental locations, and so on
- Notices to repair/parts shops
- Service bulletins
- Notices included with product replacement parts/accessories
- Notices to day care centers
- Notices to thrift stores

The Compliance staff must review and agree upon each communication that a company intends to use in a product recall before publication or dissemination. It is, therefore, imperative that companies give the staff advance drafts of all notices or other communications to media, customers, and consumers. Following are some specific suggestions for communicating recall information.

News Releases

Unless a company can identify all purchasers of a product being recalled and notify them directly, the Commission typically issues a news release jointly with the firm. The Compliance staff develops the wording of the release with the recalling company and in conjunction with the Commission's Office of Information and Public Affairs. The agreed-upon language for the news release provides the foundation for preparing other notice documents. The Commission discourages unilateral releases issued by companies because they create confusion among the media and public, particularly if CPSC is also issuing a release on the same subject.

The Office of Information and Public Affairs sends the news releases to national wire services, major metropolitan daily newspapers, television and radio networks, and periodicals on the agency's news contact mailing list. News releases from the Commission receive wide media attention and generate a good response rate from consumers.

Each recall news release should use the word *recall* in the heading and should begin, "In cooperation with the U.S. Consumer Product Safety Commission (CPSC). . . ."

Recall news releases must include the following:

- The name and location of the recalling firm
- The name of the product
- The number of products involved
- A description of the hazard
- The number of deaths, injuries, and incidents involving the product
- Detailed description of the product, including model numbers, colors, sizes, and labeling
- A line drawing or photograph of the product
- Major retailers and where and when the product was sold and retail cost
- Complete instructions for consumers on how to participate in the recall

CPSC posts recall news releases on its Internet web site and requests companies to provide color photographs of recalled products for the web site.

Video News Releases

A video news release (VNR) is a taped version of the written news release that describes the recall in audio-visual terms. Distributed via satellite to television stations nationwide, it is an effective method to enhance a recall announcement. A VNR increases the chances that television news media will air information about a recall because it effectively provides news of the recall to television news producers in the form that they need.

Commission staff works with firms to produce VNRs announcing recalls. Like news releases, VNRs need to communicate basic information clearly and concisely. VNRs should incorporate the same information as the news release, as well as video images of the product. They often also include brief statements of company officials and/or the Chairman of the Commission. When writing a VNR script, remember that, if this information is to reach consumers, television networks or local stations must pick it up—which means that the script must be written for television producers. A brief guide describing how to produce a VNR is available from the Office of Compliance upon request.

Posters

Posters are an effective means of providing continuing notice of recalls to consumers at points of purchase or other locations that they visit. Guidelines for posters and counter cards are:

- Keep them *brief* and eye-catching; in general, a poster requires far fewer words than a news release.
- Describe the hazard and tell consumers what to do.
- Use color to make the poster stand out.
- Use a print font, size, and color that provides a strong contrast to the background color of the poster.
- Include the terms *safety* and *recall* in the heading.
- Use a good quality line drawing or photograph of the product with call outs identifying product information, such as model numbers and date codes.
- The firm's toll-free telephone number should be in large size type at the bottom of the poster.
- The poster should include "Post until [date at least 120 days from recall announcement]."
- Consider tear-off sheets with each poster with information on the recall for consumers to take home.

A company that chooses to produce posters announcing a recall should contact the firms or individuals that the company wants to display the posters before the recall is announced. The company should explain the reason for the recall and the contribution to public safety that the posters provide. The company should also:

- Advise retailers or other firms to place the posters in several conspicuous locations in their stores or offices where customers will see them, for example, the area where the product was originally displayed for sale, store entrances, waiting rooms in pediatric clinics, service counters at repair shops.

- Provide sufficient numbers of posters for retailers or others to display them in more than one place in each store or location, and provide a contact for ordering additional posters.

CPSC recommends that posters be 11 × 17 inches, but in no case smaller than 8.5 × 11 inches. These two sizes are easiest to mail in bulk quantities. Larger sizes may be appropriate for repair and service shops. Also, many retailers, particularly large chains, have specific requirements for posters, including size and some product identification information. To avoid delays and having to reprint, a company producing a recall poster should take care to contact retailers in advance to see if they have any such requirements.

Other Forms of Notice

Like news releases and posters, letters, advertisements, bulletins, newsletters, and other communications about a recall need to provide sufficient information and motivation for the reader or listener to identify the product and to take the action you are requesting. They should be written in language targeted to the intended audience.

- Letters or other communications should be specific and concise.
- The words *Important Safety Notice* or *Safety Recall* should appear at the top of each notice and cover letter and should also be on the lower left corner of any mailing envelope.
- Notices to retailers and distributors should explain the reason for the recall, including the hazard, and contain all the instructions needed to tell them how to handle their product inventory, as well as instructions for displaying posters or notices, providing information to consumers, and disposing of returned products.
- All letters and other notices to consumers should explain clearly the reason for the recall, including injury or potential injury information, and provide complete instructions.

TOLL-FREE NUMBERS

A company conducting a recall should provide a toll-free (800-555-1212) telephone number for consumers to respond to the recall announcement. Generally, this number should be dedicated only to the recall.

Historically, the Commission staff has found that most company systems for handling consumer relations or for ordering products, repairs, or accessories are unable to respond effectively to callers about recall announcements, particularly during the first few weeks after the initial announcement.

When establishing a telephone system to handle a recall, be over-generous in estimating consumer response, especially during the first several days/weeks. It is easier to cut back than it is to add more capacity once a recall is announced, and consumers who are unable to get through may not keep trying.

Whether you use an automated system or live operators to answer the calls, prepare scripts and instructions for responding to questions. Operators or taped messages should begin by identifying the firm and product and explaining the reason for the recall. Most consumers who hear about a recall by radio, television, or word of mouth will not remember all the information they initially heard. Again, at its beginning, the message should reinforce the need for listeners to act, particularly if the message is lengthy. CPSC Compliance staff needs to review all scripts before the recall is announced. All automated systems should provide a number for consumers to contact the firm for special problems, for example, problems completing repairs or installing parts.

EXAMPLES OF PRODUCT RECALL NOTICES

⌐

(Brand name) Electric Irons
About 40,000 electric irons recalled because thermostats could malfunction causing the irons to overheat, which presents a fire hazard. Manufacturer: *(company)* Model: *(identified) electric irons sold nationwide by independent discount, hardware, and variety stores from November 1994 through September 1996 for about $7.* Corrective Action: *Consumers should stop using the recalled irons immediately and should return them to the stores where purchased for a full refund.*
(Brand name) Hair Dryers
Approximately 55,000 hand-held hair dryers recalled because thermostats could malfunction, causing the dryers to overheat, which presents a fire hazard, and because they do not have a full immersion protection plug to protect against electrocution if they fall into water. Manufacturer: *(company)* Model: *(brand name) that were sold nationwide by independent discount, hardware, and variety stores from May 1994 through September 1996 for about $6.* Corrective Action: *Consumers should stop using the recalled hair dryers immediately and should return them to the stores where purchased for a full refund.*

(Manufacturer) Bunk Beds

 Certain metal bunk beds recalled because they have openings on the top bunk that are too large and present a potentially lethal entrapment hazard to young children. Manufacturer: *(company)* Model: *(model numbers) distributed from July 1996 until January 1997 in California, Colorado, Illinois, Nebraska, Oklahoma, Oregon, and Texas.* Corrective Action: *Consumers should stop using the recalled beds immediately and should call the company or contact the retailer for a replacement guard rail, retrofit kit, or instructions to help eliminate the potential entrapment hazard.*

(Brand name) Chain Saws

 About 277,000 chain saws recalled because if the removable exhaust deflector is not attached properly, heat from the saw's muffler can melt the saw's front hand guard, which is designed to prevent contact with the chain and can manually activate the chain brake during a kickback. Manufacturer: *(company name)* Model: *(model numbers) with serial numbers beginning with 531 and below, all of which were sold nationwide by authorized (manufacturer) dealers from 1990 through 1995 for about $400 to $600.* Corrective Action: *Consumers should stop using the chain saws immediately and should return them to the nearest authorized (manufacturer) dealer for a free replacement muffler, which has a welded deflector: however, (manufacturer) will also replace any hand guards that show signs of heat damage.*

◢

Developing a Company Policy and Plan to Identify Defective Products and to Undertake a Product Recall

Companies whose products come under the jurisdiction of the CPSC should consider developing an organizational policy and plan of action if a product recall or similar action becomes necessary, whether it involves the CPSC or another government agency. This policy and any related plans should focus on the early detection of product safety problems and prompt response.

Designating a Recall Coordinator

Designating a company official or employee to serve as a *recall coordinator* is a significant step that a firm can take to meet its product safety and defect reporting responsibilities. Ideally, this coordinator has full authority to take the steps necessary (including reporting to the Commission) to initiate and implement all recalls, with the approval and support of the firm's chief executive officer.

The recall coordinator should have the following qualifications and duties:

- Knowledge of the statutory authority and recall procedures of the Consumer Product Safety Commission.

- Ability and authority to function as the central coordinator within the company for receiving and processing all information regarding the safety of the firm's products. Such information includes, for example, quality control records, engineering analyses, test results, consumer complaints, warranty returns or claims, lawsuits, and insurance claims.

- Responsibility for keeping the company's chief executive officer informed about reporting requirements and all safety problems or potential problems that could lead to product recalls.

- Responsibility for making decisions about initiating product recalls.

- Authority to involve appropriate departments and offices of the firm in implementing a product recall.

- Responsibility for serving as the company's primary liaison person with CPSC.

ROLE OF THE RECALL COORDINATOR

At the outset, the recall coordinator should fully review the company's product line to determine how each product will perform and fail under conditions of proper use and reasonably foreseeable misuse or abuse. Through research and analysis, product safety engineers can identify the safety features that could be incorporated into products that present safety risks to reduce their potential for future injury.

The company should institute a product identification system if one is not now in use. Model designations and date-of-manufacture codes should be used on all products, whether they carry the company's name or are privately labeled for other firms. If a product recall is necessary, this practice allows the company to identify easily all affected products without undertaking a costly recall of the entire production. Similarly, once a specific product has been recalled and corrected, a new model number or other means of identification used on new corrected products allows distributors, retailers, and consumers to distinguish products subject to recall from the new items. Until a production change can be made to incorporate a new model number or date code, some companies have used sticker labels to differentiate products that have been checked and corrected from recalled products.

RECORDS MAINTENANCE

The goal of any product recall is to retrieve, repair, or replace those products already in consumers' hands as well as those in the distribution chain. Maintaining accurate records about the design, production, distribution, and marketing of each product for the duration of its expected life is essential for a company to conduct an effective, economical product recall. Generally, the following records are key both to identifying product defects and conducting recalls:

A. *Records of complaints, warranty returns, insurance claims, and lawsuits*—These types of information often highlight or provide early notice of safety problems that may become widespread in the future.

B. *Production records*—Accurate data should be kept on all production runs—the lot numbers and product codes associated with each run, the volume of units manufactured, component parts or substitutes used, and other pertinent information which will help the company identify defective products or components quickly.

C. *Distribution records*—Data should be maintained as to the location of each product by product line, production run, quantity shipped or sold, dates of delivery, and destinations.

D. *Quality control records*—Documenting the results of quality control testing and evaluation associated with each production run often helps companies identify possible flaws in the design or production of the product. It also aids the firm in charting and sometimes limiting the scope of a corrective action plan.

E. *Product registration cards*—Product registration cards for purchasers of products to fill out and return are an effective tool to identify owners of recalled products. The easier it is for consumers to fill out and return these cards, the greater the likelihood the cards will be returned to the manufacturer. For example, some firms provide pre-addressed, postage-paid registration cards that already have product identification information, for example, model number, style number, special features, printed on the card. Providing an incentive can also increase the return rate. Incentives can be coupons toward the purchase of other products sold by the firm, free accessory products, or entry in a periodic drawing for a product give away. The information from the cards then needs to be maintained in a readily retrievable database for use in the event a recall becomes necessary.

Investigating a Potential Liability Incident

12

A product liability case starts with an incident and later evolves into an actual lawsuit. The first objective is to investigate the incident and gain all the facts while it is still in its infancy, before it formally becomes a case. The primary goal is to determine the credibility of the allegation, and if the case isn't credible, stop it in its tracks. As improbable as this may sound, it is accomplishable for a manufacturer who takes an aggressive stand toward product liability prevention. Typically when incidents are first reported to manufacturers and their insurance carriers or attorneys, rather than challenging the allegations or educating the other parties of the impossibilities, especially in cases where the evidence is circumstantial, the manufacturers remain uninvolved and the claim continues to develop.

Potential product liability incidents can be reported or communicated to a manufacturing organization in a number of ways. It can be a letter received from some other party's insurance company, or from an attorney representing another party. It can be, and many times is, a phone call from a passerby, a customer, a witness who is somehow affiliated with your company or your customer, the victim, or other sources.

One of the first problems that exists within a company is when an employee gains knowledge of an incident and doesn't know how to handle the situation or who to tell. They usually don't know what to say, or *what not to say*. Many times it is a customer service representative who first gains the knowledge of an incident. If they are not careful with what they say when such a call comes, they can create serious problems for the organization.

A customer service representative's primary goal is to show compassion toward a customer's problem and immediately service the customer in any way that they can. A dangerous potential exists for the representative to say or explain more than they should. For instance, a manufacturer recognized they improperly designed a product that's already in the field, and have already received six complaints during the past month. The company manufactures exercise equipment and sells it directly to the consumer. The piece of equipment in question is a simulated cross-country ski machine, and the design defect involves an inadequately designed resistance belt that has the possibility of suddenly breaking during workouts.

In each of the situations reported, the manufacturer told the complaining callers that they would ship them cartons to repack the units, and would then arrange for a carrier pickup. The manufacturer would then ship each customer a new unit. The current caller is different from the rest. When the belt broke on this machine, the caller seriously injured the vertebrae in his back and can hardly walk. The caller is making the call from his attorney's office. The intent is to report the problem and inquire as to the cause. They aren't sure at this point whether they have a good case against the manufacturer. The attorney is unsure whether his client may have abused the equipment, which led to the accident and injury.

When the caller connects with the manufacturer's customer service representative, he begins to explain the accident. The customer service representative stops him short because she already knows the problem. "Yes sir, I understand, do you still have the carton in which the product was shipped?" The customer replies, "No." Customer service, "What I'm going to do is ship you another carton to repack the machine, and then we'll arrange for a carrier pickup. Once we get it back we'll ship you another which won't have the problem." Customer, "Thanks, but why did this happen?" Customer service (in an attempt to have a friendly conversation with the customer, expecting this to just be another routine call), "Well, it seems our engineering department screwed up and specified the wrong size belt for the machine, but we'll take care of you right away, no problem." Customer (now being prompted by his attorney), "Have you had any other reported incidents?" Customer service, "Yes, we received about six already this month, but don't worry, we'll take care of this screw-up and get you another machine." The call ends. The customer service representative hangs up and feels she succeeded in taking care of the customer.

To the CEO's surprise, they receive a notice a few days later that they are being sued. The court complaint cites *defective design, post-sale failure to warn, negligence,* and a long list of other allegations. As they begin to inquire within the company as to whether anyone has heard of the individual named in the lawsuit, the customer service representative recognizes that it is the same person she talked to a few days earlier, but doesn't elaborate on the conversation.

The next surprise comes when counsel for the plaintiff starts holding depositions and deposes the product engineer, the customer service representative, and other key officials. Under oath, the customer service representative is reminded of the phone conversation and is drilled about everything she said. In her horror, as well as the company's, she begins to verify the fact that she said the product was designed defectively, that the company had received complaints, and that the company failed to notify the end users of the problem. In essence, the customer service representative is regretfully hanging the company.

Could this happen? Yes, it could. A different set of circumstances, but with the same end result. A potential product liability situation is reported, and someone says more than they should have in a phone conversation. It happens out of pure ignorance. It is avoided through training and awareness.

IN-HOUSE TRAINING PROGRAMS

To kick off the *Product Liability Prevention* effort, the in-house product liability expert first needs to conduct a training and awareness session with all the sales, customer service, and other management employees to begin to educate them on all the aspects of prevention. As part of such a session, they need to learn how to immediately recognize a potential product liability incident and fully document what is being told to them. In many situations, this first communiqué of an incident can be more revealing than anything else that may be said in the future. As the situation begins to develop, witnesses and participants may realize that the incident will become a lawsuit and therefore no longer want to get involved. Or an attorney may enter the picture and tell certain individuals not to have further contact with anyone. So this initial communication can be very important to the in-house product liability expert in helping to gather the real facts.

A form needs to be developed for recording such communications and effectively gathering the initial facts. The form may resemble the one shown in Figure 12.1.

Notice of Potential Liability Incident

Reported by:_____ Date:_____

Name of contact reporting incident to you:_____

Who is this contact:_____ Phone No. _____
(Customer contact, store owner, distributor, etc.)

Where is this contact located:_____

Other parties who may have knowledge of the accident or incident (if known):

_____	_____	_____
Name	*Position*	*Phone*
_____	_____	_____
Name	*Position*	*Phone*

Company Product:_____ Customer:_____

Means by which incident was communicated: ___Phone Call
___Conversation in person
___Letter or fax (attached)
___Other _____

Type of incident being reported:_____
(Personal injury, fire, property damage, etc.)

Date of incident:_____ Location:_____

Details as presented:_____

Please forward this form to our In-house Product Liability Expert

---

Figure 12.1 A form for recording calls.

PREPARING FOR AN INVESTIGATION

When the product liability expert is made aware of a potential product liability incident, depending on the nature and extent of the incident, the expert needs to make the necessary plans to investigate the situation as quickly as possible. Things explained today may not be next month. The key to possibly stopping an action in its tracks is to act fast, but the expert should not act alone.

If the situation is an insurance claim, say for instance a fire, and the company is covered by insurance (as opposed to being self-insured), then the product liability expert needs to have the company's insurance carrier assign a representative to accompany him or her. In most situations this means that the insurance carrier needs to appoint a local claims representative to handle the case (local to the incident). Once that person has been assigned, the product liability expert needs to bring the individual up to date on the case and make the necessary arrangements to meet with the other parties and investigate the incident.

If the other party already has an attorney involved, however, the product liability expert needs to bring along an attorney as well. If the company is insured, the insurance carrier will normally appoint an attorney local to that area.

The objective here, if the case is credible, is for the in-house expert to immediately get back to the operation and correct the problem. While on location, however, the expert only wants to state that they came to gather the facts, and nothing else. The expert does not want to acknowledge that the product truly does appear defective. In all probability, the other party(s) are only speculating that the product is defective, but are typically unsure. This would be the ultimate quality failure of your product. Your goal should be to get back, inform management of your findings, correct the defective condition, and start preventing additional incidents.

If, however, the in-house expert recognizes that the reported situation isn't credible, possibly because the product either isn't technically capable of doing what was described or the obvious signs of failure aren't present, then the expert needs to convince those present of the improbabilities. This is achieved not through arguing with the other parties, but by educating them on the technical aspects of the product and the reasons why the alleged scenario couldn't have happened.

MAINTAINING AN ATMOSPHERE OF COOPERATION

When the company's product liability expert first arrives at the scene or meeting place, the individual must be very diplomatic, friendly, positive, open, and nonchallenging. This is crucial if you ever hope to successfully gain all the available information surrounding the incident, and especially if you hope to convince them that the case is without merit. When all the parties first get together, none are sure what to expect of the other.

In some situations, especially personal injury cases that already involve attorneys, the attorney for the plaintiff can be extremely difficult to deal with and can shut the meeting down at the least amount of provocation. The product liability expert does not want to come across as though he is challenging the plaintiff. In these difficult situations, as the expert asks the plaintiff questions in order to understand the chain of events, the attorney for the plaintiff will often control the answers supplied. The expert wants to cooperate as much as possible in order to gain the answers to specific questions.

This won't always be the situation, however. In some situations the attorney for the plaintiff will be very open and friendly. The attorney is just trying to explain what they feel happened, and hopes that the manufacturer will agree and accept their responsibilities. This type of attorney will be more open to discussion and reason and be a better candidate for convincing of the improbability, if that ends up being the case.

Typically, a manufacturer doesn't get involved in an early investigation or spearhead such a meeting. The other parties won't be accustomed to it, nor will they know what to expect. In addition, especially when attorneys are already involved, the attorney for the other party will expect that you and your representatives have come to talk settlement. It will be a letdown when they realize that you have no such immediate intent, so you want to remain diplomatic.

GATHERING THE FACTS

Once again, the primary objective in the first investigative trip is to gather all the facts. You are concerned about potentially having a defective product, and you want to find out firsthand what happened. Where was the product? How did it get there? What happened? When did it happen? Who saw it happen? What are the actions that led up to the event? Was it properly installed/used? These are just some of the things you want to know.

As incidents continue the path into litigation, stories have a tendency to change, and some of the accounts tend to get manipulated favoring the plaintiff. Foolish actions get left out and proper and innocent actions inserted. It is critical to have the initial meeting quickly, ask all the pertinent questions, and document everything being said. The other parties may unconsciously or carelessly admit to things that catch their representatives by surprise. Always keep in mind, however, if the other attorney feels that you are beginning to interrogate their client, they may instantly become hostile and change their attitude toward this investigation and stop it from proceeding. So proceed in a sincere and cautious manner.

I have found in many of my personal injury investigations that the most revealing facts are the second-by-second reenactments of the claimant's actions leading up to the actual event or injury. Sometimes the claimant errs and admits to things that begin to put the liability in their corner. Other times the story lacks technical credibility and the expert can begin to rationalize as to what really must have happened. This again puts the cause of the accident back in the plaintiff's corner. In many cases I find that their own attorney isn't even aware of the whole story. Once I hear exactly what they supposedly did, and have viewed the product, I can begin to determine the credibility of the case.

I have had situations where the claimants in personal injury cases told their innocent stories to their attorneys, as to what they did leading up to the injury. I knew instantly that the scenario wasn't possible because the product wasn't capable of malfunctioning in the manner alleged. In one incident, after hearing the claimant, I asked if I could talk to the claimant's attorney alone. The claimant stepped out. I began to explain to the attorney why his client's story wasn't credible and demonstrated what I was saying with the product itself. At this point the attorney said something to the effect of, "Well, if that isn't what happened, then how do you explain the injury?" I then proceeded to explain step-by-step what I felt really happened, which might have involved carelessness and negligence on the part of the attorney's client. Keep in mind that at this point you're not under any oath, so what you say can't be held against you. It is an informal meeting.

Afterward, I thank them for their time and leave. In many situations, I never hear from the individuals again. In some cases, when I explained what I felt really happened, the other attorney would state, "To be honest with you, I wasn't sure if my client was really giving me the whole story."

Accomplishing such a feat is the ultimate objective. It can never happen unless you get to the scene quickly before any time or money is spent. If attorneys question the credibility of their own case and client and realize the uphill battle they will have, they may elect not to take the case.

For insurance companies and damage claims, it's a little different. Even though the expert could give a very convincing talk as to why their product wasn't responsible for the situation, and pretty much prove the product wasn't defective, the carrier suffering the loss won't want to release anyone unless they have someone else to blame.

INSPECTING THE EVIDENCE

When the initial meeting is held, the product liability expert wants to have the alleged defective product there for inspection. In cases of fire for instance, the claimant's insurance carrier, or some other forensic party, may have the product in storage or being analyzed. You want to ensure that you will have the opportunity to view the product in the first trip. Pictures of the product are not enough. You need to see the product itself.

The inspection of the product, in many situations, is the most critical element. The company's product liability expert, who should be the most knowledgeable individual of what the company's products are capable of doing even under adverse conditions, will have a definite advantage. Is the product really yours (in the case of job shop products)? Does the product appear defective? Was it manufactured to the specifications? When was it manufactured? Is it apparent to you that it is defective, and does it show definite signs of having malfunctioned, or that a component part malfunctioned? Does it appear that the product was altered, rebuilt, or reworked?

The in-house expert needs to take caution when examining the product. Many times the expert will know from experience what telltale signs indicate that the product has malfunctioned. The expert should view, touch, and possibly photograph these critical elements in a cautious and inconspicuous manner. The reason for such caution is that the other parties often don't know for sure how the product may have malfunctioned, they just allege that it did. They will be watching very closely what the expert looks at, touches, and photographs so they too can identify the exact cause. Don't be seen holding or staring at a defective component, photographing a specific area because you know that it is not per specification, attempting to operate something that clearly isn't functioning properly, or testing something with a device that will uncover in front of everyone that the product is defective. As much as your expertise can result in stopping a liability action in its tracks, it can also be the impetus for the other party to take this whole thing to a grand scale. They are going to be watching your every move, where you look, and what you touch. If you do see problems with your product, remain calm and don't draw attention to the element.

The expert should use caution when taking notes. This trip report isn't protected under attorney-client privilege, unless it is already a case and your attorney is present. Keep the defects you find in your mind and off the report. Once the case goes into litigation, counsel for the plaintiff will demand this report, so it should contain only the facts as they were stated.

After the product liability expert hears all the statements leading up to the event and has had the opportunity to inspect the product itself, if it is absolutely certain that this scenario is not credible, the expert should say so. At this point in time, the other parties aren't typically steadfast in their opinions and are open to expert opinion, even if it means they don't have a case or will be returning to square one to search for the real cause of the injury. If the expert is convincing, it will probably be the last time they hear from the other party. If the expert is not convincing, the case will continue.

This is an element of Product Liability Prevention that both parties, insurance and legal, are unaccustomed to—someone convincing the other parties in such a meeting that they don't have a case, and have them drop the issue. I have heard defense attorneys say many times, "Nobody is ever going to just drop a lawsuit," but they do. It is also one of the significant benefits of getting involved quickly. This kind of outcome is not likely to happen if you allow the insurance companies or attorneys to handle the case for you.

CREATING A REPORT

When the in-house expert leaves the meeting, the individual will need to write a report. Some key points to remember when doing this are: (1) Make sure you write down everything that was said to you. This case could continue for years and you won't remember the details if you don't write them down. (2) Thoroughly write down all of the facts; remember that they may be altered or selectively left out as the case develops. (3) Thoroughly photograph everything shown at the scene, including the product itself; don't try to go from memory or written notes. You may want to look at something at a later date that you didn't look at initially. (4) Don't include in your report defective conditions observed or your opinions, just document the facts that were presented.

Unless you have already been assigned an attorney and are protected by attorney-client privilege, these notes and reports will be some of the first documents demanded when the case is well into litigation.

IN CONCLUSION

Accident investigation is one of the best opportunities to learn the art of forensics, the science of *cause of origin* investigations in fire cases, and more about the entire legal process. It provides the opportunity to stop eventual lawsuits in their tracks and to improve your ability to critique the products and designs of tomorrow. The more you learn about how your products are used and handled, and how to gain a better perspective on *foreseeable misuse and abuse,* the better off your company will be in the future and the more money you will save.

Entering
into Litigation

When a plaintiff officially files the (court) complaint against the manufacturer and the papers are served, the litigation process starts. Prior to this, the incident may have been an insurance claim. Or an attorney representing the other party may have notified the manufacturer of an incident in the hopes that the manufacturer will quickly respond, without the attorney having to take legal action. But once the manufacturer is served the official complaint from the courts, they are now entered into litigation and are on the path to a court trial.

One of the first steps for the plaintiff in filing the complaint is to determine where they want the actual trial to take place. The complaint can be filed where the incident took place, where the defendant's corporate offices are located, or where the product was manufactured. Plaintiffs almost always file the case where the incident took place because it will be easier for the plaintiff's lawyer to handle. It puts the plaintiff in a better light with the jury as being one of them, and often makes the defendant look like a foreigner.

One of the next questions for the plaintiff to decide is the parties they should name in the lawsuit. In a lawsuit where there may be more than one party responsible for the defective product or condition, it might not be clear who to sue. The plaintiff will name all the parties known to have had some role in the creation, marketing, sales, distribution, handling, or placement of the product. This could involve the original manufacturer, the brand-named marketer, the distributor, the seller, the installer, the component supplier, and so on. Plaintiff's actions are commonly referred to as taking the shotgun approach—implicate everyone who could possibly be involved, then release certain parties as the area of responsibility narrows, and avoid letting go those perceived to have the deepest pockets.

Such practices can be bothersome for the codefendant manufacturer because each of the named defendants now has the right to name their own experts and witnesses. They can generate interrogatories not only to the plaintiff but to each of the other codefendants. They can depose any of the parties they want, and they can individually pursue settlements. For the manufacturer who is interested only in defending their product and attacking the plaintiff's case, these other parties will tend to be in the way. Nonetheless, it is important for the codefendants to cooperate with one another rather than point the finger at each other or identify defects. These findings and allegations will just help the plaintiff's case grow. The manufacturer should indemnify whatever parties makes sense, and pursue the release of others it knows couldn't be responsible.

When product liability litigation begins, attorneys for all parties seek the information and facts needed to help them with their case. This is largely accomplished through the use of interrogatories and depositions.

The attorney representing the plaintiff is typically in possession of what they believe is a defective product, but they need more information in order to build their case. They need to know more about the product, information about the manufacturer, the mechanics of the sale or distribution of the product, the product's history, technical information regarding the design and engineering, and more depending on the nature of the case.

The defense attorneys representing the manufacturer need information regarding how the product was obtained, how it was used, actions leading up to the incident, who the experts are representing the plaintiff and what their theories are, the extent of the injuries or loss claimed by the plaintiff and the credibility of the reported loss, and more.

In a way it will be similar to the central intelligence actions of two warring countries. Both parties will be involved in the investigations of the other, possible surveillance, the interrogation of the other party's key witnesses and experts, and war room strategy sessions in preparation for battle.

INITIAL DEFENSE MOVES

The first move for defense once they receive the complaint from the court is to officially deny all of plaintiff's claims and allegations, assuming, of course, they believe they're innocent. In essence, defense counterargues that the product was not defective, actions by the defendant were not negligent, and basically the accident or incident could not have happened as the result of anything the defendant did.

Once defense has denied plaintiff's first volley, it is time to launch a counterattack. There are a number of questions that need to be answered. First and foremost, did the incident really happen or in the manner in which the plaintiff claims? Was the incident the result of plaintiff's own negligent actions, or a case of *contributory negligence?* Was it the result of misuse or abuse of the product, the result of the plaintiff exposing himself to a known and obvious risk which could be classified under *assumption of risk,* or was the incident the result of alteration of the product? Who are the witnesses to the incident, and what are their claims? If the plaintiff alleges the product is unreasonably dangerous, or was defective, what is the basis of the allegation? These questions and more need to be answered by the plaintiff.

STATUTES OF LIMITATIONS AND REPOSE

Statutes of limitations were designed to allow the plaintiff adequate time to investigate their claim and file suit, but at the same time maintain a sense of fairness in consideration of the defendant. A defendant manufacturer should reach a point in time where they are no longer expected to have to resurrect evidence and locate witnesses, with the hope that they still recall what actually transpired. The limitations period starts at the time the action accrues, or normally when the injuries are incurred, except in situations where the exposure results in later injuries.

In addition, and adding some degree of confusion, one has to determine which statute of limitations applies. More than one type exists, including: statutes of limitations for tort or personal injury, specific product liability statutes of limitations, or the Uniform Commercial Code limitations provisions for breach of warranty actions. Because product liability claims are based in tort, the time period is governed under the general tort statute of limitations, unless the state maintains special statutes for product liability claims.

The general tort statutes of limitations are as follows:

Alaska	2 years
California	1 year
Delaware	2 years
District of Columbia	3 years
Georgia	2 years
Hawaii	2 years

Illinois	2 years
Indiana	2 years
Iowa	2 years
Kansas	2 years
Kentucky	1 year
Louisiana	1 year
Maine	6 years
Maryland	3 years
Massachusettes	3 years
Minnesota	2 years
Mississippi	6 years
Missouri	5 years
Montana	3 years
Nevada	2 years
New Jersey	2 years
New Mexico	3 years
New York	3 years
North Carolina	3 years
North Dakota	6 years
Ohio	2 years
Oklahoma	2 years
Pennsylvania	2 years
Rhode Island	3 years
South Carolina	3 years
Texas	2 years
Utah	2 years
Vermont	2 years
Virginia	2 years
West Virginia	2 years
Wisconsin	3 years
Wyoming	4 years

The following states have specific statutes for product liability:

Alabama	1 year
Arizona	2 years

Arkansas	3 years
California	1 year
Colorado	2 years
Connecticut	3 years
Florida	4 years
Idaho	2 years
Indiana	2 years
Michigan	3 years
Nebraska	4 years
New Hampshire	3 years
New York	2 years
Oregon	2 years
Rhode Island	3 years
South Dakota	3 years
Tennessee	1 year
Washington	3 years

In addition to statutes of limitations, some states have enacted statutes of repose which limit the ability to launch a lawsuit after an arbitrary, product-related event, such as the time of manufacture, sale, delivery, consumption, or use of the product. Stipulating that a manufacturer could no longer be held responsible for injuries caused by their products after certain time frames relieves manufacturers of the anxiety over products produced long ago. This list is as follows:

Alabama	10 years
Arizona	12 years
Colorado	10 years
Connecticut	10 years from date last parted with possession or control of product
Florida	12 years from date of delivery to original purchaser
Georgia	10 years from first sale or use
Idaho	10 years
Illinois	10 years
Indiana	10 years
Kansas	10 years

Kentucky	5 years after sale to consumer or 8 years after date of manufacture
Michigan	10 years
Nebraska	10 years
New Hampshire	12 years
North Carolina	6 years
North Dakota	10 years from date of initial purchase; 11 years from date of manufacture
Oregon	8 years
Rhode Island	10 years
Tennessee	10 years

At the end of the statutory period, the action is supposed to be barred, or a presumption arises that the product is not defective. Many of these statutes unfortunately provide for numerous exemptions and offer a defendant little benefit.

PRESERVATION, OR SPOLIATION, OF EVIDENCE

One of the first concerns of the plaintiff once the litigation process has started is to ensure the preservation of evidence. Products can be lost, tampered with, destroyed, or altered, which can affect the plaintiff's case. It is possible for plaintiff to pursue a case when in fact the product in question no longer exists or may have been destroyed in the incident or accidentally disposed. Plaintiffs would prove their case circumstantially through the use of their experts. But in most cases the evidence is available and is crucial to the case. It therefore becomes imperative for the plaintiff to closely guard the evidence, which also tends to make it harder for the defendant to gain access to it for their own inspection and verification. Should the loss of the evidence be the result of the product liability lawyer's handling of the evidence, the lawyer can expect to be on the receiving end of a professional negligence action based on spoliation of evidence.

When the in-house expert arranges the first meeting with the plaintiff and counsel, the expert should ensure that the product will be there for viewing. Pictures of the product will not suffice. At the meeting, however, the expert will only be able to view and photograph the evidence, as opposed to disassembling or disectively analyzing it. This will be allowed at a future date, when experts for all parties concerned are present, and the product can be meticulously dissected and photographed piece by piece.

INTERROGATORIES

One of the first stages of litigation, following the filing of the lawsuit with the local court and sending the notice to the manufacturer, is for the plaintiff to submit a questionnaire to the manufacturer (defendant) which asks basic initial questions. This questionnaire is known as a set of interrogatories. One party in the lawsuit submits to the other a questionnaire per se, and the receiving party is under court order to answer the questions in a short time frame.

An example is a fictitous situation where the manufacturer of a deep fryer system for the fast food industry is blamed for a fire that destroyed a restaurant, resulting in damages worth over $1 million. The insurance carrier for the restaurant hires a cause and origin expert who states that he feels the deep fryer was definitely the cause of the fire. The manufacturer of the deep fryer firmly believes their unit wasn't responsible for the fire, and that they are being wrongly accused. Nonetheless, the insurance company for the restaurant hires an attorney to launch the case against the manufacturer, and officially sends the manufacturer a set of interrogatories to answer, as well as a request for documents.

Unfortunately, because they manufacture such a high volume of deep fryers and have had units in use throughout the country for more than a decade, they have two similar incidents that have been reported in other parts of the country. In the first incident, reported almost a year ago, the insurance carrier had an in-house attorney file a complaint in order to achieve subrogation. In recent months, however, they seemed to be giving up on the case, because they couldn't uncover enough technical evidence to support their claim. Everything in the kitchen area was too badly destroyed to identify any other potential source. There hasn't been any activity on the case in almost nine months. Ironically, when the case was first reported, the manufacturer's engineering and reliability departments took a hard look at the unit's design and made number of design improvements to help eliminate any potential causes of a fire, just in case their product really was the cause of the fire.

Six months later, another incident was reported, and once again one of the parties at the scene of the fire put the blame on the deep fryer. The loss here was at least as great as the prior event. Nonetheless, the manufacturer felt confident that their unit wasn't the cause of the fire. If the fire started within the unit, it had to have been the result of user negligence or equipment abuse. This was also just an insurance claim at this point; no legal action had been taken, nor was there any indication that legal action would follow.

It is also important to note that none of the parties involved in the three incidents has any knowledge of the other two. Each believes they are singularly involved in their claim against the manufacturer and are in various stages of trying to prove it.

Now, the manufacturer is involved in litigation in the third incident and has received a set of interrogatories which it must answer within 30 days. The interrogatories are forwarded to the manufacturer's internal product liability expert. The questions on the interrogatory are as follows:

INTERROGATORY NO. 1: Identify the person(s) answering or assisting in answering these interrogatories.

INTERROGATORY NO. 2: Identify all persons retained and/or employed in the manufacture and/or marketing and/or servicing of the deep fryer units.

INTERROGATORY NO. 3: Identify all the individuals along with their job titles, whether still employed by your company or no longer with your company, known by you to have any knowledge of previous product malfunctions, design modifications, design defects, or design improvements of the deep fryer units, for as long as they have been produced.

INTERROGATORY NO. 4: Identify any and all design modifications or design improvements that have been made to the deep fryers, or any component within the unit. Include in your answer the reason for such modifications or improvements.

INTERROGATORY NO. 5: Please identify any Underwriters Laboratory listing numbers and standards applicable to the deep fryers.

INTERROGATORY NO. 6: Please identify any other standards or codes which you are required to comply with in the manufacture of the identified deep fryer which was sold to (fast food restaurant).

INTERROGATORY NO. 7: With respect to all complaints (including but not limited to lawsuits), written or oral, received directly or indirectly by (manufacturer) from any distributor, dealer, ultimate user, or any other person, entity, or regulatory body relative to fires involving deep fryers, please:

    A. Identify the person or entity making each such complaint.

    B. State the date on which each such complaint was made.

    C. State the substance of each such complaint.

    D. State your answer to each complaint and how each complaint was resolved.

INTERROGATORY NO. 8: If you have ever been sued or had claims brought against you arising out of the design, manufacture, installation, maintenance and/or sale of the deep fryer units, identify the party or parties bringing the suit or making the claim, the city, state, and court in which each such unit was brought and the docket number of each suit or claim.

INTERROGATORY NO. 9: With respect to any and all recalls and/or warnings you have ever known of, received, published or distributed with respect to the installation, maintenance, or use of any of Defendant's deep fryers, including but not limited to the subject deep fryer, please:

    A. Identify each such recall and/or warning.

    B. State the purpose and nature of each such recall and/or warning.

    C. State what corrective action or measures were taken by you as a result of such recalls and/or warnings.

INTERROGATORY NO. 10: Identify any conditions, mechanical failures, defects, or other design elements that you are aware of that could cause, or have caused, the deep fryer, or any of its components, to start a fire.

INTERROGATORY NO. 11: If you contend that any act or omission of plaintiff or another person caused or contributed to plaintiff's damages in this case, identify each such act or omission with particularity.

INTERROGATORY NO. 12: If (manufacturer) conducts its business based upon any government, industry, or professional standards or codes in the course of its business, and more specifically in the design or manufacture of its deep fryers, please identify the applicable government, industry, and/or professional standards, codes, and/or regulations.

INTERROGATORY NO. 13: If you have ever performed any repairs, maintenance and/or service on the subject deep fryer or any of its components, please:

    A. State the nature of the work performed.

    B. Identify the persons and their current employers, if known, who performed such work.

INTERROGATORY NO. 14: If at any time prior to the incident, you tested or inspected the subject deep fryer, identify all such tests including the date of such test or inspection, the person who performed the test or inspection, the conclusions or result of the test or inspection, and identity of any documents produced in connection with such test or inspection.

INTERROGATORY NO. 15: If you have ever talked to the plaintiff or any of the plaintiff's agents, servants, employees, directors, partners, or anyone in the employ of the plaintiff's regarding the incident or the subject deep fryer in question, or you have knowledge, either directly or indirectly, of any statement or admission of any kind made by the plaintiff, or anyone acting on the plaintiff's behalf, please identify the person making the statement and/or admission and describe the statement and/or admission.

Although the manufacturer feels their product wasn't responsible for the three fires reported, the interrogatories are sure to create major problems for them. First and foremost, Interrogatories 7 and 8 are going to enable all the parties to find out about each other and allow them to compare notes and share information. In situations where it appeared the other parties would probably drop their claims, it is a sure bet they won't now. If they don't take advantage of the opportunity to build an alliance with the other claimants, they will at least wait to see how the case is settled before deciding their next action.

Interrogatory # 4 is also likely to create problems. "Identify any and all design modifications or design improvements that have been made to the deep fryers . . ." The manufacturer had closely analyzed their design after the first reported incident and made some design changes related to eliminating any potential sources of fire. Depending on how they documented these changes and the reasons for the changes, they may now have some real dangerous documents waiting to be discovered.

Furthermore, in Interrogatory #3, the plaintiff demands the names of all persons who have knowledge of any design changes that have ever taken place with the product. This would include the product engineers as well as various other quality or manufacturing personnel. Now, regardless of how carefully Interrogatory #4 was answered, the plaintiff will gain the names of other key people within the organization, or worse yet, people who have left the company who have any knowledge of the design changes that took place, which will help set the stage for future depositions of these individuals.

In addition to what may have been recorded in the engineering change documents and/or other associated records, there will now be the fear of what these individuals might say when cross-examined by attorneys under oath. What were the recognized potentials of the unit catching on fire that prompted design improvements after the first incident was reported? Such information will be significant in helping plaintiff build their case.

REQUEST FOR DOCUMENTS

Along with the interrogatories, a second part of litigation will be a request for documents. The title is rather misleading. It isn't really a *request* but instead a court ordered *demand* for documents. The request for documents will ask for different documents, such as the blueprints for the product, which might even stipulate that the prints are to include drawings from two years before the product in question was produced, to the current drawings. The reason for this will be to uncover whether the manufacturer made changes prior to the accident which contributed to the accident itself, or made improvements after the accident which identifies the product produced as being defective.

The request will demand records of engineering changes which should thoroughly explain all the changes made over the years, as well as who the individuals are that were involved in the changes. They will request sales records, distribution records, records of any customer complaints ever received, possibly records of any insurance claims or other legal claims involving the product, or similar products. The records will ask for copies of letters and memos involving the product and production of the product. It will ask for copies of warranties, product warnings that were supplied, instruction and operating manuals, and records of any recalls that ever took place.

The request for documents could involve finding 20 to 30 related documents, or it could involve 100,000 documents, which has been the case in some reported automotive lawsuits.

Although the request is actually a demand, there are still defenses that can be utilized when responding to the demand. For instance, the plaintiff could demand the names, titles, (home) addresses, and (home) phone numbers of every employee that has had any involvement in the design, production, testing, marketing, sales, and distribution of the product. The defense attorney could respond to the request by objecting to the request, citing that this is an *overly broad and burdensome* request, since the manufacturer has over 5000 employees, many of which were involved in some phase of the product's development.

The same objection could be used when the manufacturer is asked for numerous records involving the product *or similar products*. The manufacturer may produce countless products that could be considered *similar* and could demand that the plaintiff be more specific in their demand, or ask the court to narrow the request to the product itself. So although the defense attorney will likely forward the interrogatories and request for documents to the in-house expert to prepare and return, the expert could consult with the attorney on some of the requests in order to see if, in fact, they really need to gather the information, or whether there is a possibility of objecting to a specific element of the request.

DEPOSITIONS

The next stage after responding to interrogatories and request for documents will be depositions. This is where both parties get the pretrial chance to question under oath all the witnesses, experts, and anyone else they can think of that might help them uncover critical facts for their case. Although the trial hasn't been scheduled at this point, those deposed will be sworn under oath, and their testimonies will be recorded by a court reporter. What they state could be revisited and used against them during the trial.

The deposition could take place at one of the attorneys' offices, the company where the individual works, or any other mutually agreed spot for all those involved.

During the actual deposition, the witnesses will be sworn under oath and asked to thoroughly identify themselves and verify their relationship to the case at hand (eyewitness, doctors, manufacturing rep, store owner, plaintiff, and so on). Then with the attorneys present representing the parties involved, the witnesses will be asked specific questions which they must answer. Although they're not in court, it will be the equivalent.

What normally happens is the attorney for the plaintiff will ask for the names of individuals within the manufacturing organization, in order to determine who they should depose. They will try to find out who the product engineer and other key manufacturing or salespeople are. This could create problems because these individuals may be scared to be deposed, or the expert and attorney could be unsure of what others might say as they're being interrogated by the opposing attorney.

Some people, for instance, fear they may go to jail or be personally fined for information they know or details they fail to make known. So they tend to not only answer the questions, but discuss everything that happened. From the opposite perspective, others may have a negative attitude toward the case and give the opposing party a piece of their mind, which ends up getting the manufacturer in deeper trouble.

As the attorney for the plaintiff is beginning to identify the manufacturing representatives they want to depose, the in-house expert, through the manufacturer's defense counsel, can offer to have the expert be the only person who testifies on behalf of everyone else. This is a highly unusual move which surprises many attorneys as possible or acceptable to plaintiffs, but it does work. Counsel for the plaintiff will normally be caught off-guard by the proposal and will inquire whether the in-house expert has the technical product knowledge to answer all the questions they will want to ask. If the defense attorney says "yes," the attorney for the plaintiff will often accept the offer.

The advantage here is that the in-house expert can be sharper in answering the questions, quite experienced in the whole process, and remain calm and confident during the deposition. If the expert is unable to answer the technical product questions, however, plaintiff will hold a second round of depositions and bring in the others.

A key element in depositions is to just answer the question. Many individuals offer more than what needs to be said or add a cliff-hanger that opens the door to more questions and revealing details. For instance, a manufacturer produces coffee making machines but has many models to choose from. Many of the models have the same internal components and assembly but have different outside housings and enclosures. A specific model coffeemaker is involved in a large fire. It is the first time this specific model has ever been involved in a fire, but other models have been involved in a number of fires over the years.

During the deposition and under oath, counsel for the plaintiff asks the manufacturer's representative, "Has this model coffeemaker ever been involved in any other fires since it was first introduced?" The right answer for the manufacturer's representative is "No" period, and not another word. Some nervous individuals might say, "We've had a number of reported fires with other models we produce, but this is the only fire that I know of with this model." Or the cliff-hanger would be, "You're just asking about this model? No, we haven't had any fires with just this model." An obvious problem is if the internal operating components are the same, and only the outside shell is different, then whatever malfunctioned on the other units could malfunction on this one too.

The in-house expert needs to learn how to testify under oath, be brief, and not open the door to other problems or plaintiff opportunities.

SETTLEMENTS

Although the author is a staunch supporter of fighting an unfounded case to the death, there will begrudgingly be times when settling the case with the plaintiff makes more economic sense. Attorneys know that roughly 96 percent of all product liability cases settle out of court. It is difficult for the fully, or mostly, insured manufacturer to insist that their insurance carrier continue to fight a $200,000 case to successful conclusion, when the estimated legal costs for the fight will amount to $50,000 and the plaintiff has just announced that they would be willing to settle for $15,000. Even though defense is pretty confident in their abilities to win the case, there is still the chance of losing, or compromise, and the potential losses far exceed the immediate cost to settle.

The author, however, is still a firm promoter of manufacturers fighting for their reputation and record in unfounded cases against their companies. Defendant should either push plaintiff into dropping their case or for the manufacturer to have their day in court, as opposed to following the trend of settling.

As a matter of fact, because almost all cases do settle out of court, the in-house expert should take a hard look at the background of the attorney selected to represent them, to ensure the attorney has sound trial experience and isn't just a good negotiator. Many unskilled defense attorneys are just as nervous about taking a case to court, as are plaintiff attorneys, and may encourage insurance carriers to settle in the final hours.

IN CONCLUSION

Litigation can be an educational experience for the in-house product liability expert who is not a lawyer. Much will happen, albeit slowly. Win, lose, or settle, there will be a lot to learn if the expert stays active and manages the litigation process.

SETTLEMENT AGREEMENT AND RELEASE

FOR AND IN CONSIDERATION OF the payment of the sum of $_____ the receipt and sufficiency of which is hereby acknowledged, I [we] hereby release, acquit and forever discharge (your company) and its administrators, representatives, officers, agents, insurers and connected companies of and from any and all claims, demands, damages, costs, expenses, compensation and causes of action on account of, or in any way relating to the incident involving _____.

IT IS UNDERSTOOD AND AGREED that this is a full and complete release of all injuries and damages which the undersigned claim to have sustained as a result of said _____ or will sustain by reason thereof, whether said injuries and damages are now known or hereafter become known, including all present injuries and damages and all future developments therefrom.

IT IS FURTHER UNDERSTOOD AND AGREED that this settlement is a compromise of a doubtful and disputed claim and that the payment and this release is not to be construed as an admission of liability on the part of the above-named parties, by whom liability is expressly denied.

IT IS FURTHER UNDERSTOOD AND AGREED that both the parties and their respective attorneys and representatives will maintain this settlement agreement and release in strictest confidence and will not divulge either the existence of this agreement, nor the amount hereinunder to any third party except as required by law or court order.

I [WE] FURTHER STATE that I [we] have carefully read the forgoing release, that I [we] have consulted with counsel as to its meaning, that I [we] fully understand its provisions and that I [we] sign the same as my [our] free act and deed.

Dated this _____ day of _____ , 200___.

_____
Plaintiff

_____
Attorney for Plaintiff

_____
Defendant

SETTLEMENT AGREEMENT AND RELEASE

FOR AND IN CONSIDERATION OF the payment of the sum of $_____ the receipt and sufficiency of which is hereby acknowledged, I [we] hereby release, acquit and forever discharge (your company) and its administrators, representatives, officers, agents, insurers and connected companies of and from any and all claims, demands, damages, costs, expenses, compensation and causes of action on account of, or in any way relating to the incident involving _____.

IT IS UNDERSTOOD AND AGREED that this is a full and complete release of all injuries and damages which the undersigned claim to have sustained as a result of said _____ or will sustain by reason thereof, whether said injuries and damages are now known or hereafter become known, including all present injuries and damages and all future developments therefrom.

IT IS FURTHER UNDERSTOOD AND AGREED that this settlement is a compromise of a doubtful and disputed claim and that the payment and this release is not to be construed as an admission of liability on the part of the above-named parties, by whom liability is expressly denied.

IT IS FURTHER UNDERSTOOD AND AGREED that an action in the Circuit Court of _____ County entitled _____ has been docketed as case number _____ and that said action will be dismissed on its merits, with prejudice and without costs, and I [we] hereby authorize my [our] attorney to sign a stipulation to accomplish this.

IT IS FURTHER UNDERSTOOD AND AGREED that both the parties and their respective attorneys and representatives will maintain this settlement agreement and release in strictest confidence and will not divulge either the existence of this agreement, nor the amount hereinunder to any third party except as required by law or court order.

I [WE] FURTHER STATE that I [we] have carefully read the forgoing release, that I [we] have consulted with counsel as to its meaning, that I [we] fully understand its provisions and that I [we] sign the same as my [our] free act and deed.

Dated this ____ day of _____ , 200___.

_____
Plaintiff

_____
Attorney for Plaintiff

_____
Defendant

Going to Trial

14

Going to trial will be the climactic end in the long life of a product liability case. It will be a tense period, but it will be a chance to have your day in court and hopefully win. It will take countless hours of planning and preparation. Realistically, it will take months of preparation for the attorney and manufacturer. Deciding who will testify, who won't, what evidence will be presented, and what facts will be brought to light all have to be carefully planned and choreographed.

As the manufacturer nears the trial date in a product liability case, it is still beneficial for the in-house expert to gain and maintain an in-depth knowledge of trial tactics, as well as for the assigned attorney to already have good knowledge of the manufacturer and the technical product. The manufacturer may be represented by their own hired counsel who has gained a degree of product expertise from the years they've been associated. Or the manufacturer may be represented by an attorney who was selected by the insurance carrier in the city where the trial is going to take place. In the latter scenario, which is the most common among insured manufacturers, the attorney selected will undoubtedly not know anything about the manufacturer's product or product type starting out, and may even be a pretty mediocre defense attorney. One of the reasons for the mediocrity is the probability that the insurer is maintaining a tight control over what they are willing to pay for the manufacturer's defense. This can be much like an HMO.

In addition to the potential mediocrity of some assigned defense attorneys, the manufacturer and in-house expert must keep in mind that 96 percent of all cases settle out of court. Unfortunately, this often means that the defense attorneys are better negotiators than experienced trial lawyers. I would encourage any defendant with assigned counsel to request a copy of the attorney's bio, or ask how many cases the attorney has taken through trial and won. This is different than asking how many product liability cases the attorney has handled, because the attorney may have been assigned to numerous cases but settled early on every one of them. That isn't the type of attorney a manufacturer wants to have defend them, unless the manufacturer is also interested in settling out of court.

Preparing for trial will be a very time-consuming process. It will require a significant amount of planning, and there are countless defense strategies to think about. It can be quite beneficial for the in-house nonlawyer expert to have a good knowledge of various trial rules, defense tactics, and winning strategies in order to not only be a good planning partner for the defense attorney, but to also ensure that the company is getting the best defense possible.

TESTIFYING VERSUS NONTESTIFYING EXPERT

One decision that should to be made between the attorney and the in-house expert is whether the expert should testify in the court case. Prior to the start of a product liability case, both parties, plaintiff and defendant, must make it known to everyone who they will have testify as experts at the trial. This announcement has to leave enough time for the other party to depose that expert and gain an insight into what they are going to say and introduce in the trial. Last minute surprises aren't normally allowed.

Depending on his or her educational background, the in-house expert might wonder whether they are qualified to be considered an *expert*, by the court. Remember the definition of the word *expert*, *One skilled in any particular art, trade, or profession, being possessed of peculiar knowledge concerning the same, and one who has given subject in question particular study, practice, or observation.* This means that even a nondegreed individual who thoroughly knows and understands the product based on years of working with the product, would qualify as being a product expert.

As stated in the previous chapter, the best strategy during the Deposition stage is to get counsel for the plaintiff to allow the in-house expert to solely be deposed in place of anyone else from the manufacturer's organization. This helps eliminate the possibility of other people within the organization panicking during the trial and *spilling their guts* about everything that ever went wrong. During the trial, however, more thought might be given as to whether the in-house expert should still testify.

The defendants have three options: (1) have the in-house expert be their prime spokesperson and testify on behalf of the manufacturer during the trial; (2) have an in-house engineer or someone else within the organization testify at trial regarding the technical product; or, (3) hire an outside expert to officially represent the manufacturer and testify at the trial, with the in-house expert assuming the role of the nontestifying expert who educates the testifying expert about the product.

The in-house expert is going to be the most well-versed individual regarding the product, and eventually the best trained in giving testimony, but could also come with problems. For instance, if there were other cases involving the product that the plaintiff never knew about, and failed to find out about during the interrogatory and deposition stages, the in-house expert would know about this information and suddenly could be asked about it during the trial. An outside expert, hired to represent the company during the trial, wouldn't know about the company's history, and therefore couldn't offer any potentially damaging information.

Even an in-house engineer or other technical management representative may not have knowledge of other incidents if the in-house expert and the corporate liability team kept such information confidential, as they should. This and other elements of concern should be carefully weighed as defense decides who would be their best candidate for testifying.

DISQUALIFYING PLAINTIFF'S EXPERT WITNESS—THE DAUBERT RULING

One of the most significant defense moves would be to have the ability to eliminate plaintiff's key expert witness, especially at the start of a trial. In the early 1990s the Supreme Court opened the door to such a possibility in the landmark *Daubert* ruling.

In the landmark case *Daubert v. Merrell Dow Pharmaceuticals Inc.,* 113 S. Ct. 2786 (1993) the United States Supreme Court addressed the admissibility of expert opinion for the first time since the adoption of the federal rules of evidence. The case itself dealt with a suit brought against Merrell Dow Pharmaceuticals regarding limb reduction birth defects affecting two minors, allegedly because their mother had once taken a drug called Bendectin for morning sickness.

The significant aspect of the case was that the theory presented by the plaintiff's experts did not reflect scientific knowledge, nor were the findings or theory derived by scientific method. The theories were presented by experts with impressive qualifications, and under the assurance that their conclusions were reliable. The credibility of such testimony has always been covered by the criteria found in the *Frye* test, which originated in the case of *Frye v. United States*, 293 F. 1013 (D.C. Cir. 1923). Although it was a criminal case, it dismissed as evidence the polygraph machine because it had not gained *general acceptance* within the particular field in which it belongs, which at the time would have been the fields of physiology and psychology. This had been held as the standard for admissibility of theory and evidence for decades, but the turning point now was the Supreme Court under *Daubert* determining that just *general acceptance* was not enough.

An example is a case where a fluorescent light ballast is alleged to have been the origin of a fire that caused considerable damage to a store. Plaintiff's expert witness may be a cause and origin expert with a significant background in metallurgy, structural design, and other unrelated fields, even listing similar cases where he had appeared as an expert witness. The expert witness could commonly even be a college professor from the school of engineering.

During cross-examination by the defense, however, counsel could bring to light the fact that the expert never specifically worked with, received thorough training or education on, or worked for any company that built ballasts. Furthermore, it may be brought to light that the expert never performed a thoroughly documented failure analysis test to prove out his theory. Therefore, the theory isn't considered scientific, nor is the expert considered credible. The Supreme Court under *Daubert* heavily emphasized the role and responsibility trial court judges must play as *gatekeepers* in screening expert testimony for relevance and reliability, and not to automatically allow it to be presented to the jury simply because it is the opinion of a so-called *expert*.

The Supreme Court explained that the expert's testimony must be *reliable*, that is, the opinion must have a *reliable basis in the knowledge and experience of the expert's discipline*. The *Daubert* factors that the courts should employ in determining whether a theory or hypothesis constitiutes *scientific knowledge* would include:

A. *Testing*—Whether the expert's theory or technique can be, and has been, tested

B. *Peer review*—Whether the theory or technique has been subject to peer review and publication

C. *Rate of error*—Whether there is a known or potential rate of error

D. *Standards*—Whether there exists, and have been maintained, standards controlling the technique's operation

E. *General acceptance*—Whether the theory or technique is generally accepted within the relevant scientific community

Other significant rules and guidelines are the Federal Rules on Evidence 403, 702, 703, and 706.

> **Fed.R.Evid. 403**
>
> The expert testimony cannot have the tendency to confuse or mislead the jury. As applied in *Daubert*, "Expert evidence can be both powerful and quite misleading because of the difficulty in evaluating it. Because of the risk, the judge in weighing possible prejudice against probative force under Rule 403 of the present rules exercises more control over experts than over law witnesses."
>
> **Fed.R.Evid. 702**
>
> Scientific experts must possess the requisite knowledge and be sufficiently reliable in order to express his or her opinions to the jury.
>
> **Fed.R.Evid. 703**
>
> The facts and/or data relied upon by the expert must be "of a type reasonably relied upon by experts in the particular field in forming opinions or inferences upon the subject."
>
> **Fed.R.Evid. 706**
>
> The court also has the ability to chose its own expert in evaluating scientific testimony.

When the plaintiff's expert witness, and evidence being presented, doesn't comply with the preceeding guidelines, counsel for the defense can ask for a *Rule 104(a) Hearing* prior to allowing the testimony to be admitted. This is basically a motion by the defense to have plaintiff's expert witness impeached by the (gatekeeper) judge. The defense tactic is to ask for a Rule 104(a) hearing late enough in the pretrial process to handicap the plaintiff, yet early enough to allow the court time to decide on the issue leaving an inadequate amount of time for the plaintiff to obtain another questionable expert.

An example of such a decision can be found in *Mark Smith v. Ford Motor Co.* which both commenced and ended on April 26, 1999, in the U.S. Southern District court in Indiana. The case concerned allegations that the steering system and gear box components in a 1993 Ford Econoline van were defective and unreasonably dangerous, thus causing a single car accident with resulting injuries and damages. The Federal Court established a case management plan which included, among other things, deadlines for disclosure of expert opinions. In compliance, the plaintiff disclosed their two testifying experts.

Through discovery it was learned that plaintiff had one expert retained to testify on design issues and another to address metallurgical issues. Through their depositions, sufficient information was obtained to call into question the expertise of both witnesses, as well as the basis for their opinions. Accordingly, pursuant to *Daubert* and *Kuhmo Tire*, appropriate motions to exclude the testimony were prepared by defense.

The judge, immediately in advance of jury selection, held a hearing on the motion as to whether plaintiff's expert witnesses should be allowed to testify. Vigorous cross-examination of both experts was undertaken. Even the judge posed a few questions of the experts. Their lack of expertise was established, as well as the lack of any scientific or engineering basis for opinions of design or manufacturing defect. After a short recess, the judge returned to the courtroom and announced that neither individual would be allowed to testify.

With defense having won this battle, they then focused on winning the war. They entered a motion to dismiss the case on the basis that plaintiff did not have the appropriate expert evidentiary basis to prove a product liability case under Indiana law. The judge agreed and dismissed the case on the first day.

Stanczyk v. Black & Decker, Inc., 836 F. Supp. 565, 566 (N.D. Ill. 1993)—The court evaluated plaintiff's expert's testimony that he could design a guard for defendant's saw that would reduce possible contact with the exposed blade. Citing the expert's admission that although he was comfortable that his design would work, his concept was not fully defined, fully proven, nor fully documented. The court's analysis of this was a textbook example of the *gatekeeper* role prescribed by *Daubert:*

Daubert teaches that the court must consider certain factors, the most important factor is whether the technique or theory being advanced by the expert can be or has been tested. The expert offered no testable design to support his concept. Furthermore, the history of engineering and science is filled with finely conceived ideas that are unworkable in practice. There is a high potential rate of error for mechanical concepts offered engineering analysis.

One must consider whether there is peer review and publication of the technique. There is none, and the closest proxy for it, industry practice, produces no evidence of the use of gravity guards for this type of saw. This rules out the possibility of general acceptance, another factor to be considered. Finally, to the extent there are controlling design standards, they offer no support to the expert's opinion.

⅃

The court concluded that the expert's testimony did not pass the criteria under *Daubert* standards, and excluded the evidence.

***Pries v. Honda Motor Co. Ltd.*, 31 F.3d 543 (7th Cir. 1994)**—In an action arising from an automobile rollover, the district court granted summary judgement for the manufacturer. In that case, it was alleged that the occupant's seat belt had come open during the course of the rollover accident. A test was performed by plaintiff's expert on a similar seat belt latch by dropping it on a hard surface to see whether it would open. Periodically it did. Subsequently, when defense counsel asked what forces had brought about this opening and whether these were commonly achieved in a crash, the expert did not know. The court held that under *Daubert*, evidence of this kind is not scientific and does not satisfy Federal Rules of Evidence 702.

***Fitzpatric v. Madonna* (Pa. Sup. Ct. 1993)**—A 16-year-old boy was killed after being struck by the propeller of a motorboat. The jury awarded more than one million dollars in damages to the victim's mother in a wrongful death and survival action.

The Pennsylvania Superior Court overturned the verdict. It found that the plaintiff's claim that a shroud over the propeller would have prevented the accident ignored the potential undesirable effects of such a device.

⌐

An outboard motor is designed to move a boat through water. It has not been designed to allow motorboats to move among swimmers. The risk inherent in such movement is readily apparent. Moreover, it cannot be said with any degree of certainty that the risk of injury will be reduced by a safety guard, for the presence of a shroud over the propeller presents its own risks to swimmers. For example, a shroud creates a larger target area. In addition, the possibility exists that human limbs may become wedged between a shroud and the propeller, exposing a swimmer to even greater injury.

A competent person knows that he or she must stay clear of the churning blades of an outboard motor in the same way as a person avoids airplane propellers, chain saw teeth, and lawn mower blades.

⌐

If either party is successful in rebutting the other expert's analysis prior to or during trial, such a tactic would have substantial impact on the case, or that individual's credibility with the jury and the grounds for their case. Such a move would be a devastating blow to the plaintiff's case. If counsel for the plaintiff is cognizant of such a potential move, they may try to change their facts and opinions just prior to court. If this should happen, and plaintiff's expert presents a whole different scenario, defense would want to motion that the court either suppress this new theory, or allow for additional depositions and discovery.

PRETRIAL CONFERENCE

Just prior to the actual trial, the courts may require a pretrial conference between the two parties for such purposes as the following: expediting the disposition of the action, establishing early and continuing control so that the case will not be protracted because of lack of management, discouraging wasteful pretrial activities, improving the quality of the trial through more thorough preparation, and *facilitating the settlement of the case.* This is an action that the manufacturer and in-house expert should be alert to, especially if they are fully insured. The two attorneys will have their last chance to pursue and agree on possible settlements, with a last-second check with the insurance carrier and plaintiff. The upsetting element could be that the in-house expert is in-flight to the city where the trial is going to take place, totally prepared for them to win the case, when the two attorneys suddenly agree to an eleventh-hour settlement and bring an end to the entire process. If the manufacturer is fully insured, the insurance claims representative may not have to gain the manufacturer's permission to agree to a settlement, unless such a stipulation is written in their contract. If the manufacturer is self-insured, this wouldn't be a factor, and if the manufacturer has a deductible, it would just need to be reviewed whether there is any provision allowing for this.

JURY SELECTION

This is the final stage of going to trial. Jury selection takes place either the day before, or the morning of, the trial. Jury selection is an art, if the attorneys involved treat it as one. There are many cases in large trials where the defense attorneys hire consultants to help them with the process and selection. It is interesting to study the process and hear experts teach seminars on the art and technique of selecting jury members. If the defense attorney selected has little trial experience, and logically little experience going to product liability trial techniques seminars, they probably won't have much knowledge regarding the science of picking jurors.

Sitting with the defense attorney during the jury selection process could be another enlightening and educational experience for the in-house product liability expert.

IN CONCLUSION

Going to trial in a product liability case will likely be an emotional experience, but it will also be an educational experience for the in-house expert, regardless of the outcome.

Case Studies

The following case studies are referenced in order to support many of the elements contained in this book. They are also offered for their educational value for the manufacturer's management team. As shown and demonstrated in various chapters, many decisions made by the courts and defenses offered take place based on other legal precedents. The precedents mentioned in some of the following case studies may also be good reference material for the in-house expert to share with counsel for the defense.

SUBCONTRACTOR CREATED LIABILITIES

In all my years of speaking around the world, I have had many opportunities to meet with individuals and hear their product liability horror stories. One story dealt with a major manufacturer of bread toasters. After years of producing different models and probably millions of toasters, the manufacturer suddenly began to run into problems with one model that accidentally started on fire due to a defective thermostat.

Within a month the toasters resulted in numerous fires and four to five deaths. The company was taken to court and sued for millions in the cases and lost. The company quickly recalled all the products in the field through various media means. In the end the recall effort resulted in approximately five railroad cars full of the packaged toasters. The company determined that the toasters weren't worth what it would cost to disassemble and replace the thermostat, so they worked out an agreement with a small salvage company to have certain parts removed and reused. Basically, the toasters now belonged to the salvage company, and all the manufacturer wanted back were the cartons and instruction manuals. The salvage company could do what they wanted with the toaster components.

The verbal agreement was worked out between certain parties in the manufacturer's purchasing department and the individual who owned the privately held salvage company. The only problem was that shortly after reaching the agreement, the owner of the salvage company died. His son wasn't part of the discussions and didn't fully understand what the problem was with the toasters. The son tried a few of the units and they seemed to work fine. Now that they belonged to the salvage company, the son offered them to a major discount department store chain, at half the normal price. The department store bought them and offered them for sale in the next available Sunday newspaper sale section. The manufacturer had no knowledge of the sale. Within three days one person was already dead from a fire, and within a week to ten days two more people had died in fires. The son instantly closed the salvage company and claimed bankruptcy, and the manufacturer was once again sued for millions in the new deaths and had to perform another recall.

DESIGN DEFECTS

Napolean v. Products Finishing Corp.

Napolean, 31, was injured when a luggage rack bungee cord with metal hooks on the ends came loose from his portable luggage cart and hit him in the eye. As a result, Napolean suffered an enucleation of his right eye and missed three years of work as a messenger because of his injuries.

Napolean sued the manufacturer of the cart and cord alleging a defective cart design which failed to possess a restraint device to keep the end of the bungee cord attached to the cart. The lawsuit also claimed a failure to warn of potential serious injuries arising out of use of the powerfully elastic bungee cord. At trial, Napolean showed that the defendant had been sued 15 times prior to this incident for injuries relating to the bungee cord and cart and that the defendant subsequently changed the design of the cart following Napolean's accident. The parties settled during trial for $850,000.

Uniroyal Goodrich Tire Co. v. Martinez, Tex., No. 95-1159 (1998)

Roberto Martinez was badly injured when he was struck by an exploding Goodrich 16" tire that he was mounting on a 16.5" rim. The tire had a prominent warning label that included pictures and stated:

Ⴁ

DANGER

NEVER MOUNT A 16" SIZE DIAMETER TIRE ON A 16.5" RIM.
Mounting a 16" tire on a 16.5" rim can cause severe injury or death.
While it is possible to pass a 16" diameter tire over the lip or flange of a
16.5" size diameter rim, it cannot position itself against the rim flange.
If an attempt is made to seat the bead by inflating the tire, the tire bead
will break with explosive force.

NEVER inflate a tire which is lying on the floor or other flat
surface. Always use a tire mounting machine with a hold-down device
or safety cage or bolt to vehicle axle.

NEVER inflate to seat beads without using an extension hose
with gauge and clip-on chuck.

NEVER stand, lean or reach over the assembly during inflation.

Failure to comply with these safety precautions can cause the
bead to break and the assembly to burst with sufficient force to cause
serious injury or death.

⅃

Martinez ignored the warnings. According to the court, he leaned over the assembly and attempted to mount a 16" tire on a 16.5" rim without a tire mounting machine, a safety cage, or an extension hose. It should be noted, however, that Martinez testified that he thought he was mounting a 16" tire on a 16" rim, because he had removed a 16" tire from the rim.

The Martinezes sued Goodrich, rim designer Ford Motor Co., and rim manufacturer Budd Co. The Martinezes did not claim the warning was inadequate. Instead, they alleged both negligence and strict liability claims for manufacturing and design defects. Ford and Budd settled prior to trial.

A jury found Goodrich 100 percent liable for Martinez's injuries. It awarded $5.5 million in actual damages and $11.5 million in punitives. The trial court reduced the actual damages to $4.1 million and the punitive damages to about $4.1 million to reflect a pretrial agreement between the parties.

Afterward, Uniroyal Goodrich Tire Company appealed and took the case to the Texas Supreme Court. The high court rejected the argument by Uniroyal Goodrich that the tire was not defective because an *unambiguous and conspicuously visible* warning appeared on the side about the dangers of mounting on wrong-sized rims. Citing the recently released *Restatement (Third) of Torts: Product Liability,* the court said where a warning leaves risks in place that a safer design can correct, the safer design is required if it can be implemented reasonably. The court concluded that the plaintiffs presented sufficient evidence to the jury that an alternative bead design would have been safer and prevented the accident.

DECISIONS UNDER *DAUBERT*

Kuhmo Tire Co. v. *Carmichael* 119 S.Ct. 1167 (1999)

Facts: Petitioners were injured in a car accident that occurred when a tire blew out. They relied on an expert's testimony that the tire was defective. The district court granted Respondents motion to have the expert disqualified because his methodology, visual and tactile examination of the tire, did not satisfy the *Daubert* reliability factors (testing, error rate, acceptability, and peer review). The Eleventh Circuit reversed holding that *Daubert* only applies to scientific expert testimony. The U.S. Supreme Court reversed holding that *Daubert* not only applies to scientific expert opinions, but also applies to technical expert opinions (for example, engineers).

William Avelar v. *CMI Corporation,* Case Civil No. 1:98CVI, in the United States District Court, District of Utah, Central Division

On July 13, 1999, Judge Boyce of the United States District Court of Utah granted, in part, a motion to exclude the proffered testimony of a mechanical engineer regarding the design of a CMI concrete placer/ spreader. The plaintiff was injured when his arm was caught between a return roller and a conveyor belt running underneath the placer/ spreader. The plaintiff sued CMI originally alleging strict liability and negligence for defective design and inadequate warnings/instructions in the operator manuals for the machine.

The plaintiff offered the testimony of a mechanical engineer who opined that: (1) the placer/spreader is defectively designed because no guard or rubber scraper guards the roller in question, and (2) the warnings and instructions in the manuals are inadequate. CMI moved to exclude the testimony based on Kumbo analysis, pointing to the absence of any testing, peer review, and general acceptance of plaintiff's expert's opinions.

After review of briefs and the entertainment of oral argument, Judge Boyce excluded the plaintiff's expert's testimony, in part. The expert may not offer any opinions relating to the alleged defect due to a lack of guarding, the failure to use an alternative design, or the content of the warnings and instructions contained in the manuals. The only testimony allowed was related to general engineering principals of design criteria and what the expert observed when he inspected the placer/speaker more than two years after the accident in question.

Guild v. G.M. Corp., 1999 U.S. Lexis 9690 (W.D.N.Y. 1999)

Product liability case based on an allegedly *uncrashworthy* seat belt. GM sought to exclude plaintiff's expert's testimony regarding inertial seat belt unlatching because NHTSA published a report stating that the seat belts were safe and because the expert's methodology was unsound. The court admitted the testimony stating that *Kumbo* applies *Daubert* to technical fields such as engineering and the expert is published and qualified. Also, his testimony will be helpful to the jury. The court stated that the conflicting NHTSA report is a question of credibility for the jury to decide.

Pillow v. G.M. Corp., 184 F.R.D. 304 (E.D.Mo.)

Product liability action where plaintiff avers that defendant defectively designed the brake system on her van. The court excluded plaintiff's expert's testimony because he failed to satisfy the four *Daubert* factors.

Hickman v. Sofamor-Danek Group, Inc.,
1999 U.S. Dist. Lexis 4384 (9th Cir.)

Products liability action arising from plaintiff's injury which allegedly resulted from a spinal fixation device used in his spinal surgery. Court granted defendant's motion for partial summary judgement because plaintiff's expert on spinal surgeries was not qualified and his methodology did not satisfy *Daubert* because it was no more than general scientific reports and his own subjective belief as to causation.

FAILURE TO WARN CASES

Marcon v. K-Mart Corp. et al., 573 N.W. 2d 728 (Minn. Ct. App.1998)[1]

A 12-year-old boy was riding a sled down a hill on his knees when he struck a bump and was thrown from the sled. As a result, the boy sustained serious injuries and was rendered quadriplegic. The boy's family sued K-Mart, where they had purchased the sled, as well as Paris Manufacturing Corporation, the manufacturer of the sled.

Normally, when an *innocent* seller of a product is made a defendant in a product liability suit, the seller may be dismissed pursuant to Minnesota statutory law by filing an affidavit identifying the manufacturer of the product. If, however, the manufacturer is not able to satisfy the judgement, then the seller can be brought back into the suit. In this case, the manufacturer of the sled had gone bankrupt before the suit was filed. Therefore, K-Mart remained a party in the suit.

Plaintiffs brought claims against K-Mart and Paris Manufacturing alleging strict liability for failure to warn. Plaintiffs argued that the sled contained no labels warning that sledding on one's knees would increase the likelihood of injuries. Plaintiffs also brought a separate claim against K-Mart based on its failure to test the products it was selling.

The jury found that the sled was defective because it failed to provide adequate warnings or instructions for safe use. The jury attributed 100 percent of the causal fault for the boy's injuries to Paris Manufacturing and awarded approximately $8 million in damages. The jury found that K-Mart was not negligent in failing to test the sled. The trial court, however, held K-Mart and Paris Manufacturing jointly and severally liable for the awarded damages.

K-Mart appealed the decision arguing that since it was not found negligent, it could not be held jointly liable for the verdict. The Minnesota Court of Appeals affirmed the trial court. The Court of Appeals analyzed the facts of the case under the three-part test to prove strict liability in Minnesota:

1. That the defendant's product was in a defective condition and unreasonably dangerous for its intended use
2. That the defect existed when the product left the defendant's control
3. That the defect was the proximate cause of the injury sustained

---

[1]As reported by Rider, Bennett, Egan & Arundel.

The Court of Appeals found all three elements present in the *Marcon* case. First, the jury found that the sled was in a defective condition due to its lack of warnings. Second, the jury found that K-Mart sold the sled without warnings. Third, the jury found that the lack of warnings was the proximate cause of the boy's injury. Accordingly, the Court of Appeals held that plaintiffs were entitled to a strict liability recovery from K-Mart for the failure to warn. Furthermore, because Paris Manufacturing had gone bankrupt and was unable to satisfy its portion of the judgement, K-Mart was found fully liable for the $8 million verdict. (K-Mart had not secured an indemnification agreement with the manufacturer.)

Lakey v. Sta-Rite Industries, NC SuperCt, WakeCnty, No. 94-CVS 00425

Lakey, age 5, was injured in a wading pool at a recreational club in North Carolina. Because the cover had been removed, the suction pulled out large portions of her intestines when Lakey sat on the drain. Sta-Rite Industries manufactured the drain cover, which had been removed from the pool at the recreational club before the child's accident.

The plaintiffs argued the manufacturer should have made the cover with permanent warnings stating the risks of removing it and should have modified the design to prevent removal.

Sta-Rite maintained that misuse of the drain cover caused the injuries. The manufacturer said swimming pool employees knew the cover had to be screwed in place.

After a two-month trial and three hours of deliberation, a jury in the North Carolina Superior Court awarded $25 million to Valerie Lakey and her parents, finding Sta-Rite's negligence caused the child's injuries.

Erxleben v. Sears Roebuck & Co., Ore CirCt (1996)

Yvonne Erxleben was riding a mountain bike when she was thrown over the handle bars, landing on her head. Erxleben sustained permanent brain injuries as a result of the accident and suffers from speech problems, memory loss, headaches, and fatigue. The bicycle was made by Roadmaster Corp., assembled by Huffy Service First.

Erxleben alleged the accident was caused by a defective rear brake, loose wheel bearings, and a loose headset—a bearing collar assembly that secures the bicycle fork to the frame. She also contended that the bicycle was poorly assembled, and that the rear brake failed to slow the bicycle as it should have.

Sears argued that there was nothing wrong with the brakes and no evidence that Erxleben ever applied them. The company also noted that she was not wearing a helmet.

After six days of deliberation, the jury in Oregon Circuit Court found the bicycle brakes were defective and awarded the plaintiff $650,000 in noneconomic damages, $200,000 in lost earning capacity, and $79,000 in medical costs.

INDEX